D0368083

On Being Human

FAITH AND CULTURES SERIES

An Orbis Series on Contextualizing Gospel and Church

General Editor: Robert J. Schreiter, C.PP.S.

The *Faith and Cultures Series* deals with questions that arise as Christian faith attempts to respond to its new global reality. For centuries Christianity and the church were identified with European cultures. Although the roots of Christian tradition lie deep in Semitic cultures and Africa, and although Asian influences on it are well documented, that original diversity was widely forgotten as the church took shape in the West.

Today, as the churches of the Americas, Asia, and Africa take their place alongside older churches of Mediterranean and North Atlantic cultures, they claim the right to express Christian faith in their own idioms, thought patterns, and cultures. To provide a forum for better understanding this process, the Orbis *Faith and Cultures Series* publishes books that illuminate the range of questions that arise from this global challenge.

Orbis and the *Faith and Cultures Series* General Editor invite the submission of manuscripts on relevant topics.

Also in the Series
Faces of Jesus in Africa, Robert J. Schreiter, C.PP.S., Editor
Hispanic Devotional Piety, C. Gilbert Romero
African Theology in Its Social Context, Bénézet Bujo
Models of Contextual Theology, Stephen B. Bevans, S.V.D.
Asian Faces of Jesus, R. S. Sugirtharajah, Editor
Evangelizing the Culture of Modernity, Hervé Carrier, S.J.
St. Martín de Porres: "The Little Stories" and the Semiotics of Culture, Alex García-Rivera
The Indian Face of God in Latin America, Manuel M. Marzal, S.J., Eugenio Maurer, S.J., Xavier Albó, S.J., and Bartomeu Melià, S.J.
Towards an African Narrative Theology, Joseph Healy, M.M., and Donald Sybertz, M.M.
The New Catholicity, Robert Schreiter, C.PP.S
The Earth Is God's: A Theology of American Culture, William A. Dyrness
Mission & Catechesis: Alexandre de Rhodes and Inculturation in Seventeenth-Century Vietnam, Peter C. Phan
Celebrating Jesus Christ in Africa, François Kabasele Lumbala
Popular Catholicism in a World Church: Seven Case Studies in Inculturation, Thomas Bamat and Jean-Paul Wiest, Editors
Inculturation: The New Face of the Church in Latin America, Diego Irarrazaval, C.S.C.
The Bible on Culture, Lucien Legrand

FAITH AND CULTURES SERIES

On Being Human

U.S. Hispanic and Rahnerian Perspectives

Miguel H. Díaz

ORBIS BOOKS

Maryknoll, New York 10545

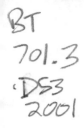
BT
701.3
·D53
2001

The Catholic Foreign Mission Society of America (Maryknoll) recruits and trains people for overseas missionary service. Through Orbis Books, Maryknoll aims to foster the international dialogue that is essential to mission. The books published, however, reflect the opinions of their authors and are not meant to represent the official position of the Society. To obtain more information about Maryknoll and Orbis Books, please visit our website at www.maryknoll.org.

Copyright © 2001 by Miguel H. Díaz

All rights reserved. No part of this publication may be reproduced or transmitted in any form or by any means, electronic or mechanical, including photocopying, recording, or any information storage or retrieval system, without prior permission in writing from the publisher.

Queries regarding rights and permission should be addressed to: Orbis Books, P.O. Box 308, Maryknoll NY 10545-0308.

Published by Orbis Books, Maryknoll, NY 10545-0308
Manufactured in the United States of America.

Orbis/ISBN 0-57075-402-0

Díaz, Miguel H.
    On being human : U.S. Hispanic and Rahnerian perspectives / Miguel H. Díaz.
        p.cm. — (Faith and cultures series)
    Includes bibliographical references and index.
    ISBN 1-57075-402-0 (pbk.)
    1. Man (Christian theology)   2. Hispanic American theologians   3. Rahner, Karl, 1904—Contributions in Christian doctrine of man.   4. Catholic Church—Doctrines.   I. Title.   II. Series.

BT701.3.D53   2001
233—dc21   2001036742
                                                                CIP

JESUIT - KRAUSS - McCORMICK - LIBRARY
  1100 EAST 55th STREET
  CHICAGO, ILLINOIS 60615

To

My spouse, Marian K. Díaz,
for teaching me what it means to be human in the image of God.

And to my children,
Joshua, Ana, and Emmanuel,
who mediate for me ordinary encounters with the life of grace.

Contents

Foreword

As the twenty-first century gets under way, it becomes increasingly apparent that the themes of theological anthropology—the Christian understanding of what it means to be human—will increasingly loom large on the theological agenda. The forces of globalization and the turbulence of migration have made identity more and more problematic in many parts of the world. How are we to understand the cosmopolitan identities of those who profit from and live a lifestyle in tune with economic neoliberalism? What do the overlapping, fragmentary identities of persons and communities of immigrants to the megalopolises of the world mean? And perhaps most importantly, what of the majority of the world's population who lose autonomy and what little means they have as the gap between rich and poor grows more widely? As the local reasserts itself in resistance to the trenchant homogenizing waves of the global, how does one gauge identity as difference and identity as a commonly shared humanity?

The continuing conflict within nations shatters societies and jeopardizes the possibility of people living as neighbors after overt conflict has come to an end. What will a possible reconciliation look like? How can just societies be constructed that will diminish the chances of warfare again breaking out? How can human rights and a global ethic inform a more peaceful and ecologically sustainable life together on this planet?

Questions regarding the human are being raised daily in bioethical research. And what of the triage of medical goods and services in the world so profoundly divided between rich and poor? Is economic profit to be the sole arbiter of who receives help and who does not? What vision of the human informs all these questions?

These are some of the profound questions about the human that are very much with us today: questions of identity, of human dignity, of the right to a decent life, of moral responsibility. In a time when difference is rightly such an important category, the negotiation of difference and commonality, of catholicity and of unity becomes an area of anthropology that needs careful and extended exploration.

Miguel Díaz offers two important perspectives in this book that address a number of the questions that have just been raised. He brings together, first of all, the theological reflection on the human that has been accumulating over a period of twenty-five years by Hispanic theologians in the United States. Their exploration of themes of the human in the various Hispanic communities is an important venue for examining the dimensions of theological anthropology in the twenty-first century. They represent a dramatically growing population in the United States. Some of them were within the United States territory long before this nation was even conceived. Others are more recent arrivals. They present among themselves (peoples from some twenty-two countries are represented among them) nearly all the variations on the themes of life in a time of globalization. Some of them are long settled, and are trying to negotiate the centrifugal forces of globalization. Others have been arriving as economic migrants, and as refugees and exiles from war-torn countries. All experience discrimination and racism; all experience being defined by others (the problematic terms "Hispanic" and "Latino"—examined by Díaz here—are emblematic of this dilemma). Many are struggling with the transition from collective to individualist styles of culture. Many, too, worry about what will become of their children and grandchildren in the cultural globalization sweeping through youth culture. They negotiate streams of cultural distinctiveness, integration, and assimilation in the larger culture. They are becoming a major force in politics. In the Roman Catholic Church, they already constitute a substantial population, but one underrepresented in positions of decision-making, leadership, and power.

Not only are their visions of the human important for their own communities and for the United States, but they are an example of what is happening in many parts of the world today. They carry with them a colonial heritage that must be re-examined in a postcolonial time. They confound the racial categories of the nineteenth and twentieth centuries, as the U.S. 2000 Census has shown. They do not aggregate easily into convenient categories of the "other." They—and other populations like them—represent rather what much of the future of humanity will look like, and they are likely to become the norm rather than the exception, as the majority populations of North America and Europe age and dwindle. Their encompassing of *tiempos mixtos*—premodernity, modernity, and postmodernity—is illustrative of what is happening in much of the world today.

So we have a great deal to learn from the Hispanic communities and how, in the context of their faith, they have learned to fashion a vision of the human in the midst of the diversity they represent and the contexts in which they are finding themselves.

Second, Díaz takes the vision of the human that emerges from these rich reflections and brings it into dialogue with the thought of the greatest and most influential Catholic theologian of the twentieth century, Karl Rahner. Rahner's work starts from a very different place. His transcendental anthropology articulates a picture of what is common in the human quest for God. Difference and marginality do not figure prominently in his theology. For that reason, many theologians have questioned whether Rahner's theology, all-embracing as it is, can really engage and illuminate the struggles that are marking the situation of the church in the twenty-first century. In his last years, Rahner seemed to sense and to support those who were exploring areas he himself had not examined. His sketch of the future of a genuinely world church, his support of Gustavo Gutiérrez in his troubles with the Vatican, and phrases here and there in his writings all give hints as to how he might have engaged the issues that were beginning to emerge. Díaz draws upon them here and shows, for the first time, how Rahner's work might be engaged from these perspectives. In doing so, he forges a link between Rahner's vision and what is taking shape in a world church today. This bodes well for the daunting task of articulating a Christian view of the human in the very changed circumstances of the twenty-first century.

What Díaz presents us here, then, is an example of the best of bringing together theologies of the human that represent two of the most important dimensions of what must characterize our reflections on Christian faith in the new millennium: the integrity of difference and the enduring importance of the commonly held; the voices of the marginalized and the perspective of a shared center; the emerging new communities and the long-standing gatherings in faith. This book provides a benchmark against which to measure discussions of theological anthropology in the future.

Robert J. Schreiter, C.PP.S.

Introduction

"But today, in the age of a uniform humanity, a humanity that seeks
to accord all its members equal rights and majority of age, the
Church may no longer permit itself to remain a European Church
exporting Western Christianity to the whole world. Now it must
really become a world Church."

—Karl Rahner[1]

As a result of the Second Vatican Council's invitation to "read the
signs of the time," and to interpret these signs in light of Christian faith
and doctrine, Catholic thought has witnessed the explosion of numerous
contextually rooted theological visions. Among other things, a wide range
of gender, social, political, and cultural experiences have informed these
visions. This book studies one of these visions. It explores emerging U.S.
Hispanic Catholic theological anthropology, and sets this vision in conversation with the leading Catholic theologian since the Council, namely,
Karl Rahner. This conversation will increase the understanding of U.S.
Hispanic theological anthropology, especially with respect to the way
this anthropology fits—in a unique way—into the Catholic tradition.

U.S. Hispanic theological anthropology can be read as being in fundamental continuity with central Rahnerian themes; and in some cases, as a
result of the particular socio-cultural location of U.S. Hispanic theology,
this theology concretizes, challenges, and moves beyond Karl Rahner.
This claim should not in any way be taken to mean that this anthropology represents a contextual "offspring" of Karl Rahner. That claim would
be untenable. The theological sources and methodologies of U.S. Hispanic theologians would immediately preclude anyone from arriving at
such a position. While Rahner is cited in the footnotes of U.S. Hispanic
theologians, and many of his ideas have explicitly or implicitly found
their way into the writings of these theologians, it would be simply mis-
leading to conclude from the latter that U.S. Hispanic theological anthropology is essentially Rahnerian.

---

[1]Karl Rahner, *The Love of Jesus and the Love of Neighbor* (New York: Crossroad,
1985), 78.

Rather, what I will argue is that the central elements that comprise U.S. Hispanic theological anthropology, which are rooted in a particular context and derived from a variety of methodologies, are not inconsistent with Rahner's anthropological vision. In fact, Rahner would welcome the specific contribution of U.S. Hispanic theological anthropology as not only a valid but also a necessary development of his anthropological premises. What Rahner argued relative to the theology of his student and friend Johann Baptist Metz, could be, *mutatis mutandis,* argued relative to emerging U.S. Hispanic theological anthropology:

> Metz's critique of my theology (which he calls transcendental theology) is the only criticism which I take very seriously. I agree in general with the contribution in Metz's book. In so far as the critique by Metz is correct, every concrete mystagogy must obviously from the very beginning consider the societal situation and the Christian praxis to which it addresses itself. If it is not sufficiently done in my theory of mystagogy . . . then this theory must be filled out. However it is not therefore false. For it has always been clear in my theology that a "transcendental experience" (of God and of grace) is always mediated through a *categorical experience in history, in interpersonal relationships, and in society* . . . If one not only sees and takes seriously these necessary mediations of transcendental experience but also fills it out in a concrete way, then one already practices in an authentic way political theology, or, in other words, a practical fundamental theology. On the other hand, such a political theology is, if it wishes to concern itself with God, not possible without reflection on those essential characteristics of man [sic] which a transcendental theology discloses.[2]

The thesis of this book is, therefore, as follows: U.S. Hispanic theological anthropology can be systematically, philosophically, and theologically enriched by engaging in an explicit conversation with Karl Rahner, and Karl Rahner's theological anthropology can be deepened, developed, and critiqued from the perspective of U.S. Hispanic visions. While U.S. Hispanic theology does not lack philosophical and theological foundations, this conversation with Karl Rahner will broaden the philosophical and theological partners of U.S. Hispanic theology, and bring to this contextual project further grounding within the Catholic tradition. Given the breadth and scope of Karl Rahner's work, to enter into conversation with him is also implicitly to enter into conversation with some central

---

[2]Karl Rahner, in the introduction to James J. Bacik, *Apologetics and the Eclipse of Mystery: Mystagogy According to Karl Rahner* (Notre Dame: University of Notre Dame Press, 1980), ix-x. Emphasis added.

philosophical and theological voices that have constituted past and present Catholic traditions.

Chapter one of this book offers some brief observations on modernity's turn to the subject and its recent evolution into the contextualized subject. It then explores some fundamental issues and concerns with respect to U.S. Hispanic theology and the subjects that comprise its reflections. Chapter two elucidates the U.S. Hispanic Catholic contribution to contemporary theological anthropology. It proposes seven central themes that comprise U.S. Hispanic visions of humanity. These are: 1) the Galilean identity of Jesus; 2) accompaniment; 3) cultural humanization; 4) human praxis and struggle; 5) engendered relationships; 6) creaturehood; and 7) trinitarian relationships. In order to facilitate a discussion of these themes, I will survey the writings of seven central figures in U.S. Hispanic Catholic theology, whose work reflects a concern with primarily one of these themes: Virgilio Elizondo, Roberto S. Goizueta, Orlando O. Espín, Ada María Isasi-Díaz, María Pilar Aquino, Alejandro García-Rivera, and Sixto J. García.

The choice and number of theologians included in chapter two are not intended to be exclusive of the various ways in which one could approach a discussion of U.S. Hispanic theological anthropology. Since my primary goal is to engage the thought of Karl Rahner, a Catholic theologian, I have decided to engage only Latino/a Catholic theologians. My hope however is that, in the spirit of what Justo González has characterized as a "new ecumenism" among U.S. Hispanic Catholics and Protestants,[3] this discussion framed primarily within a Catholic vision of what is human may find points of intersection with the literature that is emerging among Protestant Latino/a theologians. Indeed, a recently published essay on U.S. Hispanic theological anthropology by Protestant theologian David Maldonado reflects many of the themes that frame the discussion in chapter two of this book.[4]

Chapter three will explore the central sacramental expression of U.S. Hispanic Catholic approaches to the human reality, namely U.S. Hispanic popular Catholicism. I will then shift the theological context and content in chapter four to provide a discussion of Rahner's theological understanding of what it means to be human. The following three themes will be explored: 1) Rahner's theology of grace; 2) his theology of person and community; and 3) the socio-practical implications of Rahner's thought, especially evident in his writings after the Council. This threefold the-

---

[3]See González, "Hispanics in the New Reformation," in *Mestizo Christianity* (Maryknoll, New York: Orbis Books, 1995), 238-259.

[4]See David Maldonado, "Doing Theology and the Anthropological Questions," in *Teología en Conjunto: A Collaborative Hispanic Protestant Theology* (Louisville: Westminster John Knox Press, 1997), 98-111.

matic structure will be used to facilitate a more systematic arrangement of the distinct visions that comprise the U.S. Hispanic understanding of what it means to be human. They will also provide the basis for conversation in chapter five of this book.

Chapter five concludes this book with a Rahnerian-U.S. Hispanic conversation in theological anthropology. This conversation will provide an opportunity to interrelate two very distinct cultural encounters of grace, one that affirms the openness of the human person to the "always and everywhere" experience of grace (Rahner), the other which, without denying the universality of God's self offer, prefers instead to speak of the encounter of grace in light of very particular persons and their specific social, cultural, political, and gender contexts (U.S. Hispanic theological anthropology). Moreover, as a result of engaging Karl Rahner's thought, this conversation will also situate U.S. Hispanic theological anthropology in continuity with some of the most important contemporary developments in Catholic theological anthropology. To facilitate this conversation, answers to the following questions will be explored. What can Rahner's transcendental anthropology contribute to the ongoing emergence of U.S. Hispanic theological anthropology, and what can U.S. Hispanic theological anthropology contribute, both critically and constructively, to contemporary understandings of Rahner's transcendental anthropology?

U.S. Hispanic theology has emerged in recent times as a new and important theological vision. Demographic research, such as the recent U.S. 2000 Census, witnesses to the growing number of Latinos/as in this country. With respect to the U.S. Catholic presence, it is predicted that in a few years Latinos/as will comprise the majority of this ecclesial body. Thus, this effort to systematically examine U.S. Hispanic anthropology and to situate this anthropology within recent developments in Catholic theology represents a timely contribution. I hope that in the spirit of *mulataje/mestizaje,* that is, the U.S. Hispanic ethos that seeks inclusion of the other, the following pages can elicit conversation with other contemporary voices in theological anthropology. In so doing, the hard task of bridging differences and fostering a more authentic catholicity *among* and *from* the plurality of communities that comprise the church, academy, and society will have been well served.

This work began as a dissertation on U.S. Hispanic theological anthropology.[5] I want to express my sincere thanks to my dissertation director, Dr. Mary Catherine Hilkert, O.P., for her support and suggestions throughout the research and writing phases of the dissertation. I want to thank professors Thomas O'Meara, O.P., Robert Krieg, and J. Matthew

---

[5] "A Study in U.S. Hispanic Theological Anthropology, 1972-1999" (Ph.D. diss., University of Notre Dame, 2000).

Ashley for their contributions as well. I want to thank the Academy of Catholic Theologians of the United States (ACHTUS), and in a special way Professor Orlando O. Espín for the encouragement I received to initiate and complete this project. I thank my former colleagues and students at the University of Dayton and my present colleagues and students at St. Vincent de Paul Regional Seminary. My gratitude is also extended to Robert Ellsberg, editor-in-chief of Orbis Books, and to Susan Perry and the staff of Orbis Books, who have worked with me on editing this manuscript for publication. Gratitude is also due to Professor Robert J. Schreiter, C.PP.S., for agreeing to include this work in the Faith and Culture Series and writing a foreword to the book. Last, but certainly not least on my list is *mi familia*, especially my spouse, who has accompanied me throughout this entire process. Thank you, Marian, for your support, trust, and encouragement. Without you this book would not have been possible.

1

Exploring What Is "Hispanically" Human

Fundamental Issues and Concerns

BEYOND THE TURN TO THE SUBJECT:
THEOLOGY IN NEW CONTEXTS

Modernity is characterized by the "turn to the subject" and the "turn to historical consciousness." Building upon this methodological shift, contemporary Catholic theologians have underscored the fundamental importance of anthropology in theology.[1] In the writings of Karl Rahner, for instance, "Feuerbach's axiom, 'theology is anthropology,' is given a counter-interpretation and undergoes an inversion."[2] For Rahner, the human, as the expression of God's very self, is understood to be "for all eternity the expression of the mystery of God which participates for all eternity in the mystery of its ground."[3] This contemporary shift to anthropology does not invalidate the classic theocentric orientation of theology. Indeed, it is still the case today that any attempt to speak *theologically* about the human reality "cannot speak about the human reality without referring this reality back to God, that is, without considering the human as the subject destined to participate in divine life."[4]

---

[1]Rahner, "Theology and Anthropology," in *Theological Investigations*, vol. IX, trans. David Bourke (New York: Crossroad, 1983), 28-45.

[2]Stephen J. Duffy, *The Dynamics of Grace: Perspectives in Theological Anthropology* (Collegeville: The Liturgical Press, 1993), 262.

[3]Karl Rahner, *Foundations of Christian Faith: An Introduction to the Idea of Christianity*, trans. William V. Dych (New York: Crossroad, 1990), 225.

[4]See M. Flick and Z. Alszeghy, *Antropologia Teologica* (Salamanca: Ediciones Sígueme, 1989), 18-19. My translation.

Working within this paradigm shift, other contemporary theologians have moved to situate the human subject within specific historical experiences. The "turn to the subject" has precipitated a "turn to the contextual subject." The term "contextual theology" has emerged in reference to theologies that have *consciously* acknowledged specific social, racial, cultural, and gender experiences as places or loci of theological reflection. Embracing a variety of empirical and philosophical tools in their search to explore the humanity of historical subjects, contextual theologies have offered very specific understandings of the relationship between theology and anthropology.

Thus, European political theologies and Latin American liberation theologies in the 1960s have pointed out the importance of the socially constituted subject. Within these theologies the "suffering" subject has received special attention, as has the emancipatory and liberative nature of human praxis.[5] Similarly, but working within their own human experiences, Native American, Asian, African, and Black theologies have focused on issues related to the socially and culturally situated subject, and have emphasized the importance of the latter for understanding the mediation of grace.[6] Finally, various feminist theologies, rooted in the sociocultural experiences of women, have critiqued androcentric biases in theology, retrieved women's experiences as a source of theological reflection, and theologically reconstructed the symbols of Christianity.[7] In turning to gender experience as a locus of divine revelation, feminist theologies

---

[5]As examples of European political theologians see Johann Baptist Metz, *Faith in History and Society,* trans. David Smith (New York: Seabury Press, 1980); and Jürgen Moltmann, *Theology of Hope: On the Ground and the Implications of a Christian Eschatology,* trans. James W. Leich (New York: Harper & Row, 1967). For examples of Latin American liberation theologians, see Gustavo Gutíerrez, *A Theology of Liberation,* ed. and trans. Sister Caridad Inda and John Eagleson (Maryknoll, New York: Orbis Books, 1988); and Leonardo Boff, *Trinity and Society* (Maryknoll, New York: Orbis Books, 1988).

[6]For instance, on African theologies see Benézét Bujo, *African Theology in Its Social Context* (Maryknoll, New York: Orbis Books, 1992); John Parratt, *Reinventing Christianity: African Theology Today* (Grand Rapids: William B. Eerdmans Publishing Company, 1995); Robert J. Schreiter, ed., *Faces of Jesus in Africa* (Maryknoll, New York: Orbis Books, 1991); and F. Eboussi Boulaga, *Christianity without Fetishes* (Maryknoll, New York: Orbis Books, 1984). On Asian theologies, see K. Koyama, *Waterbuffalo Theology* (Maryknoll, New York: Orbis Books, 1974, rev. ed. 2000); and G.H. Anderson, ed., *Asian Voices in Christian Theology* (Maryknoll, New York: Orbis Books, 1976). On Native American theologies see Jace Weaver, ed. *Native American Religious Identity: Unforgotten Gods* (Maryknoll, New York: Orbis Books, 1998). On Black theologies see the various reflections on the Catholic reception of black theology in *Theological Studies* 61/4 (2000).

[7]Anne E. Carr, "The New Vision of Feminist Theology," in *Freeing Theology: The Essentials of Theology in Feminist Perspective,* ed. Catherine M. LaCugna (San Francisco: HarperCollins, 1993), 9-12.

have also expanded upon and challenged the relationship between anthropology and theology.[8]

These renewed efforts to draw attention to the contextualization of theology are in continuity with the theological vision of the Second Vatican Council and subsequent papal exhortations such as Pope Paul VI's *Evangelii Nuntiandi*. At the heart of these contextual visions in theological anthropology is an incarnational understanding of faith already present at the Council. This understanding recognizes the centrality of human historicity, and its importance relative to any attempt to speak about the reality of God. As the Council so well expressed in a now oft-cited assertion from *Gaudium et Spes*,

> At all times the Church carries the responsibility of reading the signs of the time and of interpreting them in the light of the Gospel, if it is to carry out its task. In language intelligible to every generation, she should be able to answer the ever recurring questions which men [sic] ask about the meaning of this present life and of the life to come, and how one is related to the other. We must be aware of and understand the aspirations, the yearnings, and the often dramatic features of the world in which we live.[9]

To respond to the perennial questions in "language intelligible to every generation" is the cornerstone of the contemporary "turn to the subject," and, in particular, the turn to the contextually defined subject. If theology, to recall its classic definition, is faith seeking understanding, it is an understanding that always arises from, and is most intelligible within, specific contexts. As Robert J. Schreiter argues, "Local theologies make us aware that 'understanding' itself is deeply colored by cultural context. Indeed, even the epistemological forms for understanding can have a strong cultural tint, reminding us that to start with 'universal' anthropology means starting with a local anthropology extended beyond its cultural bound-

---

[8]See, for example, Mary Daly, *Beyond God the Father: Toward a Philosophy of Women's Liberation* (Boston: Beacon Press, 1973); Letty M. Russell, *Human Liberation in a Feminist Perspective—A Theology* (Philadelphia: The Westminster Press, 1974); Elizabeth A. Johnson, *She Who Is: The Mystery of God in Feminist Theological Discourse* (New York: Crossroad, 1992); Sallie McFague, *The Body of God: An Ecological Theology* (Minneapolis: Fortress Press, 1993); Ann O'Hara Graff, ed., *In the Embrace of God: Feminist Approaches to Theological Anthropology* (Maryknoll; New York: Orbis Books, 1995), Ursula King, ed., *Feminist Theology from a Third World Perspective* (Maryknoll, New York: Orbis Books, 1994).

[9]Pastoral Constitution of the Church in the Modern World (*Gaudium et Spes*), n. 4. On the Council's understanding of the historicity of human subjects see M.-D. Chenu, "The History of Salvation and the Historicity of Man in the Renewal of Theology," in *Theology of Renewal: Proceedings of the Congress on the Theology of the Renewal of the Church; Centenary of Canada, 1867-1967*, vol. 1, ed. L.K. Shook (New York: Herder and Herder, 1968), 160-166.

aries."[10] In other words, historical and social factors necessarily inform expressions of, and critical responses to, faith.

Contextual theologies have, therefore, rekindled an awareness of the historical framing of the very "doing" of theology. They have persuasively underscored the social, engendered, and cultural framing of knowing, and have noted how these experiences impact the naming of the human reality as it exists in relationship to God (or what is perceived to be "of" God).[11] In the process of providing new theological visions, contextual theologians have brought about important shifts in theological methodology.[12] One such vision, with its accompanying methodological particularity, is U.S. Hispanic theology, a theology that has emerged in the last thirty years in response to a particular U.S. context.

MAPPING THE U.S. HISPANIC CONTEXT

Although "Hispanic-American"[13] roots are among the oldest in the U.S. landscape, as a result of various social, political, and religious practices that have gradually prevailed, little is known of this cultural heritage.[14] When we think of the founding ethos of the U.S. landscape, rugged individualism and Anglo-Protestantism generally come to mind. This vision is in stark contrast to the communally oriented and medieval Spanish Christian Catholic ethos, which originally informed Latin America and most of the Southeastern and Western parts of what is now the United States.[15] Glossing over any U.S. history text would be sufficient to realize

---

[10]See Robert J. Schreiter, *Constructing Local Theologies* (Maryknoll, New York: Orbis Books, 1985), 75.

[11]See Schreiter, *Constructing Local Theologies*, 75-94.

[12]Stephen B. Bevans provides an excellent introduction to the central theological and methodological issues involved in doing contextual theology. See Bevans, *Models of Contextual Theology* (Maryknoll, New York: Orbis Books, 1994), especially chapters 1 and 2.

[13]The term "Hispanic-American" is here being used in its broad sense in reference to those persons connected to the fifteenth and sixteenth century Spanish Empire. Hereafter, the term "Hispanic-American" will acquire a more specific connotation connected with communities that permanently reside in the U.S. and whose roots lie primarily within this heritage.

[14]See Justo L. González's insightful discussion of "U.S. Hispanic identity," and his critique of "Manifest Destiny" in his *Mañana: Christian Theology from a Hispanic Perspective* (Nashville: Abington Press, 1990), 31-42.

[15]Note the relationship between Catholicism and Latin American culture, and the communal anthropology suggested in the following observation by Joseph Fitzpatrick: "when a Latin American said he [sic] was *católico*, or, more commonly *muy católico* [very catholic] . . . he simply meant he was a member of a people, a *pueblo*, which was Catholic." See Fitzpatrick, *Puerto Rican Americans: The Meaning of Migration to the Mainland* (Englewood: Prentice-Hall, 1971), 116; cited also in Caleb Rosado, "The Concept of *Pueblo* as a Paradigm for Explaining the Religious Experience of Latinos," in *Old Masks, New Faces: Religious and Latino Identities*, ed. Anthony M. Stevens-Arroyo and Gilbert R. Cadena (New York: Bildner Center Publications, 1995), 78.

the historical biases that favor "Anglo-American" cultural perspectives.[16] Sadly, but truly, other cultural and religious traditions have been to a large extent suppressed. The following remarks by the leading Protestant U.S. Hispanic theologian, Justo L. González, have invited a more just retrieval and re-envisioning of "American" traditions.

> When I began teaching in Atlanta, Georgia, I opened my first lecture by telling my students that there was a time when Havana—not Savannah, Georgia, but Havana, Cuba—was the capital of Georgia. And then I went on to say, "Welcome, y'all furriners." This was intended only as a joke, but it may also serve to point out a fact often forgotten: As far as time is concerned, it is not the Hispanic-American but the Anglo-American who is the newcomer to this country. Nineteen years before the British founded their first colony in the land that Sir Walter Raleigh called Virginia, the Spanish based in Cuba founded a city that still exists in Saint Augustine, Florida. And twelve years before the Pilgrims landed on Plymouth Rock, the Spanish founded the city of Santa Fe, New Mexico.[17]

My central concern does not entail an effort to rewrite U.S. culture and history. Nor do I want to provide a history of the "Hispanic" presence, especially of its Catholic component in this country. Others have already begun to address both of these issues.[18] I am, however, interested in deepening at the theological level the understanding of communities whose ancestors have contributed to some of the oldest Christian traditions in this country. That relatively few theological projects in this area have been undertaken in the past perhaps witnesses to the suppression (intentional or unintentional) of the memory of these cultural and religious traditions woven unto the very fabric of this nation and of the U.S. Catholic Church.[19] The emergence of U.S. Hispanic-American theologies which

---

[16]For instance, when one hears about Manifest Destiny we are generally told how the "West" was won, yet one hardly hears at what cultural, religious, social, and political cost this landscape was lost.

[17]González, *Mañana*, 31.

[18]See Moises Sandoval, *On the Move: A History of the Hispanic Church in the United States* (Maryknoll, New York: Orbis Books, 1990); Anthony M. Stevens-Arroyo, *Prophets Denied Honor: An Anthology on the Hispano Church in the United States* (Maryknoll, New York: Orbis Books, 1980); Allan Figueroa Deck, *The Second Wave: Hispanic Ministry and the Evangelization of Cultures* (New York: Paulist Press, 1989); and David A. Badillo, "Latino/Hispanic History since 1965: The Collective Transformation of Regional Minorities," in *Hispanic Culture in the U.S.: Issues and Concerns*, ed. Jay P. Dolan and Allan Figueroa Deck (Notre Dame: University of Notre Dame Press, 1994), 50-76.

[19]For a complete list of theses and dissertations dealing with U.S. Hispanic-American religious topics see Anthony M. Stevens-Arroyo and Segundo Pantoja, *Discovering Latino Religion: A Comprehensive Social Science Bibliography*, vol. 4 (New York:

hinge upon a more critical reading and appropriation of past and present "Hispanic" contexts is indeed a timely and overdue theological moment.

Perhaps the most central claim that U.S. Hispanic theologians make is that U.S. Hispanic theology is self-consciously rooted in and reflects the "U.S. Hispanic context."[20] Given the centrality of this claim, it seems reasonable to raise and explore the following questions: What do U.S. Hispanic theologians understand by U.S. Hispanic context? Who are the persons primarily associated with this context? What is the significance of the year 1972 in the emergence of Latino/a theology? And finally, what are theological reasons that U.S. Hispanic theologians give to justify a common group categorization (e.g., Latino/a and Hispanic)? In exploring answers to these questions, a wide spectrum of U.S. Hispanic theological writings will be surveyed.[21]

THE PLACE AND TIME FRAME

The geographical coordinate of this contextual theology is the "United States of America." While few U.S. Hispanic theologians would question the fact that it is impossible, and in fact undesirable, to separate the theological issues that arise with communities that constitute the various "American" landscapes, their theology is not about "Latin-Americans" in the U.S. Rather, their theology reflects upon the contextual experiences of subjects who reside permanently in the U.S., yet whose roots (whether by birth or by familial heritage), lie in Spanish-speaking Latin America.

U.S. Hispanic theologians also underscore the fact that this contextual project is "not the stepchild of any other theological movement."[22] Un-

---

Bildner Center for Western Studies, 1995), 125-135. The two most recent and significant dissertations in U.S. Hispanic Catholic theology are Virgilio Elizondo's *"Mestissage, violence culturelle, annonce de l'évangile"* (Ph.D. diss., Institut Catholique, Paris, 1978); and Eduardo C. Fernandez, "U.S. Hispanic Theology (1968-1993): Context and Praxis," (Th.D. diss., Pontificia Universita Gregoriana, 1994).

[20]For instance, see Roberto S. Goizueta, "U.S. Hispanic *Mestizaje* and Theological Method," in *Concilium: Migrants and Refugees*, ed. Dietmar Mieth and Lisa Sowle Cahill (Maryknoll, New York: Orbis Books, 1993/4), 22-23. See also, Ada María Isasi-Díaz and Yolanda Tarango, *Hispanic Women: Prophetic Voice in the Church* (Minneapolis: Fortress Press, 1992), 1-3.; and Sixto García, "Sources and Loci of Hispanic Theology," *Journal of Hispanic/Latino Theology* 1/1 (1993): 39.

[21]I will restrict my reflections and examples to U.S. Hispanic/Latino(a) theological literature. The literature from the social sciences, however, is vast and growing. For an introduction to this literature, see Anthony M. Stevens-Arroyo, "The Emergence of a Social Identity among Latino Catholics: An Appraisal," in *Hispanic Culture in the U.S.: Issues and Concerns*, 77-130; and Gerardo Marín and Barbara VanOss Marín, *Research with Hispanic Populations*, Applied Social Research Methods Series 23 (Newbury Park, Calif.: Sage Publications, 1991), 18-23.

[22]Arturo Bañuelas, *Mestizo Christianity: Theology from the Latino Perspective* (Maryknoll, New York: Orbis Books, 1995), 3.

doubtedly, the careful reader of U.S. Hispanic theological writings will discover a number of convergences between Latin-American liberation and emerging U.S. Hispanic theological anthropology.[23] Indeed, U.S. Hispanic theologians would readily acknowledge that the two have had a kind of "sibling" relationship.[24] Still, as Allan Figueroa Deck has pointed out, Latin-American liberation theologian Gustavo Gutiérrez suggested over and over again to Hispanic theologians that "it was not a question of replicating the work of Latin Americans in the considerably different North American context, but of taking their *method* seriously—that is, doing theology out of *this* particular U.S. Hispanic reality."[25]

The first U.S. Hispanic Catholic theologian[26] to highlight the social, cultural, and religious experiences of U.S Hispanics and to inter-relate these experiences was Virgilio P. Elizondo, a priest of the diocese of San Antonio and now widely acknowledged as the founder of U.S. Hispanic theology.[27] A little over a quarter of a century ago, Elizondo pioneered the beginning of what has come to be known as U.S. Hispanic theology. Although not the first nor the most important of his publications, Elizondo's 1972 article *"Educación religiosa para el Mexico-Norteamericano"*[28] is an important landmark in U.S. Hispanic theologi-

---

[23]For instance, both are deeply rooted in context and praxis. Yet even after recognizing this methodological similarity, there are differences that have emerged in the meaning of "praxis" and "reflection," and how they relate to one another. See Ada María Isasi-Díaz who writes: "We do not accept the understanding that contemplation and practice together constitute the *first act*; theologizing is the *second act.*" For us, this division is artificial not only because of our understanding of the intrinsic connection between reflection and practice in praxis but also because for us the sacred is an integral part of our daily lives." In Ada María Isasi-Díaz, *En la Lucha/In the Struggle: Elaborating a Mujerista Theology* (Minneapolis: Fortress Press, 1993), 178.

[24]For instance, see Allan Figueroa Deck, ed., *Frontiers of Hispanic Theology in the United States* (Maryknoll, New York: Orbis Books, 1992), xiv-xv. See also Gilbert R. Cadena, "The Social Location of Liberation Theology: From Latin America to the United States," in *Hispanic/Latino Theology: Challenge and Promise*, ed. Ada María Isasi-Díaz and Fernando F. Segovia (Minneapolis: Fortress Press, 1996), 167-182.

[25]Deck, *Frontiers of Hispanic Theology*, xv.

[26]Among Protestant U.S. Hispanic theologians the contextual theology of Orlando E. Costas must also be acknowledged. For instance, see Costas, *Liberating News: A Theology of Contextual Evangelization* (Grand Rapids: Wm. B. Eerdmans Publishing Co., 1989); idem, "Evangelism from the Periphery: A Galilean Model," *Apuntes 2/3* (1982): 51-59.

[27]To date, Elizondo's greatest contribution is his work on the theological significance of *mestizaje* (a concept that points to the biological, cultural, racial, and religious mingling of peoples). In his various writings on this topic, Elizondo provides a "cultural re-reading of the Gospel," and a "Gospel re-reading of culture," from the perspective of Mexican-American *mestizaje*. See especially his *Galilean Journey: The Mexican-American Promise* (Maryknoll, New York: Orbis Books, 2000).

[28]In *Catequesis Latinoamericana* 4/14 (1972): 83-86. An English translation appears

cal reflection for both historical and theological reasons.[29] Rooted in Mexican-American cultural and popular religious experiences, Elizondo's brief reflections in this 1972 article capture, thematically and methodologically speaking, what would become central in U.S. Hispanic theology, namely, the focus on U.S. Hispanic culture and religious experiences. Commenting on the groundbreaking work of Elizondo, Deck writes,

> It would be difficult to exaggerate the importance of Elizondo's contribution to U.S. Hispanic theology. In addition to the work on *mestizaje*, Elizondo was one of the first theologians to view popular religiosity as a *locus theologicus*. In this he pioneered an implicit theological method that takes the anthropological concept of culture quite seriously. Undoubtedly this interest was the fruit of Elizondo's reading of *Guadium et Spes*, especially paragraphs 56 and following.[30]

Elizondo's groundbreaking work has become the historical marker that points to the beginning of a U.S. Hispanic/Latina/o theology, and more specifically, to a U.S. Hispanic theological anthropology. His particular attentiveness to the socio-cultural location of Mexican-Americans and his emphasis on their social and cultural marginalization set an important precedent for all other U.S. Hispanic theologians.

NAMING AND COMMUNAL IDENTITY

A quick perusal of U.S. Hispanic sources suggests that various names have been used to refer collectively to the persons that permanently reside in the U.S., and whose humanity has been deeply informed by a Spanish-speaking Latin-American cultural and religious heritage. Latino/a, Hispanic, and Hispanic-American are the most commonly used names. Presently, little consensus exists on the question of naming.[31] Most of these persons, however, would prefer to name themselves in relation to

---

inTimothy Matovina, ed., *Beyond Borders: Writings of Virgilio Elizondo and Friends* (Maryknoll, New York: Orbis Books, 2000), 58-61.

[29]Note that Elizondo's publication of this piece can be seen in light of a greater theological movement in the Americas, especially Latin-America. Elizondo's article came just a few years after Gustavo Gutiérrez's speech, *Hacia una teología de la liberación*, and the Latin-American bishops' reflections at Médellin (both of the latter occurred in 1968). Note too how this publication came the same year that he founded the Mexican-American Cultural Center (MAAC). The year 1972 also marks the first *Encuentro Nacional Hispano de Pastoral*. The *Encuentro* represents the first time that an attempt was made to reflect on the faith of U.S. Hispanics. Elizondo offered one of the keynote addresses at that first *Encuentro*.

[30]Deck, *Frontiers of Hispanic Theology in the United States*, xiii.

[31]See Fernando F. Segovia's excellent discussion on issues of nomenclature. What

their country of origin, that is, Cuban-American, Mexican-American, Puerto Rican, and the like.

A number of theological arguments have emerged to justify the use of an encompassing name, although most U.S. Hispanic/Latino/a theologians would agree that each of these names carries inherent theological limitations. The choice of names is ultimately rooted in issues related to self-identity.[32] Given the centrality of context within this theological project, the basic question that one must address is: What is the appropriate name to express the communal identity of this people? Thus far, the answer to this question remains inconclusive.

Those among us who argue for the use of names such as "Hispanic" or "Hispanic-American" generally do so on the basis of one or more of the following factors: religion, language, culture, and gender. For instance, U.S. Hispanic theologian Roberto S. Goizueta argues that the term "Hispanic" or "U.S. Hispanic" underscores the linguistic basis of a common group identity.[33] This connection is further justified by the fact that the nominative or adjectival form of "Hispanic" is a transliteration of the Spanish adjective *hispánico/a,* and therefore suggests not only a shared linguistic tradition but also a shared cultural heritage.[34] The importance of Spanish heritage and, consequently, of the Spanish Catholic Christian traditions that have significantly informed the humanity of the persons under consideration cannot be denied.[35] From a theological and specifically incarnational perspective, the name "Hispanic" underscores the importance of "language" for U.S. Hispanic theology. "Language," here, is being used in a broad sense to connote cultural traditions, communal values, and other essential human realities that have to be considered in any theological understanding that seeks to remain faithful to the particular human experiences that comprise the human reality.

Beyond linguistic and cultural concerns, some of us maintain that in English the terms "Hispanic" or "Hispanic-American" are gender inclu-

---

follows is deeply indebted to the reflections found in "Aliens in the Promised Land: The Manifest Destiny of U.S. Hispanic American Theology," in *Hispanic/Latino Theology,* 31-42.

[32]See Jorge J. E. Gracia, *Hispanic/Latino Identity: A Philosophical Perspective* (Malden: Blackwell Publishers, 2000), esp. 1-69.

[33]Roberto S. Goizueta, *Caminemos con Jesús: Toward a Hispanic/Latino Theology of Accompaniment* (Maryknoll, New York: Orbis Books, 1995), 13.

[34]The term "hispánico/a" comes from "Hispania," a word used by the Romans to refer to the Iberian peninsula ("land of rabbits"). It is generally believed that gradually, especially after the *Reconquista* and the success of Castelian hegemony, the term *Hispania* gave way to its Castelian form *España.* See Gracia, *Hispanic/Latino Identity,* 2.

[35]On U.S. Hispanic popular Catholicism see Orlando O. Espín, "Popular Catholicism among Latinos," in *The Faith of the People: Theological Reflections on Popular Catholicism* (Maryknoll, New York: Orbis Books, 1997), 111-155.

sive, and therefore more appropriate in theological usage.[36] Since U.S. Hispanic theology is a theology that strives for theological pluralism and inclusivity at all levels, especially with respect to gender issues, the term Hispanic would appear to be more appropriate in this theological discourse.[37]

Undoubtedly, the names "Hispanic" and "Hispanic-American" also have theological limitations. Given the methodological goal to reflect as closely as possible upon the concrete historical and cultural circumstances that mediate the presence of God, it would be a gross injustice, as far as Hispanic-Americans are concerned, to deny African and Amerindian roots.[38] Among other things, the use of "Hispanic" or "Hispanic-American" masks other linguistic and cultural traditions that have informed and mediated our experience of the divine. Thus, theological inclusivity must apply not only relative to gender issues but to socio-cultural issues as well. Moreover, as some point out, without an explicit "U.S." qualifier in front of "Hispanic" or "Hispanic-American," these terms are not sufficiently socially restrictive.[39] In other words, any person living in Spanish-speaking Latin America is also an Hispanic/Hispanic-American.

By way of contrast, some among us have argued that the name "Latino," although not gender inclusive, can easily be made to be so (that is, by adding an "a" as in "Latino/a" or "Latina/o").[40] There are also some sociological reasons that could be cited in support of the use of this term. "Latino/a" has the advantage of being a self-identifying name, which has been increasingly used and embraced by the largest group of U.S. Hispanics (Mexican-Americans).[41] And other factors have been noted in favor of its usage. For instance, some who favor using this name argue that it is culturally neutral (that is, less Eurocentric), and more nuanced relative to the political, geographical, and historical links that exist with Latin-American communities. This argument would be especially appealing when consideration is given to the fact that the

---

[36]Goizueta, *Caminemos con Jesús*, 13.

[37]On U.S. Hispanic pluralism, inclusivity, and the role of Latina theologians within this theological discourse see María Pilar Aquino, "Theological Method in U.S. Latino/a Theology," in *From the Heart of Our People: Latino/a Explorations in Catholic Systematic Theology*, ed. Orlando O. Espín and Miguel H. Díaz (Maryknoll, New York: Orbis Books, 1999), 6-48.

[38]See Goizueta, *Caminemos con Jesús*, 12; and Segovia, "Aliens in the Promised Land," 41.

[39]See Segovia, "Aliens in the Promised Land," 36-37.

[40]Note that I use interchangeably both Latina/o or Latino/a in order to avoid any gender bias that would subordinate the qualifier (a or o), to the dominant noun Latina or Latino, and hence would still preserve a certain sex-linked nominal preference.

[41]See Stevens-Arroyo, "The Emergence of a Social Identity among Latino Catholics," n. 2.

word "Latino" references the Latin-American link, over and against the Spanish connection present in any variation of the name "Hispanic."[42]

Theologically speaking, however, the weaknesses and strengths of using "Latino/a" as a common name also begin to appear. For instance, while the name Latina/o carries the advantage of being a consciously self-adopted name and implies for some a closer link to the Latin-American continent and socio-cultural reality, the word, like "Hispanic," is unable to connote linguistically the link that these communities have to their African and Amerindian traditions. Moreover, "Latino/a," as opposed to "Hispanic," can be equally applied to U.S. communities with ties to the various Romance-languages.[43] Finally, Latino/a "is by no means culturally or racially neutral, or to put it another way, it is no more and no less Eurocentric than the label 'Hispanic.'"[44] And not unlike the term "Hispanic" which was universally imposed upon various communities in the U.S. since the 1970s, "without respect for legitimate differences,"[45] the term Latino/a was created and imposed without distinctions by the French "to distinguish non-Anglo America from Anglo-America."[46] Thus, in the end the linguistic roots of both terms point to socio-cultural ambiguities and to their European connections.

The issue of naming gets even more complex when we consider those names that arise from specific U.S. gender and socio-cultural contexts not embraced or common to all Latinos/as. For instance, in searching to name themselves, Latina theologians have been split between self-identifying terms such as Latinas, *feministas hispanas* (feminist Hispanic women), Latina feminists, and *mujeristas*. Presently, no consensus has been reached among "Latina" theologians.[47] From a socio-cultural perspective, a number of Mexican-American theologians insist on self-consciously identifying themselves as Chicana theologians. While the name "Chicano/a," reminiscent of the Mexican-American struggles of the 60s

---

[42]See Segovia who notes this argument in "Aliens in the Promised Land," 37-38.

[43]Hence, the argument that in the Northeast of the United States, "Latino" includes Italians, Portuguese, French, and even Romanian peoples. And so, while New Yorkers might refer to themselves in Spanish as *Latinos*, they would not do so in English for fear of being confused with all Romance-language groups. See Stevens-Arroyo, *Prophets Denied Honor* (Maryknoll, New York: Orbis Books, 1980), xv.

[44]See Segovia, "Aliens in the Promised Land," 38-39. Segovia's argument is based on the fact that "Latino/a" derives from "*Latium*," which is "an ancient name for the central region of the Italian Peninsula surrounding the city of Rome."

[45]Gracia, *Hispanic/Latino Identity*, 6.

[46]Ibid., 4.

[47]Ada María Isasi-Díaz, María Pilar Aquino, and Jeanette Rodriguez each have their own preferred terms. Isasi-Díaz introduced the term "*mujerista*," but also uses *feministas hispanas* and Latinas. Aquino prefers the term Latina or Latina feminist and has never used the term "*mujerista*" as a self-identifying term. Jeanette Rodriguez vacillates between "Latina" and "Hispanic women."

and 70s,[48] would appeal to many Mexican-Americans, it would not be appropriate for other Latinas in this country.

This brief exposition of the status of the question relative to naming issues should suffice to point out that this cannot be easily resolved. Perhaps, U.S. Hispanic/Latina/o theological literature has embraced the best alternative thus far, namely, to encourage the multiple use of these terms, while acknowledging the potential cultural, linguistic, gender, and social limitations inherent with each term. As Goizueta avers in his introduction to *We Are a People!*, " 'Hispanic,' 'Latino,' 'Hispanic American,' or 'U.S. Hispanic'—we are all these, and more."[49]

Even if we cannot agree on a preferred name, this does not mean that there are no valid arguments that justify our shared Latino/Hispanic identity.[50] Without in any way dismissing or undermining socio-cultural and religious differences that exist among the various U.S. Hispanic-American communities, there are significant fundamental shared experiences and historical relationships that draw our communities together and justify efforts to engage in a common and emerging theological vision. Most arguments in favor of a common identity hinge upon the following factors: 1) linguistic, 2) cultural, 3) social, and 4) religious perspectives.

First, whether we speak of Mexican-Americans, Cuban-Americans, Puerto Ricans, Nicaraguans, or Latinas/os connected to other parts of Spanish-speaking Latin America, U.S. Hispanic theologians have underscored common linguistic backgrounds.[51] Hence the preference among some U.S. Hispanic theologians for the name "Hispanic" because it suggests some aspects of this shared linguistic component. As I noted above, this linguistic component refers not only to spoken and written language bonds but also includes the set of cultural symbols and rituals through which Latinos express and constitute themselves as human. In contempo-

---

[48]For instance, see Andrés Guerrero, *A Chicano Theology* (Maryknoll, New York: Orbis Books, 1987).

[49]Goizueta, *We Are a People!: Initiatives in Hispanic American Theology* (Maryknoll, New York: Orbis Books, 1992), vii.

[50]See Fernando F. Segovia, "Two Places and No Place on Which to Stand: Mixture and Otherness in Hispanic American Theology," *Listening: Journal of Religion and Culture* 27/1 (1992): 28-30; idem, "Toward a Hermeneutics of the Diaspora: A Hermeneutics of Otherness and Engagement," in *Reading from This Place: Social Location and Biblical Interpretation in the United States*, ed. Fernando F. Segovia and Mary Ann Tolbert (Minneapolis: Fortress Press, 1995), 61-65; González, *Mañana*, 33-38; Isasi-Díaz, *En la Lucha*, 11-61; and Allan Figueroa Deck, "A Pox on Both Your Houses: A View of Catholic Conservative-Liberal Polarities from the Hispanic Margin," in *Being Right: Conservative Catholics in America*, ed. Mary Jo Weaver and R. Scott Appleby (Bloomington: Indiana University Press, 1995), 88-104. For a philosophical perspective see Gracia, *Hispanic/Latino Identity*, 44-69.

[51]See Goizueta, *Caminemos con Jesús*, 13.

rary philosophical arguments, and in particular in U.S. Hispanic theology which can be read as a contextual development of those arguments, the importance of language cannot be overstated.

In contemporary philosophy one need only recall the arguments that have underscored the importance of language as a revealer of human identity. Language, to cite Heidegger's famous proposition, is "the house of being and the residence of humanity."[52] To speak of language as the "house of being" is to understand language in terms of its ability to name and reveal being. "Language is not only and primarily a phonetic and written expression of that which is to be communicated."[53] Language in the Heideggerian sense is a manifestation, a showing forth of being.[54] Language is not a tool but rather the closest neighbor that enables human beings to be who they are.[55] Language speaks.[56] It speaks specific human identity unto history.[57]

In U.S. Hispanic theological discourse, language is taken as a revealer of communal and cultural identity. Language, affirms Goizueta, is "not simply an instrument for communicating human experience; it is to some extent, that experience itself."[58] "More than any other aspect of culture, language symbolizes the communal origins of the individual person."[59] And to be more precise, as Jaime Vidal argues "language is to Hispanics what color is to Americans: the basic ground of identity by which we (Hispanics) distinguish between 'us' and 'them.' "[60] In fact, among Latinos/as language not only unites them, but also distinguishes them as being different from those that comprise their communities of origin. For instance, in parts of the Southwest a Latina/o of Mexican-American descent could

---

[52]Cited by García, "U.S. Hispanic and Mainstream Trinitarian Theologies," in *Frontiers of Hispanic Theology*, 92.

[53]Martin Heidegger, *Holzwege*, 60, cited by Walter Biemel in "Poetry and Language in Heidegger," in *On Heidegger and Language*, ed. Joseph J. Kockelmans (Evanston, Illinois: Northwestern University Press, 1972), 76.

[54]Of special significance is the evolution that takes place in Heidegger's understanding of language. In his earlier writings (especially in *Being in Time*) Heidegger conceived language as an existential structure of Being, while in his later writings language becomes the ontological ground of Being. Thus, in the latter, language is no longer under the domain of Being ("Dasein speaks") but Dasein is under the domain of language ("Language speaks"). See David E. Klemm, *Hermeneutical Inquiry* (Atlanta: Scholars Press, 1986), 136-137.

[55]Martin Heidegger, "Language" in Klemm, *Hermeneutical Inquiry*, 141.

[56]Ibid., 142.

[57]Ibid., 143 ff.

[58]Goizueta, *Caminemos con Jesús*, 12.

[59]Ibid., 52.

[60]Jaime Vidal, *Presencia Nueva* (Newark: Office of Research and Planning, 1988), 256. See also, the following sociological studies which explore issues of language among Hispanics: Aida Negrón de Montilla, *Americanization in Puerto Rico and the Public School System, 1900-1930* (Río Piedras: Editorial Edil, 1970); Antonio M. Stevens-

be easily distinguished from a Mexican by his/her spoken "amalgam" of Spanish and English.[61]

Second, closely related to issues of language is the cultural/racial "mingling" that constitutes most U.S. Hispanic communities. Commonly known as *mestizaje* or *mulatez*, this experience has framed and continues to shape the identity of U.S. Hispanics.[62] *Mestizaje* refers to the biological, cultural, and racial mingling that occurred as a result of Spanish and Amerindian interactions. Similarly, *mulatez* refers to the mingling that occurred between Spanish and African cultures. Within emerging U.S. Hispanic theologies, this experience of living "in-between" two worlds "has struck a responsive chord among Latinos and Latinas of various backgrounds."[63]

Whether from Cuba, Mexico, Puerto Rico, Nicaragua, or any other part of Latin America, every one of us embodies a particular form of *mestizaje/mulatez*. As a result of past and present interactions, U.S. Hispanics find themselves rooted, to cite a colloquial saying, *"con un pie en cada lado"* (with one foot on each side).[64] As Goizueta maintains, the *mestizo/a* "by definition inhabits the in-between world of 'both/and.' Indeed, this world is more than a habitat, it is our very identity."[65]

While U.S. Hispanic theologians underscore the importance of *"mestizaje"* in understanding Latino/a communal self-identity, increased

---

Arroyo and Ana María Díaz-Stevens, "Religious Faith and Institutions in the Forging of Latino Identities," in *Handbook for Hispanic Cultures in the United States*, ed. Felix Padilla (Houston: Arte Publico Press, 1993).

[61]See Elizondo, *Galilean Journey*, 27.

[62]The concept of *mestizaje* was systematized and made popular by the late Mexican philosopher José Vasconcelos. In his controversial book, *La raza cósmica*, Vasconcelos links culture to biology and argues for the superiority of Latin-American people. In contrast to the prevalent Darwinian ideology, which Vasconcelos saw as a scientific projection of the cultural arrogance, colloquialism, and racism of the dominant white race, he proposes Latin-American *mestizaje* as the ultimate expression of human culture. He argues that this *mestizo* community represents the climactic synthesis of a manifold of biological and cultural expressions. This bi-cultural community emerges from an emphatic pathos that would go beyond previous human efforts to create homogeneous communities. Vasconcelos hoped that this unique form of *mestizaje* would bring an end to parochial visions of community, realizing instead an all-inclusive humanity. See José Vasconcelos, *La raza cósmica: mision de la raza iberoamericana* (Paris: Agencia Mundial de Libreria, 1925), 17-18. For a critique of Vasconcelos' notion of *mestizaje*, see R. Goizueta, *Caminemos con Jesús*, 120-122. For a study tracing the development of this concept, see Claudio Esteva-Fabregat, *Mestizaje en Iberoamerica* (Tucson: University of Arizona Press, 1995).

[63]Justo L. González, "Hispanic Worship: An Introduction," in *¡Alabadle!: Hispanic Christian Worship*, ed. Justo L. González (Nashville: Abington Press, 1996), 15. See also Elizondo, *"Mestizaje* as a Locus of Theological Reflection," in *Frontiers of Hispanic Theology*, 104-123; and John P. Rossing, *"Mestizaje* and Marginality: A Hispanic American Theology," *Theology Today* 45/3 (1988): 293-304.

[64]Isasi-Díaz, *En la Lucha*, 15.

[65]Goizueta, *Caminemos con Jesús*, 17.

attention has been given not to idealize this experience. Most Latino/a theologians are keenly aware that this U.S. Hispanic "hybrid" identity emerged, for the most part, from the subordination of one culture, race, and language over another. The *mestizo* heritage of Latinos/as of meso-American descent, and the *mulatto* heritage of those with Caribbean background has to some extent been tainted by non-egalitarian relationships.[66] Many Latino/a theologians would also agree, based on past and ongoing experiences within the present U.S. landscape, that "mingling" often occurs at a great cultural cost.[67] Indeed, "melting-pot" immigrant models (to which a number of Latinos/as are subjected) are built on the implicit or explicit assumption of the superiority of one people and culture over another. In the name of "unity" the immigrant is expected to give up his or her cultural particularity in order to become an "American." What is conceived as "American," however, emerges from and reflects the dominant ethos, culture, religion, and communal identity of the nation. This univocal understanding of "American" is gradually loosing ground. Instead, the recognition and affirmation of the gifts that diverse cultures and peoples offer is becoming the key in defining what an American is and understanding how to foster an authentic union within the peoples that comprise the "United" States.

Third, beyond linguistic and cultural experiences, social experiences also contribute to our shared Latina/o identity. U.S. Hispanic theologians have noted how whether by choice, or by imposition, U.S. Hispanic-Americans share a common experience of exile. For some, exile resulted from their (or their family's) "voluntary" departure from a Latin-American country. For others, such as Mexican-Americans and Puerto Ricans, exile was imposed from U.S. involvement across the territories that surround the Rio Grande and the Caribbean Sea. Most, however, discover their exile by the very fact of racial, cultural and religious *mestizaje*. The both/and nature of this human identity makes Latinos/as socially unacceptable, and, as such, permanent exiles in either Latin-American or Anglo-American circles.

Various forms of cultural marginalization also contribute to our "growing sense of unity."[68] Among other things, some of us have pointed out how statistics confirm that most U.S. Hispanics are poor (especially Latina women), uneducated, underemployed, and underrepresented at the corporate and institutional levels.[69] Since social status and cultural identity

---

[66] See Goizueta, "*La raza cósmica?* The Vision of Vasconcelos," *Journal of Hispanic/Latino Theology* 1/2 (February 1994), 25. See also, *Caminemos con Jesús*, 126-127.

[67] See Isasi-Díaz, *En la Lucha*, 52-53.

[68] See González, *Mañana*, 33.

[69] See Isasi-Díaz, *En la Lucha*, 22-28; González, *Mañana*, 34-35; and F.D. Bean and M. Tienda, *The Hispanic Population of the United States* (New York: Russell Sage Foundation, 1987).

are intrinsically related,[70] these statistics also suggest the cultural margin-alization of Latinos/as. This socio-cultural marginalization has contrib-uted to what has come to be referred to as a new ecumenism among various Christian Latino/a communities.[71] What founds this new ecumen-ism is not so much doctrinal consensus, but rather a communal Latina/o solidarity that seeks to overcome present forms of marginalization.

These various linguistic, cultural, and social factors, which suggest a common Latino/a identity, converge sacramentally in what is perhaps the strongest link among U.S. Hispanic communities, namely, U.S. Hispanic popular religion (both in its Protestant and in its Catholic manifesta-tions).[72] While U.S. Hispanic communities may each have distinct reli-gious popular symbols and celebrations, this religious praxis has all been informed by a common heritage derived primarily from the "relating" of Spanish, African, and Amerindian religious factors.

Among Latina/o communities such a common heritage facilitates a better understanding of each other's way of being Christian. For instance, a Mexican-American devoted to Our Lady of Guadalupe would under-stand and embrace much more readily a Cuban-American's devotion to Our Lady of Charity (and vice versa), than one of the other European devotions to Mary. The latter does not mean that Latinos/as do not also embrace Euro-centric religious expressions. What it means, however, is that as a result of a shared socio-cultural matrix, and the impact of the latter on popular religious expressions (see chapter three), Latino/a com-munities have much more in common with each other than with their Anglo-American Christian neighbors. Thus, Mark Francis notes the bind-ing aspects of Latino popular Catholicism, and distinguishes the latter from Euro-centric popular devotionalism:

> Unlike the devotionalism of the pre-Vatican II European and U.S. Churches, Hispanic popular religion is not based on prayer books or the printed word but on oral traditions passed on from one genera-tion to the next. Even more importantly, the exaggerated individu-alism characteristic of the devotionalism before the council does not seem to predominate in Hispanic popular religion. On the contrary, most of the expressions of piety so dear to the hearts of Hispanics are strongly anchored in a context of *communal* struggle for identity, both religious and cultural.[73]

---

[70]See Isasi-Díaz, *En la Lucha*, 52; and Goizueta, *Caminemos con Jesús*, 2.

[71]See González, *Mañana*, 74.

[72]Note how Espín has argued that both Protestant and Catholic popular religious expressions serve as preservers of a common U.S. Hispanic identity. See his "Pentecostalism and Popular Catholicism: Preservers of Hispanic Catholic Tradition?" Presidential Address at the 1992 Colloquium of the Academy of Catholic Hispanic Theologians of the United States, published in ACHTUS Newsletter, Vol. 4 (1993).

[73]Mark R. Francis, "Popular and Liturgical Reform in a Hispanic Context," in

To summarize: in spite of recognized legitimate differences that exist among the various Latino/a communities, there are sufficient common interactions at the level of linguistic, cultural, social, and religious experiences that warrant a common identity. The formation of various Latina/o professional theological organizations,[74] the initial search for the roots of an Hispanic philosophical tradition,[75] and the very emergence of U.S. Hispanic theology have witnessed to this conviction. Furthermore, the *Encuentro* process (1972-1985), which gave a chance for U.S. Hispanics for the first time to explore "the question of Church and their place in it,"[76] and the various bishops' documents on U.S. Hispanics[77] have only but confirmed a sense of being an "Hispanic" people, and thereby have indirectly promoted the emergence of U.S. Hispanic theology.

This common identity among the various communities that have given rise to U.S. Hispanic theological discourse need not be understood in essentialist terms. In other words, establishing our common identity does not depend upon the presumption that there is some kind of universal "Hispanic" set of shared characteristics. Such an argument would attempt to find some kind of an "Hispanic" essence independent of the particular experiences that unite Latinos/as.[78] On the other hand, this does not mean that the particular experiences that bind Latinos/as cannot be appealed as a basis of a common socio-cultural identity. Nor does it mean that such experiences must be interpreted as merely accidental or superficial to the constitution of the Hispanic self.

It is true that within the U.S. Hispanic context some experiences can be more strongly appealed to than others as the basis for a common iden-

---

Dialogue Rejoined: Theology and Ministry in the United States Hispanic Reality (Collegeville: The Liturgical Press, 1995), 171. Emphasis in original.

[74]In 1988, a group of Catholic theologians founded the Academy of Catholic Hispanic Theologians of the United States (ACHTUS); in 1991 a group of mainly Protestant theologians founded the *Asociación para la Educación Teológica Hispana* (AETH); and in 1993 an ecumenical group of Latino/a theologians founded *La Comunidad* at the American Academy of Religion. U.S. Hispanic theological journals were also launched in the 80s and 90s (respectively, *Apuntes* and the *Journal of Hispanic/Latino Theology*). Most recently, the Hispanic Theological Initiative (HTI) was founded to promote theological scholarship among Latinos/as.

[75]Gracia, *Hispanic/Latino Identity*, 130-192.

[76]Ana María Pineda, "Personal and Ministerial Formation in a Hispanic Context," in *Dialogue Rejoined*, 150. On the *Encuentros* see Office of Hispanic Affairs, *Proceedings of the I Encuentro Nacional Hispano de Pastoral*, 1972; United States Catholic Conference, *Proceedings of the II Encuentro Nacional Hispano de Pastoral*, 1978; United States Catholic Conference, *Prophetic Voices: The Documents on the Process of the III Encuentro Nacional Hispano de Pastoral*, 1986.

[77]See National Conference of Catholic Bishops, *The Hispanic Presence: Challenge and Commitment: A Pastoral Letter on Hispanic Ministry*, 1983; and *The Bishops Speak with the Virgin: A Pastoral Letter of the Hispanic Bishops of U.S.* (1981).

[78]See Gracia's rejection of the notion of identity understood in essentialist terms in *Hispanic/Latino Identity*, 190. I agree with him on the need to avoid essentialism, but

tity (for instance, the way most U.S. Hispanic communities relate to God at the popular level). Still, all of these experiences should be approached as being "essential" with respect to the constitution of a particular self, as this self exists ultimately in his or her relationship to God. Indeed, in U.S. Hispanic theological discourse relationships that derive from geographical locations and from social, gender, cultural, and racial experiences are not accidental, but intrinsic to the ongoing constitution of the U.S. Hispanic self. Theologically speaking, the issue is the ancient dilemma of relating the particular to the universal, and ultimately, how particular human experiences constitute persons in history and serve as mediations for the offer of grace.

THE "DOING" AND "ROOTING"
OF U.S. HISPANIC THEOLOGY

U.S. Hispanic theology, in all of its varying methodological approaches[79] and hermeneutical principles,[80] is self-consciously rooted in a Latina/o context. Reflecting the modern turn to the subject, and its natural evolution into the turn to the contextual subject, U.S. Hispanic theology takes very seriously the task of "faith seeking understanding" within a specific socio-historical context. Or perhaps, to be more accurate, U.S. Hispanic theology combines this traditional approach to theology with the praxis-oriented approach of "faith-seeking social justice," and the aesthetic-oriented approach of "faith seeking adoration."[81] Rather than being a detached reflection about, for, on behalf, or in the name of faceless subjects, U.S. Hispanic theology is a reflection on faith that emerges from within the engaged "accompaniment" of engendered subjects who are socially and culturally situated.[82] Thus, Allan Figueroa Deck writes,

> Latino theology, in its current manifestations, is decidedly a form of *contextual* theology. That is, it is explicit about the social class and cultural location on which it is grounded. It is a form of ethnic

---

as a theologian I would give a greater transcendental weight to what he terms "historical relations."

[79]U.S. Hispanic theologians have embraced a wide range of approaches. For instance, note the following: 1) philosophical (Goizueta, García), 2) narrative (Rodriguez, Elizondo), 3) cultural-sociological (Espín, Isasi-Díaz), and 4) semiotic (García-Rivera).

[80]See Aquino, "Theological Method in U.S. Hispanic Latino/a Theology," in *From the Heart of Our People*, ed. Orlando O. Espin and Miguel Díaz (Maryknoll, New York: Orbis Books, 1999), 6-48.

[81]See Gerald O'Collins, *Retrieving Fundamental Theology: The Three Styles of Contemporary Theology* (New York: Paulist Press, 1993), esp. 7-15.

[82]Roberto S. Goizueta, "U.S. Hispanic *Mestizaje* and Theological Method," in *Concilium: Migrants and Refugees*, 22-23. Emphasis in original. See also, Isasi-Díaz and Tarango, *Hispanic Women: Prophetic Voice in the Church*, 1-3; and García, "Sources and Loci of Hispanic Theology," 39.

theology in that it assumes the cultural identity of Latinos as a place for beginning one's reflection. Moreover, Latino theology is *experiential*. It makes human experience in some form or other the starting point of the reflection. In this it is not different from many other contemporary theologies. It stresses, however, the *particular* experience of Latinos in several coordinates: social class, ethnic, racial, and gender.[83]

The contextual rootedness of this theology undergirds the U.S. Hispanic theological claim that U.S. Hispanic theology must be judged "from within." That is, the theoretical quality and basic structure of our reflections, principles of coherence, and the articulation and rationality of our arguments depend ultimately upon how faithful we reflect upon U.S. Hispanic experiences.[84] A number of U.S. Hispanic theologians have pointed out how we do not reject whatever can be found to be of value in "dominant" methodologies. What we reject is the "dominant culture's conceptualist and instrumentalist models of reason and criteria of reasonableness."[85]

U.S. Hispanic methodology has incorporated in a variety of ways the challenge initiated by Virgilio Elizondo for U.S. Hispanics to think with their own minds and to feel with their own senses.[86] In taking up this challenge, U.S. Hispanic theologians have embraced epistemological approaches that conform to U.S. Hispanic experiences. Broadening our understanding of what counts as "rational," we have argued that a "theology that truly reflects 'the Hispanic mind' will do so not only in content but also in form."[87] Thus, knowing must engage the mind as well as the body, and must be derived from the performed and iconically perceived word as much as from the written word.[88] In its effort to reflect a more integrated approach, U.S. Hispanic theology has increasingly embraced theological aesthetics as essential to the development of this contextual project.

To date, María Pilar Aquino has provided the most systematic and comprehensive reflections on U.S. Hispanic theological method. Most recently, Aquino has discussed various theological characteristics and

---

[83]Deck, "Latino Theology: Year of the 'Boom,' " *Journal of Hispanic/Latino Theology* 1/2 (1994): 54-55.

[84]See María Pilar Aquino, "Directions and Foundations of Hispanic/Latino Theology: Toward a *Mestiza* Theology of Liberation," in *Journal of Hispanic/Latino Theology* 1 (1993): 5-21.

[85]Goizueta, "United States Hispanic Theology and the Challenge of Pluralism," in *Frontiers of Hispanic Theology in the United States*, 17-18. Cited in Aquino, "Directions and Foundations of Hispanic/Latino Theology," 195.

[86]See Aquino, "Directions and Foundations of Hispanic/Latino Theology," 193.

[87]Goizueta, "U.S. Hispanic Popular Catholicism as Theopoetics," in *Hispanic/Latino Theology*, 269.

[88]See Goizueta, "In Defense of Reason," *Journal of Hispanic/Latino Theology* 3/3

hermeneutical principles that guide U.S. Hispanic theology.[89] Relative to characteristics, Aquino underscores how Latino/a theology: 1) situates itself within the greater Catholic tradition, especially within the tradition of Latin-American liberation theology; 2) affirms the historicity of all theological reflection; 3) welcomes the need to engage in intercultural theological conversations; 4) critiques dominant intellectual traditions; and 5) redefines and broadens the terms of theological discourse. Relative to hermeneutical principles, Aquino has emphasized the centrality of popular Catholicism, the option for the poor, and liberating praxis in U.S. Hispanic theological reflection.

Beyond these defining specific characteristics and principles of reflection that comprise U.S. Hispanic theology, one has to note the use of traditional sources in U.S. Hispanic theological reflections. In his article entitled "Sources and Loci of Hispanic Theology,"[90] Sixto J. García distinguishes and relates the traditional sources and specific loci of U.S. Hispanic theology. Among the traditional sources of U.S. Hispanic theology, García lists the Scriptures, Tradition, liturgy, and human experience. Among the specific loci of U.S. Hispanic theology he lists the socio-cultural experiences of U.S. Hispanics, their stories and myths, their concrete forms of oppressions, and their Marian devotions. García argues that the sources "can be found only as they 'perform' (in Jürgen Habermas' sense of the word) in a given cultural context. . . ." That "very same cultural context in its diversity and complexity," García goes on to argue, "will also offer the loci for Hispanic theology, or, at the very least, will point toward them."[91]

García's reflections basically delineate how U.S. Hispanic theology critically and contextually appropriates the Christian, and in particular, Catholic traditions.[92] The "historical coordinates" of U.S. Hispanic subjects (mainly, *mestizaje*, poverty, and vanquishment)[93] and the religious expressions of these subjects "qualify, shape, and condition the identity of the sources."[94] To use the image of another U.S. Hispanic theologian, the particular loci of U.S. Hispanic theology provide the "little stories," which

---

(1996): 20-22; and idem, "U.S. Hispanic Popular Catholicism as Theopoetics," in *Hispanic/Latino Theology*, 269.

[89]See Aquino, "Theological Method in U.S. Hispanic Latino/a Theology," 8-39.

[90]See *Journal of Hispanic/LatinoTheology* 1/1 (1993): 22-43. See also Espín and García, "The Sources of Hispanic Theology," in *Proceedings of the Catholic Theological Society of America* 43 (1998), 122-25.

[91]García, "Sources and Loci," 22.

[92]For a Protestant Hispanic perspective see Samuel Solivan, "Sources of a Hispanic/Latino American Theology: A Pentecostal Perspective," in *Hispanic/Latino Theology*, 134-148.

[93]On the "historical coordinates" of U.S. Hispanic theology see Aquino, "Directions and Foundations of Hispanic/Latino Theology," 197-202. See also, Isasi-Díaz, *En la Lucha*, 22-28.

[94]García, "Sources and Loci of Hispanic Theology," 23. See also, "Exploring a

embody in concrete social, cultural, and religious ways the "big" Christian story.[95]

As García suggests, popular Catholicism is an explicit religious locus that grounds the "doing" of U.S. Hispanic theology. Popular Catholicism is a prominent, if not the most prominent, locus of U.S. Hispanic theology. In a theology that stresses cultural identity, one is not surprised to find why popular Catholicism is so central to U.S. Hispanic theological reflection. Thus, Orlando Espín echoes the anthropological importance of popular Catholicism and suggests its methodological importance when he writes: "popular religiosity has been, and still is, the least 'invaded' cultural creation of our peoples, and a locus for our most authentic self-disclosure. It is through popular religiosity that we have been able to develop, preserve, and communicate deeply held religious beliefs."[96]

The characterization of U.S. Hispanic popular Catholicism as the place where U.S. Hispanics encounter the "essentials" of Christian faith further underscores the centrality of this religious experience within U.S. Hispanic theological reflections.[97] As a revealer of communal identity, U.S. Hispanic theologians see popular Catholicism as a mediator of the religious, cultural, and social location of U.S. Hispanics. To use again García's terminology, popular Catholicism serves to "qualify, shape, and condition" the Christian identity of U.S. Hispanics. I will return again to the subject of popular Catholicism in chapter three, where the sacramental and anthropological implications of this religious expression will be explored.

In carrying out the ancient task of "faith seeking understanding" U.S. Hispanic theology not only embodies a particular faith, and a particular way of seeking understanding of that faith, but it also represents a different way of carrying out this task. U.S. Hispanic theologians have come to prefer the process of attaining theological knowledge as a result of what has become known as *"teología de conjunto"* (literally meaning, doing theology jointly or communally). This methodological approach follows the conviction that theology is the expression of a people and it conforms more adequately to this expression when it emerges within the context of a theological community. Hence, U.S. Hispanic theological method might be described as a communal effort to critically and creatively appropriate the Christian tradition (the "big Christian story"), especially as mediated through the "little stories" which comprise the daily lives of U.S. Hispan-

---

Praxis-Oriented Methodology in Theological Formation," in *Dialogue Rejoined*, 90-91.

[95]See García-Rivera, *St. Martín de Porres: The "Little Stories" and the Semiotics of Culture* (Maryknoll, New York: Orbis Books), 1-39.

[96]Espín, "Grace and Humanness," in *We Are a People!*, 148.

[97]See Espín and García, "Lilies of the Field: A Hispanic Theology of Providence and Responsibility," in *Proceedings of the Catholic Theological Society of America* 44 (1989), 75.

ics. For U.S. Hispanic theologians, these little stories find sacramental expression in U.S. Hispanic popular Catholicism.

FROM U.S. HISPANIC CONTEXTS TO
U.S. HISPANIC VISIONS OF HUMANITY

Method is often the key to understanding theological content. In this chapter I have suggested that one can deepen an understanding of U.S. Hispanic theological method by: 1) considering how this methodological approach can be read as an expression of the contemporary "turn to the contextualized subject" in Catholic thought; and 2) by considering some specific foundational issues and concerns that accompany the subjects of U.S. Hispanic theology. These two factors frame, at a fundamental level, how U.S. Hispanic theologians carry out the task of "faith seeking understanding" and the theological sources that they engage in that process. This ancient task has precipitated, among U.S. Hispanic theologians, new visions that are in accordance with what is "Hispanically" human, and new ways of conceiving how this particular humanity encounters the experience of grace.

2

On Being Human
from U.S. Hispanic Perspectives

THEOLOGICAL ANTHROPOLOGY: FROM THE BROADER
CONTEXT TO THE U.S. HISPANIC CONTEXT

The Christian theological vision of what it means to be human have emerged from the joining of "scattered anthropological approaches."[1] This understanding of what is human developed in "the context of theological subsections."[2] These subsections included, among others, aspects drawn from the doctrine of creation (especially Gen. 1-3), Christology, the doctrine of the Trinity, and the doctrine of grace. Over the years, these anthropological subsections contributed to various Christian interpretations of the human reality. Recently, theologians such as Karl Rahner have called for the unification of these subsections in the discipline that has come to be known as theological anthropology.[3] Today, theological anthropology encompasses a wide range of Christian theological reflection that seeks to understand the human reality under the embrace of God.

Theological reflections seeking to understand the relationship between the human and the divine always emerged within particular histories and were reflected upon by particular human subjects. Thus, in some sense all Christian anthropologies have always been contextual anthropologies. This contextual nature of Christian anthropologies, however, invites us

---

[1]George Langemeyer, "Theological Anthropology," in *Handbook of Catholic Theology*, ed. Wolfgang Beinert and Francis Schüssler Fiorenza (New York: Crossroad, 1995), 691. See also, Luis F. Ladaria, *Introducción a la antropología teológica* (Navarra: Editorial Verbo Divino, 1996), 9-42.

[2]Langemeyer, "Theological Anthropology," 691.

[3]See Ladaria who comments on Rahner's challenge to systematize the various subsections that comprise theological anthropology in *Introducción a la antropología teológica*, 25-26.

to consider that in the search to understand what is human, care must be taken to discern which anthropological aspects of a given theological vision are more likely to reflect and mediate the divine, and which are not. Because the human is not only under the embrace of grace, but also subject to sin, it is not possible to affirm from a Christian perspective the value of all human experiences. Thus, theological understandings of the human reality must constantly be re-visited and re-evaluated in light of God's definitive self-revelation in Jesus Christ, new insights into the human reality, and the ongoing work of the Spirit.

In our times, a number of Catholic theologians have deepened the understanding of the relationship between the human reality and God.[4] They have underscored how God's self-gift to us, or grace, presupposes and is mediated by our human reality. God reveals what humans can perceive. In this sense, we can metaphorically speak of the human and the divine as being caught up in an eternal nuptial dance in which God is always initiating. But God does not invite us to dance by singing to us in a "language" we cannot comprehend. Rather, God sings to us tunes that are capable of moving us to the dance floor. The songs that God sings contain human lyrics, rhythms, and melodies. Simply put, the encounter with grace is always a human encounter.

Contextual theologians have precipitated very particular readings of the human encounter with grace. For these theologians, it is no longer acceptable to articulate the relationship between what is human and what is divine in formal and abstract terms. In light of the "turn to the contextual subject," these theologians have underscored the historical human realities that constitute persons in relationship to God. If I may be allowed to continue the metaphor above, the songs that God sings are not universal songs capable of being heard by a universally conceived hearer. Rather, the songs contain the specific lyrics, rhythms, and melodies associated with concrete human subjects.

U.S. Hispanic theological anthropology can be defined as the effort by U.S. Hispanic theologians to elucidate the relationship between God and what is "Hispanically" or *Latinamente* human. As David Maldonado points out, "a Hispanic theological anthropology requires the examination of factors within the Hispanic context which go beyond the nature and existence of the individual."[5] Indeed, one must also consider "the

---

[4]For instance, see Rahner, "Theology and Anthropology" in *Theological Investigations*, IX, trans. David Bourke (New York: Crossroad, 1983), 28-45; and Bernard Lonergan, "Theology in Its New Context," in *Renewal of Religious Thought: Proceedings of the Congress on the Theology of the Renewal of the Church; Centenary of Canada, 1867-1967*, vol. 1., ed. L.K. Shook (New York: Herder and Herder, 1968), 34-46.

[5]David Maldonado, "Doing Theology and the Anthropological Questions," *Teología en Conjunto: A Collaborative Hispanic Protestant Theology*, ed. José David Rodríguez and Loida I. Martell-Otero (Louisville: Westminster John Knox Press, 1997), 98.

examination of historical, social, and community realities, as well as economic, ethnic, racial, gender realities within which faith is known and
religious life experienced."[6] These are the realities that constitute what is
"Hispanically" human. It is within this particular human reality that U.S.
Hispanic theologians have reflected upon encounters with grace and begun
to re-envision what it means to be human from this particular context.

No single author or work provides "the" U.S. Hispanic vision on theological anthropology. Instead, one must select and survey variant voices.
Perhaps, more than any other voice, that of Virgilio Elizondo can be cred-
ited with laying down the foundations of U.S. Hispanic theological anthropology. Elizondo's understanding of the Galilean identity of Jesus provides
the initial building blocks of a Hispanic theological anthropology.

THE THEOLOGICAL ANTHROPOLOGY
OF VIRGILIO ELIZONDO

In a widely known autobiographical publication, which recounts his
personal, pastoral, and academic journey, Elizondo notes how he struggled
during his doctoral studies at the Institute Catholique in Paris, with questions related to the identity of Jesus.[7] Elizondo recalls his inability to accept theoretical constructs related to Christ, which in his opinion, spoke
little to his communal experiences. The breakthrough in Elizondo's
christological difficulties, however, came when he focused on the particular human identity of Jesus. Embracing the universality of revelation,
Elizondo argues in *The Future is Mestizo* that God's revelation in Christ
is "the answer to every human question—not just the answer to the questions that we ask."[8] But Elizondo insists on the particular and experiential basis of God's revelation by arguing that Christ is "the answer to the
question of *our* existence."[9]

Elizondo's understanding of how God's grace is experienced and mediated through Jesus offers the clue to unveiling his Christology and consequently, his theological anthropology. For Elizondo, the experience of
grace, even in the case of Jesus, is socio-culturally mediated. Consequently,
an affirmation of the Incarnation necessarily implies an affirmation of
Jesus' socio-cultural identity. Elizondo writes:

> As I tried to reconstruct his way, a previously unquestioned aspect
> started to emerge: his earthly identity. Humanly speaking, just who
> was this Jesus of Nazareth? It seemed like such an elementary

---

[6]Ibid.
[7]See Virgilio Elizondo, *The Future is Mestizo: Life Where Cultures Meet* (New
York: Crossroad, 1992), 67-86.
[8]Ibid., 70.
[9]Ibid. Emphasis added.

question, but I had never asked it before, nor had I found it studied seriously in any of the works on Christ that I knew of. His socio-cultural identity was simply passed by or idealized into a heavenly existence. The fullness of the Incarnation was not appreciated, and in many ways we Christians are still scandalized by just how human our God became.[10]

Elizondo, however, is not just interested in questions that address the socio-cultural identity of Jesus. He is also interested in doing a theological reading of Mexican-American contemporary experiences. Elizondo addresses the question of Jesus' identity and the question of Mexican-American identity in tandem. In other words, it is the socio-cultural location of Mexican-Americans, already presumed to be under the embrace of grace, which leads to Elizondo's re-reading of Jesus' socio-cultural identity in the Gospel. This re-read identity then provides the foundation from which Mexican-American socio-cultural experiences of marginalization are critiqued and re-evaluated. Thus, Elizondo's theological hermeneutics involves a dialectical movement that originates with a "faith-full" intuition[11] of Mexican-American socio-cultural reality. This intuition then enables a reading of Jesus' socio-cultural identity. The latter, in turn, triggers the return and challenge to marginalizing elements within the reality that comprises Mexican-American life.

THE LOGIC OF DIVINE ELECTION: GALILEE AND THE GALILEAN IDENTITY OF JESUS

Rejecting what he characterizes as a Western fear of confessing the Christ but forgetting Jesus,[12] Elizondo's *Galilean Journey* seeks to offer a cultural re-reading of the identity of Jesus, and subsequently, to re-read Mexican-American identity in light of the latter.[13] Following in the footsteps of E. Lohmer, R.H. Lightfoot, W. Marxsen, and Wayne Meeks, Elizondo reads the Gospels in such a way as to underscore the cultural identity of Jesus as a Galilean. While scholars may question the uncritical elements encountered in Elizondo's reading of Jesus' Galilean identity,[14]

---

[10]*The Future is Mestizo*, 75.

[11]Within U.S. Hispanic theology the term "faith-full" intuition has been coined by Orlando O. Espín. By "faith-full" intuition Espín understands "the living witness and faith of the Christian people" which is "expressed through the symbols, language, and culture of the faithful." See Espín, "Tradition and Popular Religion: An Understanding of the *Sensus Fidelium*," in *Frontiers of Hispanic Theology in the United States*, ed. Allan Figueroa Deck (Maryknoll, New York: Orbis Books, 1992), 64-65.

[12]Elizondo, *The Future is Mestizo*, 75.

[13]*Galilean Journey: The Mexican-American Promise* (Maryknoll, New York: Orbis Books, 2000).

[14]For instance, Elizondo writes: "The Galilean faith in the God of the fathers was thus

or they may differ on the meaning or degree of theological importance that can be attributed to Galilee, most, however, would agree with Elizondo that "There is no doubt that Galilee plays a key role in the life and mission of Jesus as presented in the Gospels."[15]

To be a Galilean, argues Elizondo, was to belong to a marginalized community of persons. Galilee was a crossroads of peoples, a place where cultures and religious traditions mingled. Elizondo claims that this cultural mixture, or *"mestizaje,"* became for other Jews "a sign of impurity and a cause of rejection."[16] Yet what for others may have been the cause of rejection, Elizondo sees as the cause of divine election. For Elizondo, the logic of divine election implies the embrace of *mestizaje*—a "both/and" rather than an "either/or" anthropology. In fact, Elizondo understands Jesus' *mestizaje* as one of, if not the, most important human element that enables him to transcend, challenge, and transform the exclusive and marginalizing human reality of his time. Thus Elizondo writes,

As a Galilean he demonstrates the role of a marginal person who by reason of being marginal is *both* an insider *and* an outsider—partly both, yet fully neither. And he is not just trying to get into the structures, but to change the structures in such a way that no one will be kept out, segregated, dehumanized, or exploited.[17]

Among the specific cultural and social experiences that Elizondo gives to account for Jesus' marginal *mestizo* identity include the following: First, linguistically speaking, the Galileans were mocked because of their accent and inability to pronounce certain sounds.[18] Second, Elizondo maintains that while for the Pharisees, the Galileans were a people perceived to be "ignorant of the law," for the Sadducees, they were "too lax in matters of religious attendance."[19] Third, geographically speaking, Galilee did not occupy a place of honor. "Distance from Jerusalem and daily contact with foreigners were characteristic of the Galilean Jew. The intellectual preoccupation of Jerusalem, with its various schools, hardly reached Galilee."[20] Finally, Elizondo claims that "Galilee was the home of the

---

more personal, purer, simpler, and more spontaneous." See *Galilean Journey*, 52.

[15]Elizondo, *"Mestizaje* as a Locus of Theological Reflection," in *Frontiers of Hispanic Theology in the United States,* 115.

[16]Elizondo, *Galilean Journey*, 51.

[17]Ibid., 107. Emphasis added. See also, *The Future is Mestizo,* 82-86; and John P. Meier, *A Marginal Jew: Rethinking the Historical Jesus,* vol. 1, *The Roots of the Problem and the Person* (New York: Doubleday, 1991), esp. 8-10, 350-352.

[18]Elizondo, *Galilean Journey*, 51.

[19]Ibid.

[20]Ibid., 52.

simple people—that is, of the people of the land, a hardworking people, marginated and oppressed regardless of who was in power or what system of power was in effect."[21]

THE GALILEAN IDENTITY OF JESUS AND ELIZONDO'S THEOLOGICAL VISION OF HUMANITY

For Elizondo, Galilee and the Galileans—the persons with whom Jesus identified, and the place associated with these persons—become the central loci of divine and human revelation. While he understands the *mestizo* identity of the Galileans as the unexpected cultural reality of encountering grace, he sees in their social marginalization a locus for understanding the preferential nature of this encounter. Beyond the latter, Elizondo understands the marginalizing experiences of the Galileans as something that predisposes them to receive God's grace. Elizondo does not condone these experiences. Rather, what he suggests is that such experiences historically condition a person to be more open, or as he states echoing Augustine, to become more "restless" for the presence of God. Thus, he writes:

> The apparent nonimportance and rejection of Galilee are the very bases for its all-important role in the historic eruption of God's saving plan for humanity. The human scandal of God's way does not begin with the cross, but with the historico-cultural incarnation of his Son in Galilee. The Galilean Jews appear to have been despised by all and, because of the mixture of cultures of the area, they were especially despised by the superiority-complexed Jerusalem Jews. Could anything good come out of such an impure, mixed-up, and rebellious area? Yet it is precisely within this area of multiple rejection that the restlessness for liberation and the anxiety for the kingdom of God was the greatest.[22]

The central metaphor "Kingdom of God" offers further clues into Elizondo's theological anthropology. The Kingdom of God not only sets the Christian model for human agency, but also suggests how to map specific socio-cultural landscapes.[23] Elizondo's understanding of the

---

[21]Ibid. On the economic distress and social marginalization of the Galileans, see also, Dean Brackley, *Divine Revolution: Salvation and Liberation in Catholic Thought* (Maryknoll, New York: Orbis Books, 1996), 130-134.

[22]Elizondo, *Galilean Journey*, 53.

[23]Note that contemporary theologians understand the phrase "Kingdom of God" to mean: 1) the activity that God exercises as sovereign, and 2) the spaces ruled by God. In this sense, contemporary theologians have moved away from an understanding of "Kingdom" as a place of divine activity. The purpose of this understanding, however,

Galilean identity of Jesus makes known what the Kingdom is like, and how to enable its presence in this world. The Kingdom entails activity on behalf of, and with, the marginalized. The Kingdom, suggests Elizondo in his observations above, becomes known in the face of "Galileans," and in communities that have embraced socio-cultural mixture, rather than purity.

The Galilean Jesus also offers a model for authentic human freedom. According to Elizondo, Jesus' freedom is not freedom from God, or a self-centered freedom exercised apart from communal ties. Rather, his freedom presupposes a gratuitous union with God *within the kingdoms of this world.*[24] "Intimacy with God is not an escape from the world, but rather a deeper entry into the affairs of the world."[25] Freedom, for the Galilean Jesus, emerges "from" and "within" his identification with the marginalized. "It is important to note," writes Elizondo, "that Jesus does not just *do things for* the poor, but he identifies with them in the most intimate way by being born one of them, learning from them, going to their homes, and eating with them."[26]

For Elizondo, Jesus' identification with the poor necessarily leads to a further development in the history of grace. The Galilean Jesus does not identify with the poor, and learn what their needs are, in order to offer them a spiritualized version of salvation. Rather, the Galilean Jesus tackles the source of their marginalization. Elizondo understands Jesus' "geographical break" with Galilee and the Galileans, and his entry into Jerusalem, as decisive and necessary in the history of grace, the coming of the Kingdom, salvation, and the liberation of persons. For Elizondo, Jesus' move from Galilee to Jerusalem reveals the salvific, liberative, and conflictual nature of the activity of grace in the world. Thus, Elizondo writes:

> Jesus had to attack oppression at its very roots. He had to go to the power structures. For us, Jerusalem stands as the symbol of absolutized power that cloaks the crime of the powerful in multiple ways—and worst of all, it does it in the name of God! Galilee as we have seen, was a marginated region outside the centers of power. The Galilean *has* to go to Jerusalem. It is this very tension between Galilee and Jerusalem that, culturally speaking, appears to be the dynamic core

---

has not been to divorce this activity from the concrete geographical and political landscapes that shape human lives. On the contrary, the very opposite has been the case. For instance, see Brackley, *Divine Revolution: Salvation and Liberation in Catholic Thought*, 125-126.

[24]Elizondo, *Galilean Journey*, 64.
[25]Ibid., 58.
[26]Ibid., 56. Emphasis in original.

of the liberating and salvific 'way of Jesus.' It was not just the death on the cross that was salvific, but the entire way that climaxed on the cross. It is in the conflictual tensions of the way from Galilee to Jerusalem that the full impact of the salvific way of Jesus emerges. It is not so much Jerusalem alone that is the focal point of Jesus' salvific way, as the tension between Galilee (marginal existence) and Jerusalem (established existence).[27]

The "way of Jesus" maps Elizondo's theological anthropology. Where Jesus walked and those with whom he walked offer the model for understanding the ongoing activity of grace. Elizondo's awareness of "what Galilee was and what it meant to be a Galilean so as to discover the places with similar identity and role in today's world"[28] provides the transition from the Jesus of history and the anthropological implications of his being and acting to the historical Jesus of faith and the anthropological implications for "our" ways of being and acting.

To be sure, Elizondo suggests that being like the "Galilean" Jesus today entails, as it did in his time, walking-with the marginalized, walking-within their marginalized spaces, and confronting the structures and persons who marginalize. Jesus' geographical movement from Galilee to Jerusalem and across all human boundaries in his resurrected life maps the activity of grace from past to present.[29] The "where," the "who," and "what" of Jesus' human journey become paradigmatic for all other human ways of being and acting. This logic enables Elizondo to draw a concrete analogy between the socio-cultural location of Mexicans and that of the Galileans.

Elizondo sees Mexican-Americans as contemporary "Galileans." Similar to the Galilean Jews, Elizondo argues that Mexican-Americans undergo rejection as a result of their "mixed" cultural heritage. Elizondo notes the tendencies in the U.S. to polarize issues into black or white, either Latin-American or Anglo-American, either Spanish or English, either Anglo Catholicism or Spanish Catholicism. The latter combines with Mexican-American experiences of poverty and lack of access to political and intellectual centers. These experiences ground Elizondo's justification for drawing an analogy between Mexican-Americans and Galilean Jews. For Elizondo, Mexican-Americans are "borderland rejects," who like the Galilean himself, must lovingly confront the power structures responsible for these injustices.

Elizondo's understanding of Mexican-Americans as contemporary

---

[27]Ibid., 68-69. Emphasis in original.

[28]Ibid., 92.

[29]This movement basically summarizes the three central experiences that define Elizondo's socio-cultural reading of the Gospel identity of Jesus. See *Galilean Journey,* 49-88.

Galileans further exemplifies and historically concretizes the hermeneutics of his theological anthropology. "Jesus," argues Elizondo, "revealed the truth about persons in terms of God and the truth about God in terms of persons."[30] The clue to understanding this truth lies in the Galilean identity of Jesus. This truth, suggests Elizondo, is about the who and where of grace. This truth is also about the consequences of grace. Thus, Elizondo identifies grace with "Galilean" persons and the marginalized places they inhabit. For Elizondo, these persons and places represent privileged loci of salvation.

This truth witnesses to the "worldly" nature of grace. That is, Elizondo's understanding of the Galilean identity of Jesus, which affirms the revelation of what is of God in terms of cultural social experiences, suggests very specific human ways of encountering grace. For Elizondo, these worldly experiences are not "extrinsic" to God's self-revelation. Rather, within Elizondo's thought, they appear as the historical manifestations of the face of God. Jesus' cultural *mestizaje* and his preferential identification with the Galileans exemplify an encounter of grace within a specific socio-culturally defined humanity.

"REDISCOVERING PRAXIS":
AN ANTHROPOLOGY OF ACCOMPANIMENT

Perhaps more than any other U.S. Hispanic voice, Roberto S. Goizueta's writings exemplify theological continuity with and development of the groundbreaking ideas of Virgilio Elizondo. First, like Elizondo, Goizueta also embraces the socio-cultural and geographical location of Jesus as a key "interpretative horizon."[31] Second, similar to Elizondo, Goizueta's approach correlates Jesus' experience with that of U.S. Hispanics. Finally, similar to Elizondo, Goizueta understands history—concrete human experience in their social and cultural constitution—as the very locus of God's self-revelation.[32] Notwithstanding the latter, Goizueta's anthropological contribution to U.S. Hispanic theology differs from Elizondo's. Above all, Goizueta's theology deepens, philosophically speaking, the challenge presented by Elizondo to become aware of "what Galilee was and what it meant to be a Galilean."

A discussion of Goizueta's thought will inevitably run the risk of not fully representing the depth and scope of his contributions to U.S. His-

---

[30]Ibid., 78.

[31]See Goizueta's own discussion of how Jesus (and Mary) serve as "interpretative horizons" for U.S. Hispanic theology. See *Caminemos con Jesús: Toward a Hispanic/ Latino Theology of Accompaniment* (Maryknoll, New York: Orbis Books, 1995), 47 and 191.

[32]See Goizueta, *Caminemos con Jesús*, 191. See also idem, *"Nosotros*: Toward a U.S. Hispanic Anthropology," *Listening: Journal of Religion and Culture* 27/1 (1992): 56.

panic theological anthropology. My objective here is to simply explore his most seminal contribution to U.S. Hispanic theological anthropology, namely, his anthropology of accompaniment. To date, Goizueta's *Caminemos con Jesús: Toward a Hispanic/Latino Theology of Accompaniment*[33] contains the most systematic exposition of this theme. A fourfold set of relationships structures his theological anthropology: 1) the relationship between person and community; 2) the relationship between praxis and aesthetics; 3) the relationship between private and public spaces; and 4) the relationship between the universality and gratuity of God's love, and God's preferential option for the marginalized.

THE RELATIONSHIP BETWEEN PERSON AND COMMUNITY:
"COMMUNITY AS THE BIRTHPLACE OF SELF"

"Community," argues Goizueta, "is the birthplace of self." This premise largely follows from his sacramental understanding of human persons. Persons are particular, concrete, and unique entities that mediate, embody, and reveal a universal reality.[34] Following the philosophical insights of Latin-American philosopher Juan Carlos Scannone, Goizueta argues that each person reflects and distinctly refracts the whole of reality. Goizueta notes that "the subject reflects the communities out of which it was born, yet, as in a prism, that reflection is also a refraction."[35] Ultimately, suggests Goizueta, the human person reflects and uniquely refracts the Triune community of God.[36]

When Goizueta argues that community is the birthplace of self, he does not have an abstract concept of community in mind. Rather, Goizueta intends a very concrete and socio-cultural reality. Given the fact that his focus is mainly on the socio-cultural constitution of the "Hispanic" self, it would perhaps be more accurate for him to speak of *"el pueblo"* as the birthplace of this particular self. In fact, the title of one of his books already suggests this concept.[37] For U.S. Hispanics, *el pueblo* connotes more explicitly the socio-cultural nature of community that Goizueta intends to convey.[38]

The relationship between person and community is not ethically neutral. Goizueta argues that a true family or community is one that enables the person to retain an element of otherness, an element of individual-

---

[33]See Goizueta, *Caminemos con Jesús,* esp. 47-76.

[34]Ibid., 48.

[35]Goizueta, *"Nosotros,"* 57.

[36]Ibid., 66 and 179.

[37]See *We Are a People!: Initiatives in Hispanic American Theology* (Minneapolis: Fortress Press, 1992). Were this book to be in Spanish it would most fittingly be entitled *"Somos el Pueblo."*

[38]This concept traces its root to colonial Spanish Catholicism. *"Pueblo"* has no strict equivalent in English. It refers to both a place and the community of people that embody

ity.[39] Turning to the Spanish word *nosotros*, which denotes "we," yet literally means "we-other," Goizueta argues that this word captures, anthropologically speaking, the intrinsic yet distinct relationship that each person has relative to community.[40] In authentic relationships between persons and communities, persons retain an element of individuality while also reflecting their communal origins.

Perhaps more than his U.S. Hispanic reflections on the communal nature of persons, Goizueta's main contribution has been in his understanding of "relationship." While reflecting the whole of the Christian tradition, his understanding refracts the particular socio-cultural context of U.S. Hispanics. Echoing classical arguments within the Christian tradition, Goizueta maintains that "Each person (precisely *as a* person) is defined and constituted by his or her relationships, both personal and impersonal, natural and supernatural, material and spiritual."[41] Echoing Latin-American liberation theologies, he argues that "Relationship is not something that 'happens to' someone, something one 'experiences' in a passive way, or something one 'possesses'; it is something one *does*, the most basic form of human action since through relationship, we discover and live out our identity as intrinsically relational beings."[42]

The socio-cultural particularity of Goizueta's vision emerges from his understanding of relationship as accompaniment. This understanding mainly stems from his theological articulation of the Hispanic practice of accompanying Jesus during celebrations of the triduum.[43] Goizueta argues that accompaniment is the act of relating that constitutes and defines U.S. Hispanics as persons.[44] For U.S. Hispanics, to be a human being "is to be in relationship with others, and to be in relationship with others is to be 'acompañado.' "[45] Accompaniment implies concreteness, historicity, physicality, dynamism, and directionality.[46] Moreover, Goizueta maintains that the very act of accompaniment implies ethical-political

---

cultural and religious ethos of Spanish Catholicism. Then, being a member of a place, being a member of a community, and being part of a religious tradition and culture were one and the same thing. See Caleb Rosado, "The Concept of *Pueblo* as a Paradigm for Exploring the Religious Experience of Latinos," in *Old Masks, New Faces: Religion and Latino Identities*, ed. Anthony M. Stevens-Arroyo and Gilbert R. Cedena (New York: Bildner Center for Western Hemisphere Studies, 1995), 77-91. See also Gary Riebe-Estrella, "Pueblo and Church," in Díaz and Espín, *From the Heart of Our People: Latino/a Explorations in Catholic Systematic Theology* (Maryknoll, New York: Orbis Books, 1999), 172-188.

[39]Goizueta, *Caminemos con Jesús*, 75.
[40]Goizueta, "Nosotros," 57.
[41]Goizueta, *Caminemos con Jesús*, 50.
[42]Ibid., 72. Emphasis in original.
[43]Ibid., 32-37.
[44]Ibid., 68.
[45]Ibid., 205.
[46]Ibid., 206.

action. For as he argues, implicit in this act are ethical-political questions that seek to establish the "which," "how," and "who" of the direction of this accompaniment.[47]

Goizueta's notion of human freedom follows from his notion of accompaniment. For Goizueta, freedom is not a matter of making individual choices.[48] Such a contractual view reflects the individualistic modern anthropologies that he strongly rejects.[49] Rather, freedom entails the exercise of human creativity, movement, and individuality within authentic familial/communal accompaniment.[50] "Just as community is a prerequisite for individual freedom, so too is individual freedom a prerequisite for community."[51] And freedom is never freedom from the world, but freedom "within" the world, since every act of freedom mediates the socially situated self.[52]

Goizueta's notions of person, community, relationship, and freedom are the building blocks for his anthropology of accompaniment. The philosophical corollary to his notion of accompaniment is his philosophical notion of "aesthetic praxis." This category enables Goizueta to appropriate and reject various modern and post-modern notions of the self.[53] Although indebted to Latin-American philosopher José Vasconcelos (1882-1959), Goizueta's notion of "aesthetic-praxis" avoids the idealized notion of "aesthetic" relationship, which Vasconcelos' vision inevitably reflects. Vasconcelos idealized both the process and the end result that lead to Latin-American *mestizaje*. The process, he argued, resulted from the empathic love relationships between the Spaniards and Amerindians. The end result produced a fifth race, which he saw as the culmination of other races, and the realization of an inclusive humanity.

THE RELATIONSHIP BETWEEN AESTHETICS AND PRAXIS: THE SOCIO-CULTURAL MEDIATION OF "EMPATHIC LOVE"

The second relationship central to understanding Goizueta's anthropology of accompaniment, namely, the relationship between an aesthetic

---

[47]Ibid.

[48]Ibid., 51.

[49]Ibid., 60.

[50]See Roberto S. Goizueta, "United States Hispanic Theology and the Challenge of Pluralism," in *Frontiers of Hispanic Theology in the United States*, 8.

[51]Goizueta, *Caminemos con Jesús*, 76.

[52]Ibid.

[53]In what follows we will see that critics could accuse Goizueta of blurring distinctions among and over-generalizing or caricaturing, modern and post-modern thinkers. Not all moderns, they would argue, instrumentalize human action, and not all post-moderns dehistoricize human action. Besides, such terms remain at best ambiguous. Perhaps Goizueta's thought could benefit from the kind of nuance that his argumentation employs relative to liberation theologians. For instance, see "Rediscovering Praxis: The Significance of U.S. Hispanic Experience for Theological Method," in *We Are a People!*, 61.

and liberative praxis, emerges as a result of his retrieval and critical appropriation of various notions of praxis. Goizueta retrieves Aristotle's notion of life as "action (praxis) and not production (poiesis),"[54] and critiques what he perceives to be "instrumentalist" anthropologies (both Capitalist and Marxist). In his judgment, these anthropologies conflate the Aristotelian distinction between action and production. They reduce life, the human person himself or herself, to an object. Thus, the person becomes a mere means to achieve an end, however noble the material goal or conceptual ideal may be. Goizueta writes:

> If, in capitalism, the life of the worker becomes an object to be manipulated in the service of the commodity, in Marxism the life of the worker becomes an object to be manipulated—even if by the worker himself—in the service of the future "New Person": "his own life is an object for him."[55]

Goizueta argues that "[w]hat neither ideology appreciates is that to make life an object to be worked upon is to instrumentalize life and thus, inevitably, to kill life."[56]

The important point to emphasize is that Goizueta does not completely reject the modern notion of the person as agent. I have already pointed out how his very definition of accompaniment as dynamic "act," rather than static "essence," already accepts an understanding of the human person as agent. What he rejects, however, is an instrumentalist understanding of such agency. As an alternative to the latter, Goizueta turns to Vasconcelos and in continuity with his vision proposes the notion of "aesthetic praxis." Goizueta embraces this notion, in contrast to modern instrumentalist understandings of the self as agent (homo faber), and what he considers to be the post-modern notion of the self as player (homo ludens).[57] Goizueta's "aesthetic-praxis" seeks to bridge prevailing modern and post-modern understandings of the self while at the same time avoiding their dualistic and instrumentalist pitfalls.

For Goizueta, what constitutes "aesthetic praxis" is affective accompaniment, which he understands as an end in itself.[58] Such accompaniment presupposes an embodied and holistic anthropology, since, argues Goizueta, "To relate to another as a person, I must 'fuse' with him or her, that is, we must enter into each other not only as physical bodies . . . but as whole human beings."[59] In appropriating from Vasconcelos this an-

---

[54]Goizueta, "Rediscovering Praxis," 57.

[55]Ibid., 60. See also Goizueta, Caminemos con Jesús, 80-86.

[56]Goizueta, "Rediscovering Praxis," 60.

[57]See Goizueta, Caminemos con Jesús, 137-138. See also his chapter, "Fiesta: Life in the Subjunctive," in Díaz and Espín, From the Heart of Our People, 84-99.

[58]Goizueta, Caminemos con Jesús, 105.

[59]Ibid., 92.

thropological understanding, however, Goizueta is very careful to avoid its idealization. Indeed, for Goizueta, embodiment does not just connote the physical body, but also the social body. The accompaniment of an other, the love of, feeling for, and reception of an other must assume necessarily this other's socio-cultural location. Herein lies Goizueta's strong criticism of Vasconcelos' vision. For Goizueta, aesthetic praxis "must not be seen as a leap *beyond* the ethical-political, as Vasconcelos suggests, but as a leap *into* a life of ethical-political action, *within* which (not 'beyond' which) one discovers the Beautiful."[60]

Goizueta's understanding of U.S. Hispanic *mestizaje* exemplifies this ethical and political understanding of accompaniment. For Goizueta, *mestizaje*, and its liturgical expression in U.S. Hispanic popular Catholicism,[61] represents an "aesthetic-praxis." As expected, given his critique of Vasconcelos' vision, this aesthetic-praxis does not merely involve empathic relationships among persons of different races and cultures.[62] Such an aesthetic falls into what Goizueta characterizes as "a naive cultural romanticism, or 'mestizolatry.' "[63] Rather, Goizueta argues that *mestizaje* always involves socio-economic and political mediation, since, he argues, "All human praxis is as inescapably socioeconomic and political as it is cultural."[64]

Goizueta underscores the concrete socio-cultural mediation of aesthetics, that is, the empathic love for an other. Behind the latter lies his sacramental and philosophical premise that affirms the particular as mediator of the universal. Goizueta, however, protects himself against individualistic and self-enclosed understandings of this premise. Indeed, as much as Goizueta underscores the contextual or particular mediation of love, he equally underscores the need for the particular to transcend itself, to be open to other particular mediations of empathic love. Thus, Goizueta affirms that "If human praxis is indeed, intrinsically relational, or intersubjective, then it is also intrinsically open to self-transcendence, or universality." That openness, continues Goizueta, "presupposes an intellectual, as well as an affective and ethical-political openness beyond one's particular experience."[65]

---

[60]Goizueta, *"La raza cósmica?* The Vision of Vasconcelos," *Journal of Hispanic/ Latino Theology* 1/2 (1994): 24. Emphasis in original. See also idem, *Caminemos con Jesús*, 121-126.

[61]"If Latino culture is defined by an aesthetic mestizaje, popular religion is the liturgical form of that mestizaje." Goizueta, *Caminemos con Jesús*, 132.

[62]Note how Goizueta criticizes Hans Urs von Balthasar's theological aesthetics because it is not rooted in concrete socio-historical praxis. See *Caminemos con Jesús*, note 36; see also idem, "U.S. Hispanic Popular Catholicism as Theopoetics," in *Hispanic/Latino Theology: Challenge and Promise*, ed. Ada María Isasi-Díaz and Fernando F. Segovia (Minneapolis: Fortress Press, 1996), 267, note 21.

[63]Goizueta, *"La raza cósmica,"* 6.

[64]Ibid., 25.

[65]Goizueta, *Caminemos con Jesús*, 152.

THE RELATIONSHIP BETWEEN PUBLIC AND PRIVATE SPACES:
THE PRIVATE AS A LOCUS OF AESTHETIC PRAXIS

An aesthetic vision, such as that of Goizueta, which takes socio-economic and political mediations of the self very seriously, must also consider the concrete places where such mediation occurs, since human persons by definition are spatial beings. Goizueta is very mindful of the relationship between public and private places, and of its anthropological implications. Goizueta sees as a consequence of "the modern instrumentalization of human action . . . the exclusion of domestic life, as an end in itself, from the sphere of human action."[66] Thus, the modern reductionistic understanding of the human person as an agent of history (*homo faber*), and the identification of such agency with public places, leaves little room for the home. Home is the place of feeling, aesthetics, and empathic love, the public is the place of production and accomplishment. Goizueta observes:

> . . . to be a human being is to participate in public life because that is the locus of production. Conversely, domestic life and its "private" relationships are not only depreciated but, indeed excluded from the notion of human praxis altogether: since what makes one's life "human" is one's public accomplishments, one's family or "personal" life is ultimately irrelevant to the understanding of human action or the human person. Only in public does a person "make" history; what he or she does in the home is ultimately outside the realm of human history, and therefore insignificant, except insofar as the home life supports the person's public, productive achievements.[67]

This reductionistic notion of the human person as an agent of production and the understanding of where such production takes place have implications relative to the marginalization of women, elderly, and children, since these persons are commonly, and oftentimes stereotypically, associated with "private" places conceived to be unable to contribute to the making of history. For Goizueta, domestic life mirrors the instrumentalist anthropology present within "public" spaces. Goizueta argues that the "separation between private and public realms merely masks the underlying reduction of domestic life itself to but a form of poiesis, or production; the instrumentalization of the worker in the market place is replicated in the instrumentalization of women in the home."[68]

Consistent with his anthropological vision that bridges aesthetics (em-

---

[66]Ibid., 111.
[67]Ibid., 112.
[68]Ibid., 114.

pathic relationships) and ethics (political and economic relationships), Goizueta understands public and private spaces as "distinct though intrinsically interrelated dimensions of human praxis."[69] The private is not a mere extension of the public, but, avers Goizueta, "[r]elationships in the family always take place within and are, thus, conditioned by socioeconomic structures and relationships. . . . "[70] The private, to borrow Goizueta's anthropological metaphor, "accompanies" the public (and vice versa). Just as private relationships (particular) presuppose public relationships (universal), so do public relationships presuppose private ones.

The Relationship between the Universality and Gratuity of God's Love, and God's Preferential Option for the Marginalized

How Goizueta relates what is Hispanically human to God provides the final, and undoubtedly most important relationship, that determines his theological anthropology. Similar to Elizondo, Goizueta embraces a universal, yet particular or more precisely, preferential understanding of grace. For Goizueta, God's accompaniment of humanity, God's love of, feeling for, and reception of us as "other," is mediated by the face of the marginalized, especially the socio-culturally marginalized. Goizueta grounds this preferential understanding of grace, not in the marginalized and the poor, but rather in God's very self. Goizueta suggests that the birthing forth of authentic community, which reflects ultimately the communal nature of God,[71] requires the presence of God's action (grace) to be located preferentially (not exclusively) among those who lie outside community. God's love or grace, insists Goizueta, "must" take the side of the marginalized.[72] To be in the image of God is to overcome the exclusion of the marginalized.

The communal life of God is intrinsically open to all. The life of God as any "authentic community is inclusive not exclusive; it is, of essence, open to 'the other' as a unique human person."[73] This universal openness requires a "scandalous" and "preferential" accompaniment of those who have been excluded from community. "God's grace," writes Goizueta, "is associated not with barriers and gates but with bridges and thoroughfares . . . not with 'staying in one's proper place' but with 'spilling over' . . . not with the 'closed and deadened spaces of the suburbs' but with the 'messy and open qualities of heterogeneous urban spaces.' "[74] Consistent

---

[69]Ibid., 117.

[70]Ibid., 116.

[71]Goizueta characterizes the Trinity as "the theological symbol for the intrinsically and constitutively communal character of God. See *Caminemos con Jesús*, 66.

[72]Ibid., 176.

[73]Ibid., 201.

[74]Ibid., 203.

with his intent to preference the spaces that have been undermined by modernity, Goizueta's theology of grace locates God's "aesthetic-praxis" preferentially in the homes and barrios where the poor reside. Echoing the Galilean challenge of Jesus, Goizueta concludes: "To walk with Jesus is thus to walk with the wrong persons in the wrong places."[75]

AN ANTHROPOLOGY OF CULTURAL HUMANIZATION

While Goizueta's interests lie primarily in "rediscovering" an anthropology of praxis through his theology of accompaniment, Orlando O. Espín has been mainly concerned with rediscovering a Latino/a theology of grace by underscoring the importance of socio-cultural humanization. Though in some of his later reflections on grace, Espín has given more attention to socio-economic aspects, hence what he terms "the socialized experience of the divine,"[76] Espín's essay, "Grace and Humanness: A Hispanic Perspective,"[77] to date reflects the most systematic exposition and appropriation of this classical Christian theme.

CULTURE AS THE "WOMB" OF PERSONHOOD

According to Espín, culture is an historically, socially, and geographically situated reality wherein persons are born and sustained. He describes culture as the "womb from which there is no birth, because we are already born into it."[78] But culture does not merely birth human persons. Culture is also the product of life. For Espín, culture is "the dynamic sum of all that a human group does and materially and symbolically creates in order to prolong its life in history within geographical contexts."[79] Thus, culture is not a static human reality that never changes, but a dynamic process of socialization. Intrinsically connected to persons, as their birthing context, expression, and creation, culture can be, as is the case of persons themselves, described but never fully categorized.

Because human beings are historical, no one person, argues Espín, is "ever outside of culture."[80] Unlike a coat or jacket, culture cannot be put

---

[75]Ibid., 191.

[76]See Espín, "Popular Catholicism: Alienation or Hope," in *The Faith of the People: Theological Reflections on Popular Catholicism* (Maryknoll, New York: Orbis Books, 1997), 92-96, and his "An Exploration into the Theology of Grace and Sin," in *From the Heart of Our People*, 121-52.

[77]See Espín, "Grace and Humanness: A Hispanic Perspective," in *We Are a People!*, 133-163.

[78]Espín, "Grace and Humanness," 143. See also his "A 'Multicultural' Church? Theological Reflections from 'Below,' " in *The Multicultural Church: A New Landscape in U.S. Theologies*, ed. W. Cenkner (Mahwah, N.J.: Paulist Press, 1995), 54-71.

[79]Espín, "Grace and Humanness," 143.

[80]Ibid., 142.

on and off; culture essentially constitutes us as humans. Culture provides a lens through which we perceive, learn, and understand ourselves and those around us. We "see" events and "live through" experiences as cultural beings.[81] "What is commonly catalogued in our society as 'human,' as 'experience,' and as 'God,' " writes Espín, "is all culturally allowed."[82]

For Espín, human persons "become" more fully that which they already are (images of the Triune God), in and through culture.[83] Espín calls this process humanization.[84] Conversely, Espín associates deculturalization with sin. This does not mean, however, that Espín idealizes cultural expressions. Thus, while Espín underscores familial and communal relationships as essential in understanding a "Hispanically" situated process of humanization,[85] he acknowledges the presence of ideological elements within these relationships (for instance, the machismo and the stereotyping of women as mothers, which prevail in U.S. Hispanic culture).[86]

Espín's understanding of culture partly resembles what Robert Schreiter has characterized as an integrated concept of culture.[87] Espín's understanding is also partly influenced by post-colonial critical theories of culture.[88] With respect to U.S. Hispanic communal issues, Espín appears to stress an integral approach. The latter is made evident by his emphasis on cultural identity as the womb of personhood, and the locus for encountering the mediation of grace. With respect to issues relative to the relationship between U.S. Hispanic cultures and the more "mainstream" U.S. cultural experiences, Espín appears to hold a post-modern understanding of U.S. Hispanic culture. The latter accords well with Schreiter's post-modern characterization of the fragmentation experienced by minority groups and the way such groups disrupt "the homogeneous narratives of the powerful."[89]

The cultural face of grace. Echoing Karl Rahner's Christocentric anthropology that underscores human reality as a symbol of the Logos,

---

[81]Espín, "The God of the Vanquished: Foundations for a Latino Spirituality," in *The Faith of the People*, 17.

[82]Ibid.

[83]Espín, "Grace and Humanness," 139 and 145.

[84]Ibid., 139.

[85]Ibid., 154.

[86]Ibid., 150.

[87]According to Schreiter, integrated concepts of culture understand culture "as patterned systems in which the various elements are coordinated in such a fashion as to create a unified whole." Schreiter goes on to observe that in such an understanding wisdom is valued above analysis and harmony above differentiation. See his *The New Catholicity: Theology between the Global and the Local* (Maryknoll, New York: Orbis Books, 1997), 47-53.

[88]On post-modern theories of culture and their theological importance see Kathryn Tanner, *Theories of Culture: A New Agenda for Theology* (Minneapolis: Fortress Press, 1997), esp. 38-92.

[89]See Schreiter, *The New Catholicity*, 51-54.

Espín argues that "human beings are that which God is when God expresses God's self outside of the sphere of the divine."[90] Since what is
human is necessarily historical, and since no historical being is ever
acultural,[91] Espín's argument suggests that grace has a cultural face. God's
self expression, argues Espín, is necessarily cultural because "we" ourselves are cultural.[92] Moreover, since cultures differ, so will the experience
of grace. Espín argues that "the experience of grace possible to U.S. Hispanics, in order to be authentically an experience of the *God-for-us* must
be culturally Hispanic."[93]

For Espín, authentic humanization, therefore implies, if we may be
allowed the expression, the experience of "grace as in-cultured." Again,
Espín does not argue that every cultural experience is graced. That would
ignore the sinfulness that necessarily accompanies humanity, and culture
as its matrix and creation. What Espín does affirm, however, is that because we are essentially cultural beings, we must, therefore, experience
grace in cultural ways. Thus Espín writes,

> If the ultimate will of God for us is that we become that which we are
> from creation (that is, truly human, images of the God who is love),
> then this divine will must include our cultural dimension, since we
> cannot be human without culture. Or put another way, it must be the
> will of God that each of us humanize him or herself in the manner in
> which we are humans, and that manner is specifically cultural.[94]

The U.S. Hispanic face of grace. A number of U.S. Hispanic theologians have explored specific cultural experiences and suggested ways by
which the latter mediate the presence of grace. For instance, Espín himself argues that "Whatever else can be said about a Hispanic understanding of what it means to be human, this necessarily must include the familial and communal dimensions."[95] Like Goizueta, Espín contrasts the
communal and familial anthropology of U.S. Hispanics with what he
characterizes as a prevailing "Anglo-style individualism."[96] Espín suggests that the former anthropology, as opposed to the latter, is more trans-
parent to, more capable of mediating a Christian understanding of grace.
In this sense, Espín's notion of U.S. Hispanic culture can be seen as a dis-

---

[90]Espín, "Grace and Humanness," 138. On Rahner's theology of symbol, see chapter four.

[91]Ibid., 142.

[92]Ibid. 145.

[93]Ibid., 147. Emphasis added.

[94]Ibid.

[95]Ibid., 154. On the importance of family within U.S. Hispanic culture see Virgilio
Elizondo, *Christianity and Culture* (Huntington: Our Sunday Visitor, 1975), 158-164;
and D.T. Abalos, *Latinos in the United States: The Sacred and the Political* (Notre
Dame: University of Notre Dame Press, 1986), 62-80.

[96]Espín, "Grace and Humanness," 154.

ruption of what he perceives to be the prevalent narrative of society, a narrative that he implies has been constructed upon the ideal of individualism.[97]

Espín's more explicit theological understanding of the U.S. Hispanic emphasis on familial and communal relationships comes in his metaphorical use of Trinity. For Espín, "Trinity" stands for the intrinsic relationship that exists between oneness and community, divine unity and solidarity with an other. Espín argues that trust of an other and solidarity with that same other are the "pillars" that constitute the unity of any authentic family or community.[98] Similarly, Christian tradition has understood communal solidarity as a necessary dimension of the very unity or oneness of God. For Espín, familial trust and solidarity with an other—love of neighbor—are pillars that stem from and image the very life of God. As he goes on to affirm, "the need to love God and the need to love neighbor are intimately linked at the depth of our being human because oneness and community are unconditionally linked in God." [99]

A very different cultural approach to the mediation of grace is provided by the post-modern reflections of Fernando F. Segovia. For Segovia, what is "Hispanically" human derives from the fundamental U.S. Hispanic cultural experience of being an "other," being an exile.[100] Segovia characterizes this experience as that of being "in two worlds and yet of none," an experience of being "at home in two cultures and in neither one."[101] The exile is someone for whom "belonging" and "otherness" have become "thoroughly intertwined."[102] This exile or diaspora experience results, according to Segovia, in a very conflictual and ambiguous understanding of this world and of the otherworld.

The world of the exile is a world deeply divided between a fatalistic resignation to experience injustice and an equally hope-filled and "irrepressible thirst for well-being and justice."[103] For Segovia, the latter experience mediates at best an ambiguous experience of grace. Thus, Segovia conceives the other world of the exile as "transcendent, yet clearly immanent."[104] The God of the exile is someone who "seems not to bother" but

---

[97]Compare with Schreiter, *The New Catholicity*, 54.

[98]Espín, "Grace and Humanness," 154-155.

[99]Ibid., 157.

[100]Segovia's theological anthropology can be basically drawn from the following three essays: "Two Places and No Place on Which to Stand: Mixture and Otherness in Hispanic Theology," *Journal of Religion and Culture* 27/1 (1992): 26-40; idem, "Toward a Hermeneutics of the Diaspora: A Hermeneutics of Otherness and Engagement," in *Reading from This Place: Social Location and Biblical Interpretation in the United States*, ed. Fernando F. Segovia and Mary Ann Tolbert (Minneapolis: Fortress Press, 1995), 57-73; and idem, "In the World But Not of It: Exile as Locus for a Theology of the Diaspora," in *Hispanic/Latino Theology: Challenge and Promise*, 195-217.

[101]Segovia, "In the World But Not of It," 212.

[102]Ibid., 203.

[103]Ibid., 213-213.

[104]Ibid., 215.

"who must be bothered and does bother."[105] The relationship that exists between the world and the otherworld follows this same exilic vision. Segovia writes:

> The relationship between world and otherworld, humans and God, thus forged in exile is a relationship of absence and presence, uncertainty and certainty, limitation and power. It is a relationship built on sustained unreliability yet proven commitment. Such is the human-divine relationship that emerges out of my diaspora: a profoundly ambiguous relationship vis-à-vis God in the world—a relationship that often despairs of bothering with the otherworld and yet looks upon such bother as both essential and dependable.[106]

Yet another face of U.S. Hispanic culture is found in the reflections of Allan Figueroa Deck and Jaime Vidal. Focusing on issues of communication these two theologians provide complementary descriptions of U.S. Hispanic culture. Following the cultural anthropology of Walter Ong, Deck characterizes U.S. Hispanic culture as a premodern culture of orality. Deck argues that in oral cultures, communication is always embodied "in the teachings of elders, in art, music, and popular refrains."[107] Deck maintains that such forms of communication presuppose a communal rather than an individualistic anthropology.[108]

Similarly, but drawing on the anthropological insights of Edward Hall, Vidal argues for a high contextual understanding of Hispanic culture. By "high context" Vidal means a culture that is interested not only in the "what" of one's expression, but more importantly, the "how" of one's expression. "The high context person or group," writes Vidal, "will not assimilate the message, or be motivated to act on it, on the strength of the words alone; if they are to be effective, the words must be wrapped in a matrix of tone, emphasis, gesture (facial and bodily), body contact, etc."[109]

While the reflections of Deck and Vidal do not explicitly contain a theology of grace, their arguments are indispensable for understanding what Espín characterizes as that which is "Hispanically" human. What their reflections invite us to consider is that given the "highly contextual"

---

[105]Ibid., 216.

[106]Ibid., 216.

[107]Allan Figueroa Deck, "A Pox on Both Your Homes," in *Being Right: Conservative Catholics in America*, ed. Mary Jo Weaver and R. Scott Appleby (Bloomington: Indiana University Press, 1995), 97.

[108]Ibid., 98. See also, idem, *The Second Wave: Hispanic Ministry and the Evangelization of Cultures* (New York: Paulist Press, 1989), 34-48.

[109]Jaime Vidal, "Popular Religion among the Hispanics in the General Area of the Archdiocese of Newark," in *Presencia Nueva: Knowledge for Service and Hope, A Study of Hispanics in the Archdiocese of Newark* (Newark: Office of Research and Planning, 1988), 258.

nature of U.S. Hispanics, U.S. Hispanic theologies of grace must not only take seriously the Hispanic "what" and "where" of grace, but also the "how" and "who" of grace. In other words, it is not enough to simply explore what grace is and where we find its presence. The holistic nature of U.S. Hispanic anthropology demands attentiveness to the forms that embody grace: the persons, the symbols, the celebrations, the music, the dances, and the oft-cited aphorisms of U.S. Hispanic experience. The aesthetic component of U.S. Hispanic theological anthropology is something that most U.S. Hispanic theologians readily recognize.

AN ANTHROPOLOGY OF *LA LUCHA*

U.S. Hispanic experience, or more precisely, the "lived-experience" of Latina women is the starting point for understanding Ada María Isasi-Díaz's contribution to U.S. Hispanic theological anthropology. For Isasi-Díaz "lived experience" concerns not only "what a person has endured or made happen" but most importantly, what a person has reflected upon in his or her attempt to seek self-understanding and self-agency.[110] To be sure, Isasi-Díaz situates the process that leads to Latina questioning and self-understanding within the embrace of grace. As she argues, "Because of the centrality of religion in the day-to-day life of Hispanic Women, our understandings about the divine and about questions of ultimate meaning play a very important role in the process of giving significance to and valuing our experience."[111]

Isasi-Díaz's understanding of the "lived-experience" of Latina women can be primarily explored through what she terms "an anthropology of *la lucha* (the struggle)." For Isasi-Díaz, "An anthropology developed out of the lived-experience of Latinas, centers on a subject who struggles to survive and who understands herself as one who struggles."[112] The primary source for this anthropological vision, argues Isasi-Díaz, is the ordinary question, "How are you?" and the Latina response, "*Ahí, en la lucha*" ("There in the struggle.").[113]

As an alternative to a Christian anthropology that would highlight the value of suffering, Isasi-Díaz offers this anthropology of *la lucha*. "To consider suffering as what locates us," she affirms, "would mean that we understand ourselves not as moral subject but as one acted upon by the oppressors."[114] For Isasi-Díaz, anthropology has to do with praxis. What concretely defines this praxis is the struggle for Latinas' self-determination and self-definition:

---

[110]Ada María Isasi-Díaz, *En la Lucha/In the Struggle: Elaborating a Mujerista Theology* (Minneapolis: Fortress Press, 1993), 73.

[111]Ibid.

[112]Ibid., 168.

[113]Ibid.

[114]Ibid.

As long as our voices are not heard, as long as the role we play in history is not recognized and its specificity is not appreciated, we will not be able to become full moral agents, full persons in our own right. This is why we insist that a *mujerista* anthropology has to center on Hispanic women as human beings in time and history; it is an anthropology "from within" and "from below." It recognizes that anthropology is not about an idealized type of humanity or about an abstract understanding of humanity, but that anthropology rises out of a context. Since Latinas are an intrinsic part of that context, our self-understanding cannot be ignored.[115]

Isasi-Díaz's anthropology of struggle has much in common with Latin-American liberation anthropologies. Similar to Latin-American theologians, Isasi-Díaz understands praxis to include the following: 1) the socio-historical constitution of persons; 2) the intersubjective nature of human reality; and 3) the creative capacity for humans to "shape" reality so as to attain liberation.[116] As a result of her focus on gender and her distinct socio-cultural location, however, Isasi-Díaz's anthropology differs from Latin-American anthropologies.

First and most importantly, unlike most Latin-American liberation theologies, Isasi-Díaz emphasizes the relationship between the social construction of the self and the intentional choosing of ethnic identity. "The ethnic identification of any given person is not necessarily a constant," she argues, "but a dynamic self-understanding and self-identification that can vary over time."[117] She understands *mestizaje*, an experience that embraces human difference. This experience she sees as being essential in Latina/o self-understanding and self-constitution. Parting ways with most U.S. Hispanic theologians, she understands this socio-cultural experience not as a given, but rather as a cultural experience that Latinos/as must opt for in their struggle for self-identity and liberation.[118]

Isasi-Díaz's anthropology is primarily concerned to address issues related to the continuity and survival of cultural identity. "Survival has to do with the struggle *to be* fully."[119] For Isasi-Díaz, "being designates existence in time and space; it means physical survival, and it means cultural survival, which depends to a large extent on self-determination and

[115]Ada María Isasi-Díaz, "Elements of a *Mujerista* Anthropology," in *Mujerista Theology: A Theology for the Twenty-First Century* (Maryknoll, New York: Orbis Books, 1996), 133.

[116]For a discussion of these three dimensions in Latin-American theological anthropologies see Stephen J. Duffy, *The Dynamics of Grace: Perspectives in Theological Anthropology* (Collegeville: The Liturgical Press, 1993), 354.

[117]Isasi-Díaz, *En la Lucha*, 11.

[118]Ibid., 186-204. See also, Isasi-Díaz, "*Mujerista* Theology: A Challenge to Traditional Theology," in *Mujerista Theology*, 79-82.

[119]Isasi-Díaz, *En la Lucha*, 16.

self-identity."[120] Because they suffer multiple forms of oppression, the cultural survival of Latina women must include the struggle against personal and social, physical and the non-physical forms of oppression.[121] Survival, argues Isasi-Díaz, requires the struggle against classism, ethnic prejudice, and sexism, which Isasi-Díaz claims threaten the "very existence" of U.S. Latinas.[122] Perhaps, nowhere does she exemplify better this threefold oppression than in her discussions on the sexual objectification, cultural negation, and labor exploitation of Latina bodies.[123]

Second, whereas Latin-American theologians understand praxis as the ground for reflection, that is, praxis is first, reflection is second,[124] Isasi-Díaz wants to hold these two aspects of theological discourse in closer tension. Fearing that human praxis itself would not be seen as inherently reflective or rational, she argues that "Praxis is both intellectual enterprise as well as action. . . . "[125] Thus, what defines Isasi-Díaz's anthropology is not simply intentional action, but rather intentional "critical and reflective action" that struggles to transform society and liberate Latina women from socio-cultural forms of oppression.[126]

Third, whereas for most Latin-American liberation theologians, "public" spaces and "social" relationships provide the locus for realizing the intersubjective nature of praxis, like Goizueta, Isasi-Díaz underscores the importance of ordinary life experiences *(lo cotidiano)*. *Lo cotidiano* is not something that shapes and describes the lives of Latinas a priori. In other words, it is not a metaphysical reality into which Latinas fit their daily life.[127] Nor is *lo cotidiano* intended to be an abstract and purely intellectual category. Rather, starting from the concrete and experiential level, Isasi-Díaz affirms daily ordinary experiences as the theological locus that unveils who Latinas are, and who they become. Because these daily experiences often involve oppression and marginalization, *lo cotidiano*, she argues, constitutes Latina women's social location from the "underside of history."[128]

---

[120]Ibid.

[121]Ibid., 17.

[122]Ibid., 16.

[123]For instance, see Isasi-Díaz, "Elements of a *Mujerista* Anthropology," 143.

[124]Note Gustavo Gutiérrez's argument: "Theology is reflection, a critical attitude. Theology *follows;* it is the second step. What Hegel used to say about philosophy can likewise be applied to theology: it rises only at sundown." See Gutiérrez, *A Theology of Liberation: History, Politics, and Salvation* (Maryknoll, New York: Orbis Books, 1988), 9.

[125]Isasi-Díaz, *En la Lucha*, 170.

[126]Note that this understanding of praxis as primarily "reflective action" in the service of liberation comes dangerously close to the instrumentalist notion that Goizueta's anthropology of "aesthetic-praxis" seeks to critique. See pp. 35 ff., above.

[127]Isasi-Díaz, "*Mujerista* Theology," 67.

[128]Ibid., 69.

In spite of these differences, Isasi-Díaz's anthropology of human struggle reflects liberationist ways of relating salvation and liberation, reign of God and social realities, love of God and love of neighbor. Her specific socio-cultural vision enables her to do a critical appropriation of these central themes found in most Christian theological anthropologies. Her understanding of the relationship between Latinas' historical project and the reign of God, and her understanding of charity as solidarity are central in understanding this appropriation.

LATINAS' HISTORICAL PROJECT AND THE "KIN-DOM" OF GOD

Isasi-Díaz uses the term *proyecto histórico* to refer to Latinas' struggle for "liberation and the historical specifics needed to attain it."[129] As the word "project" suggests, Isasi-Díaz has been influenced by post-Enlightenment anthropologies that stress the human capacity for self-making.[130] Indeed, as pointed out above, Isasi-Díaz's anthropology is one that underscores persons, and more specifically Latina women, as historical agents engaged in the process of self-determination and liberation, and the struggle to preserve cultural identity (hence, the importance Isasi-Díaz places on the Spanish language and Latinas' popular religion).[131]

While critics could charge that Isasi-Díaz overemphasizes the human side of the equation (struggle for preservation of self-identity and liberation from oppressive experiences) and underemphasizes the divine side (the grace needed to attain that same liberation and self identity), in fairness to Isasi-Díaz it is important to point out how she rejects what she calls "false notions" or dualistic ways of relating the spiritual and historical, the body and the soul, liberation and salvation, and the like. As the title of her essay "To Struggle for Justice Is to Pray" suggests, she takes for granted the intrinsic relation between grace and history.[132]

Isasi-Díaz exemplifies her close link to Latin-American liberation theologies by arguing that Latinas' *proyecto histórico* "is based on an understanding of salvation and liberation as two aspects of one process." Isasi-Díaz correlates Latinas' *proyecto histórico* (liberation) with the coming of the "kin-dom," (salvation). To avoid the error of conflating the two realities, she draws on traditional dialectical models and argues that historical events are, and are not, the "kin-dom."

While the historical project of Latinas "forces options" and envisions the creation of a different social order, this project, even if fully realized, is not *the* "kin-dom." This project, though intrinsically related to the liberation and salvation of Latinas (in so far as it prompts a multifaceted

---

[129]Isasi-Díaz, *En la Lucha*, 34.
[130]See Goizueta, *Caminemos con Jesús*, 85.
[131]See Isasi-Díaz, *En la Lucha*, 45-54.
[132]In *Mujerista Theology*, 29-34.

denunciation of and change relative to all that oppresses them),[133] remains an historically limited event. At most, the project provides "eschatological glimpses" which Isasi-Díaz considers to be *part of the unfolding of the kin-dom which we do not make happen* but which requires us to take responsibility for making justice a reality in our world."[134]

For Isasi-Díaz, *mestizaje* provides a culturally rooted "eschatological glimpse" of this gender-inclusive community ("kin-dom" of God) that "is" within worldly experiences, and yet "is still" to come. [135] As "the going forward of humankind," *mestizaje* represents a way of relating among distinct communities that "necessarily precludes" the subordination of one community to another.[136] Again, Isasi-Díaz does not understand this socio-cultural experience as a given. Rather, it is a way of relating that must be chosen in response to grace. As a moral option, *mestizaje* envisions a community founded upon diversity and human differences.[137] As a communal image *mestizaje* is par excellence, an Hispanic social image of the activity of grace.

CHARITY AS SOLIDARITY

Reinterpreting the meaning of Christian charity, Isasi-Díaz considers solidarity as the true meaning of charity, and the *"sine qua non* of salvation."[138] Though her socio-cultural methodology forbids any ontological connotations, her use of terms such as "mandate" and "commandment" reveal the ethical imperative she gives to solidarity. In fact, it would be reasonable to conclude that Isasi-Díaz would not hesitate to affirm that the way human persons image who God is, is through solidarity with neighbor. In so doing, persons receive and actively live out their salvation. Isasi-Díaz writes:

> From a Christian perspective the goal of solidarity is to participate in the ongoing process of liberation through which we Christians become a significantly positive force in the unfolding of the 'kin-dom' of God. At the center of the unfolding of the kin-dom is the salvific act of God. Salvation and liberation are interconnected.

[133]Isasi-Díaz, *En la Lucha*, 36-37.
[134]Ibid., 35. Emphasis added.
[135]Note the use of the word "kin-dom" as opposed to "kingdom." For Isasi-Díaz, the term "kin-dom" connotes both gender inclusivity and familial ties. Thus she writes: "The word 'kin-dom' makes it clear that when the fullness of God becomes a day-to-day reality in the world at large, we will all be sisters and brothers—kin to each other; we will indeed be the family of God." See *Mujerista Theology*, 103, n.8.
[136]Ibid., 15. See also, Elizondo, *Galilean Journey*, 124.
[137]Isasi-Díaz, "*Mujerista* Theology," 81.
[138]Isasi-Díaz, "Solidarity: Love of Neighbor in the Twenty-First Century," in *Mujerista Theology*, 88.

Salvation is gratuitously given by God; it flows from the very essence of God: love. Salvation is worked out through the love between God and each human being and among human beings. This love relationship is the goal of all life—it constitutes the fullness of humanity. Therefore, love sets in motion and sustains the ongoing act of God's salvation in which each person necessarily participates, since love requires, per se, active involvement of those who are in relationship.[139]

For Isasi-Díaz, solidarity is a "reflective-action," which in response to grace, is both humanizing and salvific. Solidarity has to do with understanding patterns of oppression and fostering "cohesiveness" among communities that struggle to overcome such patterns.[140] Solidarity is "a union of kindred persons . . . grounded in 'common responsibilities and interests' which necessarily arouse shared feelings and lead to joint action."[141] Charity as solidarity requires active relationship and participation in the life of an other. Charity as solidarity echoes the Latin-American conviction that the love of neighbor is a precondition for knowing and loving God, and the ongoing activity that constitutes us as human persons.[142]

AN ANTHROPOLOGY OF EGALITARIAN AND EMBODIED GENDER RELATIONSHIPS

María Pilar Aquino, like Isasi-Díaz, has been interested in questions that address the socially generated "non-personhood" of Latinas, and their multi-level struggle for liberation (e.g., relative to class, race, and gender).[143] Arguing against subordinationist, androcentric, dualistic, idealistic, and uni-dimensional anthropologies, Aquino proposes an egalitarian or "dialogical" anthropology that underscores a human-centered, unitarian, realistic, and multi-dimensional approach to human reality. Aquino seeks an understanding of the human reality that does not suffocate women but allows their fulfillment. Following Karl Rahner, she argues that because theology expresses a person's self-understanding in relation to God's mystery . . . theology implies an anthropology."[144] For Aquino, that anthropology must be ultimately rooted in "the fundamental structure of revelation as dialogical—one of mutuality (the I-thou of

---

[139]Ibid., 89.

[140]Ibid.

[141]Ibid.

[142]Ibid. See also Gustavo Gutiérrez, *A Theology of Liberation*, 110-116.

[143]María Pilar Aquino, *Our Cry for Life: Feminist Theology from Latin America* (Maryknoll, New York: Orbis Books, 1993), 37.

[144]Ibid., 83.

God's self-communication to humanity: women and men and both to each other)."[145]

Rejecting subordinationist anthropologies, Aquino argues for a human-centered approach that places both men and women at the center of history.[146] In theological support of the latter, she argues for an inclusive understanding of the Incarnation. "Through the incarnation," writes Aquino, "all human flesh is assumed in God so that it becomes God's temple and dwelling place. . . . "[147] Rejecting dualistic anthropologies, Aquino embraces a unitarian anthropology that bridges material and spiritual realities. Following Ivone Gebara, Aquino argues that the human person is "inseparably material and spiritual."[148] This unitarian anthropology leads her to affirm a singular understanding of history (sacred and profane),[149] and an inclusive understanding of nature (human as well as other creaturely nature).[150]

Rejecting idealistic and uni-dimensional understandings of the human person, that would either deny the complexity of the human condition (conflicts, contradictions, and contingencies) or reduce the human to "essentialist" definitions, Aquino embraces a realistic and multi-dimensional anthropology, deeply rooted in historical experiences.[151] Although Aquino emphatically affirms that "persons are not just an idea or definition, but historical faces marked by space and time,"[152] she rejects what she characterizes as the "neo-liberal anthropological view," which envisions the competitive individual as the basis for all social structure.[153] Thus, Aquino takes a critical approach to history; she does not embrace all human experience as capable of revealing the dialogical nature of Christian anthropology.

Aquino's anthropology also carries implications not only relative to the "what" but also relative to the "where" of personhood. First, Aquino's unitarian vision, which affirms the intrinsic unity between both spiritual and material reality, presupposes embodiment since, as Aquino herself argues, "This (the body) is where the human person does both spiritual

---

[145]Ibid.

[146]For a linguistic manifestation of this subordination see Aquino's arguments against the generic use of the "masculine" in the Spanish language in her article "Including Women's Experience: A Latina Feminist Perspective," in *In the Embrace of God: Feminist Approaches to Theological Anthropology*, ed. Ann O'Hara Graff (Maryknoll, New York: Orbis Books, 1995), 53.

[147]Aquino, *Our Cry for Life*, 86.

[148]Ibid., 87.

[149]Ibid.

[150]See Aquino, "Doing Theology from the Perspective of Latin American Women," in *We Are a People!*, 79.

[151]Aquino, *Our Cry for Life*, 88-89.

[152]Ibid., 89.

[153]María Pilar Aquino, "Directions and Foundations of Hispanic Theology," *Journal of Hispanic/Latino Theology* 1/1 (1993): 15.

and material things and nowhere else." Second, her insistence upon the fact that it is often women's faces, women's bodies that constitute the "underside of history" suggests her preferential and engendered approach. Indeed, for Aquino, history has irrupted into "women's life and consciousness" and into the places marginalized by androcentric relationships and power structures.[154]

Similar to Isasi-Díaz and Goizueta, Aquino relates public and private places, and emphasizes the anthropological significance of daily life experiences *(lo cotidiano)*. For Aquino, these ordinary relationships exemplify how macro (public) and micro (private) worlds are intrinsically connected. Daily relationships, argues Aquino, replicate the split between private and public, the depolitization of the domestic, the subordination of women to men, and the stereotyping of gender roles. *Lo cotidiano* reveals the lack of authentic dialogue among persons in the multiple worldly spaces they abide. Aquino observes:

> If ways of living together, values and behavior are first learned at home, when the home models unequal relationships between men and women, it becomes the crucial place for the perpetuation of hierarchical models. Daily relationships become the basis and image of all social relations. This is why analysts stress that daily life permeates the public as well as the private spheres, because the activities carried out in both spheres "imply a level of dailiness, daily actions that confer upon this oppression, day after day, an air of naturalness." This is why women stress the need to change the way things are done in daily life in order to construct equal models of interhuman relationships.[155]

Aquino's anthropology of "dialogical relationships" therefore seeks to create bridges between men and women, between the human and the divine, between the material and the spiritual, between human creatures and all other creatures, between the public and private spheres, and between sacred and profane history. Her theological anthropology, similar to the others already discussed, represents a holistic and historically minded understanding of the human, the divine, and the way that they relate with one another. Aquino is careful, however, not to blur legitimate distinctions.[156] Her anthropology hinges upon recognizing human differences

---

[154]Aquino, *Our Cry for Life*, 30-41.

[155]Ibid., 40. See also, Aquino, "Perspectives on a Latina's Feminist Liberation Theology," in *Frontiers of Hispanic Theology*, 33.

[156]For instance, relative to men and women, she argues that their "[e]quality does not depend on one person being a copy of another but on the individuality of each . . . Diversity is what makes us alike and should not become a reason for diminishing the humanity of others." See Aquino, *Cry for Life*, 94.

rather than assimilating such differences under a universal and ahistorical humanity. An emphasis on the distinctiveness and diversity of the "human" reality lies at the heart of Alex García-Rivera's anthropology of creatureliness—the next voice to be considered in the present survey of U.S. Hispanic anthropological visions.

AN ANTHROPOLOGY OF CREATURELINESS

Drawing on a semiotics of culture (especially the work of Robert Schreiter) and the subaltern method of Antonio Gramsci, and building upon the pioneering insights of Elizondo, Alex García-Rivera offers an anthropology of creatureliness that re-interprets in a socio-culturally sensitive way the "little" stories of St. Martin de Porres.[157] Although his method is aimed primarily at uncovering the subaltern message of St. Martin's little stories,[158] it is quite evident that his arguments carry implications for U.S. Hispanics. García-Rivera's contribution not only serves to underscore the importance of cosmology within U.S. Hispanic theology, but also the fact that in U.S. Hispanic theology what is human is never divorced from other aspects of creation. In other words, García-Rivera's theology serves as a powerful reminder that U.S. Hispanic theological anthropology is not just a theology that addresses human nature, but is perhaps more accurately, a theology of the human in his or her relationship to God and all of God's creatures.

García-Rivera's anthropology of creatureliness hinges upon the issue of recognizing and embracing human differences. Difference—being both Anglo-American and Latin-American *(mestizaje)*, being of two worlds yet of no world (exile)—is a central theme that predominates in U.S. Hispanic theological anthropology. García-Rivera capitalizes on this theme primarily through his notion of asymmetrical relationships. For García-Rivera, the human person is a creature defined not so much by reason, but rather by the ability to discover his or her identity within a "garden of fecund asymmetries." The human creature is not part of a Pseudo-Dionysian hierarchy of being. Rather, he or she is part of a horizontal fellowship of creaturely differences. Thus, García-Rivera writes,

The nature of the *criatura* is revealed in the cosmic eucharistic-like fellowship provided by St. Martín. The *criatura de Dios* is not some rung in a cosmic ladder but part of a cosmic fellowship. True human

---

[157]For an explanation of García-Rivera's method and his acknowledgment of the influence of Elizondo on his thought see Alex García-Rivera, *St. Martín de Porres: The "Little Stories" and the Semiotics of Culture* (Maryknoll, New York: Orbis Books, 1995), 1-39.

[158]On this point see his understanding of the concept of "hegemony" in García-Rivera, *St. Martín de Porres*, 15-18.

differences are not variations along a vertical scale of value but elements of a horizontal fellowship of sacramental grace. This I call the anthropology of creatureliness.[159]

Similar to Isasi-Díaz, García Rivera's anthropological vision challenges commonly accepted understandings of charity. For García-Rivera, charity involves an act of love toward an "asymmetric" other.[160] As was the case with Isasi-Díaz, García-Rivera understands this act as capable of imaging who God is. "The creaturely *imago Dei*" writes García-Rivera, "is not so much the stamp of rationality or intellect (although it includes that) but the capacity to form fellowship across true, asymmetric differences, fellowship similar to that which exists between the asymmetric Creator and creature."[161]

This process of creating fellowship across human differences leads, in García-Rivera's judgment, to humanization. Bridging together creation and redemption, he understands grace as a "healing" presence that encompasses the entire cosmos.[162] García-Rivera's understanding echoes Augustine's *gratia sanans*, except that for the former, healing involves the whole of the created order, while for the latter, healing primarily involves the human person. For García-Rivera, healing enables participation "in the creatureliness of each other and of the cosmos," and leads to knowledge of self and of God because "the Creator of the human creature is also the One who created the cosmos."[163]

By way of contrast, García-Rivera understands sin as the action that breaks fellowship with others, and thereby causes a loss of self-knowledge. Subsuming "differences under the conditions of symmetry is ultimately a violent act, an act against the cosmic order which was created not so much as a hierarchy but as a fecundity of different creatures."[164] Acting on behalf of cosmic order involves fostering right relationship with all of God's creatures. "What is human" affirms García-Rivera, "cannot be known without reference to God, and that reference lies not with the distinctiveness of the human but with the connectedness of creation."[165]

The authentic free person does not subordinate or exclude others, but

---

[159]Ibid., 99.

[160]For García-Rivera, asymmetry is a notion that carries sacramental underpinnings and is associated primarily in his writings with the recognition of creaturely differences and the embrace of an other, especially a marginalized other. See García-Rivera, "San Martín de Porres: Criatura de Dios," *Journal of Hispanic/Latino Theology* 2/2 (1994): 40-41.

[161]See García-Rivera, "San Martín de Porres," 52.

[162]García-Rivera, *St. Martín de Porres*, 104.

[163]Ibid., 102.

[164]Ibid., 101.

[165]Ibid., 94.

rather he/she "crosses" boundaries so as to create fellowship with a distinct other. In García-Rivera's anthropology of creatureliness, authentic freedom has to do with the willingness to accept creaturely differences as constitutive of the order of creation and redemption. Free persons are those who through acts of love participate in the sacramental fellowship of grace by establishing communion with other "asymmetric" selves.[166]

García-Rivera's anthropology of creatureliness is, therefore, defined by the capacity of humans to form fellowship across "asymmetric differences." This capacity, García-Rivera claims, is the way humans can image who God is. Such an idea is not at all foreign to Christian thought. Indeed, anthropologies that engage the Christian doctrine of God have much to say about the way we humans image the God who *is* as a result of communion or relationships among distinct others. In a more explicit trinitarian appeal, Sixto J. García's understanding of functional and dysfunctional social relationships makes explicit the trinitarian basis of U.S. Hispanic theological anthropology. García is mainly concerned with relating the life of God with the life of human societies.

A TRINITARIAN U.S. HISPANIC ANTHROPOLOGY

U.S. Hispanic theology is not unlike most contextual theologies that seek to re-envision Christian anthropology in light of traditional themes and doctrines. Among other things, the above reflections have already demonstrated re-conceptions of Christology and grace in light of the socio-cultural experiences of U.S. Hispanics. Given the communal and socio-practical nature of U.S. Hispanic theological anthropology, the presence of some reflection on trinitarian life and U.S. Hispanic experience does not come as a surprise. If the doctrine of the Trinity is indeed the signpost by which Christian life is to be ultimately critiqued and constructed,[167] U.S. Hispanic theological anthropology would naturally be expected to gravitate toward trinitarian theology as a source of its anthropological premises. Regarding the latter, García's reflections on the Trinity have begun to pave the way in this direction.

García embraces the Trinity as a "perichoretic" model for personal and social relationships.[168] As García observes, perichoresis refers to "the dynamic of loving dialogue" among the divine persons of the Trinity (Father, Son, and Spirit).[169] Following Rahner's classic trinitarian axiom (the

---

[166]Ibid.

[167]See Catherine M. LaCugna, *God for Us: The Trinity and Christian Life* (San Francisco: HarperCollins, 1991), esp. 377-417.

[168]Sixto J. García, "United States Hispanic and Mainstream Trinitarian Theologies," in *Frontiers of Hispanic Theology in the United States*, 88-103; and idem, "A Hispanic Approach to Trinitarian Theology: The Dynamics of Celebration, Reflection, and Praxis," in *We Are a People!*

[169]García, "United States Hispanic and Mainstream Trinitarian Theologies," 98.

economic Trinity is the immanent Trinity and the immanent Trinity is the economic Trinity), García affirms the socio-political manifestation of God's trinitarian life. Thus, García writes:

> The important concept for our purposes here is the economic-trinitarian dialogue of love which penetrates human history, offering liberation, renewal, hominization. The Trinity thus stamps its profile on every human being's personal reality and by extension on every human society and political structure. There is a perichoretic activity in society in whose structures the trinitarian God images godself. The original source of this imaging is the trinitarian dialogue of love which grounds the divine oneness in its tripersonality.[170]

García characterizes "trinitarian dysfunctionalism" as the failure of human persons and human structures to image this perichoretic relationship. "Our society," argues García, "defaces the image of the Trinity in and through its oppressive structures. The image of the Trinity becomes, as it were, dysfunctional."[171] Turning to the U.S. Hispanic context, García notes the following experiences as examples of such trinitarian dysfunctionalism: economic injustice, rejection of destitute migrants, sexism, religious intolerance, materialism, and cultural/racial discrimination. These examples suggest, in the words of García, the "dimming" of Jesus' "dangerous voice."[172]

The human face of Jesus, however, reveals a "dangerous memory" that challenges these and other dysfunctional social images of the Trinity. The "retrieval and reformulation of the true face of Jesus Christ," writes García, "presents dangers to our society's conventional wisdom and comfort."[173] He goes on to affirm that "[t]his danger is nothing less than actualizing God's demand for a renewal of the covenant, given in personal and communitarian justice and love."[174]

García's trinitarian hermeneutics precludes the individualization or privatization of what is human. Thus, similar to the other Latino/a voices we have examined, García's theological anthropology, which emerges from his trinitarian hermeneutics, embraces both personal and communal realities, and the private and public spaces associated with these realities. Moreover, similar to these other Latino/a voices, García's trinitarian anthropology preferences the activity of grace among personal and communal realities that have been, to use García's preferred term, "defaced" by sin. This trinitarian hermeneutics enables García to affirm the face of Christ, as God's "sacrament of a healing and redeeming love," as "God's

---

[170]Ibid., 99.
[171]Ibid., 100.
[172]Ibid., 99-100.
[173]Ibid., 100.
[174]Ibid.

transcendental ultimate victory over the structures of oppression" and as "the permanent presence of God the Father in community."[175]

GATHERING THE SCATTERED PIECES OF U.S. HISPANIC THEOLOGICAL ANTHROPOLOGY

This survey would be incomplete without some initial attempt to bring together the visions that comprise U.S. Hispanic theological anthropology. The task at hand is really not as difficult as it may seem. These visions reflect in various contextual refractions central themes that have accompanied Catholic theological anthropologies of the past. More than anything else, these contextual refractions have attempted yet again to carry forth the ancient task of re-appropriating and re-envisioning Christian faith. Within this particular re-envisioning and re-appropriation, U.S. Hispanic visions have one thing in common: to underscore very specific social, gender, cultural, and political experiences as loci for encountering grace.

The focus on particular U.S. Hispanic experiences and how the latter serve as loci of grace, re-envision within this contextual project what the Catholic tradition has generally characterized as nature, grace, and sin. Within U.S. Hispanic theology, "nature" is not an abstract reality. Nor is nature understood as a formal and ontological structure of being (as is the case, for instance, with Aquinas who defines nature in terms of a principle of operation that defines not only what a thing is but also how a thing acts with respect to its end-purpose). In U.S. Hispanic theology, concrete historical experiences become essential in defining who people are and who they become as they encounter and respond to grace *within their history*. Thus, nature is revealed in and through concrete historical subjects and all other creatures who constitute the "fecund garden of asymmetries."

Grace is perhaps the most common thread that runs throughout the visions we have examined. These visions exemplify how the experience of grace is not only cultural (as Espín affirms), but is also a social and engendered experience. The "Galilean" face of grace, *mestizaje*, *acompañamiento*, the historically minded notions of the "kin-dom" of God, the notion of charity as solidarity, the notion of exile, the "highly contextual" nature of U.S. Hispanic experience, *la lucha*, the garden of asymmetries, and the "functional" social image of Trinity, all suggest this contextual approach. In all of these, grace is encountered in the ordinary *(lo cotidiano)* private and public spaces of U.S. Hispanic experiences.

Similarly, U.S. Hispanic understandings of sin also follow this contextualization. Without undermining the personal face of sin, U.S.

---

[175]Ibid., 99 and 101.

Hispanic theological anthropology underscores the social nature of human sinfulness. The notion of Jesus' identification with the marginalized Galileans, the "accompaniment" of persons in their marginalized places, "deculturalization," the ethnocentric and social analysis of the multiple forms of Latinas' oppression, the concept of "symmetric relationships," and the "defacing" of the social image of the Trinity, all unveil this contextual approach to social sin.

The social nature of persons and the social experience of grace and sin are central themes in U.S. Hispanic theological anthropology. Goizueta's concept of *acompañamiento*, García-Rivera's concept of "asymmetric relationships," and García's notion of "functional" trinitarian relationships are especially helpful in unveiling an Hispanic understanding of these themes. Goizueta's notion of *"acompañamiento"* refracts in a Hispanically human way the Christian understanding of person as relation, even while underscoring how socio-political experiences are essential dimensions of personhood. Beyond also representing a relational anthropology, García-Rivera's concept of "asymmetric relationships" also carries socio-political implications. In affirming creaturely difference as part of God's plan to create and save humanity, García-Rivera invites us all to become co-creators of a more inclusive vision of society. Finally, García's reflections on trinitarian relations specifies our paricipation in the life of God in light of the intersection between social structures and the trinitarian life of grace. García suggests that because social structures owe their existence to human persons, they can and should image the trinitarian life of God.

Concomitant with any understandings of nature, grace, and sin is an understanding of human agency, of human praxis. While readily acknowledging the need for grace, U.S. Hispanic theological anthropology underscores the need to embrace grace. Thus, an overall emphasis on praxis characterizes U.S. Hispanic theological anthropology. Praxis, however, is always understood as communal and as gift. Freedom is always freedom exercised "within the kingdoms of this world in response to grace." The Galilean activity of Jesus, the *mestizo* notion of "aesthetic-praxis," the "struggle" to build a more just society, and the praxis of crossing social boundaries to create communion with other asymmetric selves all exemplify the praxiological emphasis of U.S. Hispanic theological anthropology.

This emphasis on human praxis has undoubtedly impacted U.S. Hispanic notions of love and relationships. Thus, relationship is not merely a given. Relationship is accompaniment. Accompaniment implies ethical action—not only in light of a personal dimension, but also mindful of social factors (political and economic). Similarly, charity or love is a gift of God, but this gift manifests itself in the act of solidarity with an other, especially and preferentially the marginalized other.

The focus on the preferential accompaniment of grace runs throughout U.S. Hispanic visions of humanity. Jesus, the Galilean, is the one who accompanies the poor in their marginalized places. He accompanies persons who are "restless" to receive a salvific word that liberates. The kindom comes to all, but it comes first and foremost to the marginalized and their marginalized spaces. Everyone and everything is open to receive grace and the trinitarian life of God, but, suggest Hispanic theologians, openness lies most with the persons and places associated with poverty, marginalization, and oppression. Thus, U.S. Hispanic theological anthropology makes what is ordinary and absent from "historical" recognition (e.g., women, the oppressed, the home, and urban spaces) the preferred locus of divine self-encounter.

These then are the visions that comprise U.S. Hispanic theological anthropology. Informed by particular human experiences, they represent socio-politically sensitive appropriations of traditional approaches to how the human reality encounters the life of grace. As I noted at the beginning of this chapter, Catholic theological anthropology has been informed by a variety of sources that have yielded numerous visions of what it means to be Christianly human. U.S. Hispanic theological anthropology offers its distinctive contribution in the various ways it has correlated critically traditional Christian themes and U.S. Hispanic theological concerns.

Recognizing the manifold scattered pieces that comprise theological anthropology, the late Karl Rahner hoped that they could somehow be brought together in a more systematic fashion.[176] In so doing, Rahner believed that some common or fundamental point of departure could be established so as to tie together the various themes that today comprise theological anthropology. The manifold contextual visions that have emerged in theological anthropology may make Rahner's goal a difficult if not undesirable one to achieve. One can no longer speak of the human and his or her encounter with grace in categories that presume a universal subject and monolithic experience of grace. Given the emergence of contextual visions one must now ask questions such as: What is the concrete humanity at issue? What are the concrete experiences that mediate or interfere with an experience of grace? What is this community's experience of grace? How has this community conceptualized the experience of grace?

Rahner, however, was not ignorant of the emerging pluralism of the church, the manifold questions, and the many answers facing contemporary theological anthropology.[177] Even if one recognizes shortcomings in his vision, Rahner's way of piecing together a coherent Catholic theologi-

---

[176]See Karl Rahner, "*Anthropologie, Theologische A.*," in *Lexicon Für Theologie Und Kirche* (Freiburg: Verlag Herder, 1957), 622. See also his "Theology and Anthropology," in *Theological Investigations*, IX, trans. David Bourke (New York: Crossroad, 1983), 28-45.
[177]Ibid.

cal anthropology can model a way by which to further piece together the U.S. contextual appropriations of key anthropological Christian themes. Chapters four and five of this book will propose and follow a Rahnerian *theological structure* that will help deepen the understanding of how U.S. Hispanic theological anthropology uniquely fits into the Catholic understanding of what it means to be human.

The next chapter explores the sacramental side of U.S. Hispanic theological anthropology. Deeply connected to the everyday experiences of U.S. Hispanics, U.S. Hispanic popular Catholicism serves as the main sacramental expression and explicit religious source of U.S. Hispanic theological anthropology. As a result of the prevalence of popular devotions to Mary within U.S. Hispanic culture, this symbol will receive special attention. The devotion to Our Lady of Guadalupe and Our Lady of Charity will provide specific test cases.

3

Human being is relation in popular catholicism.

On Being Human from U.S. Hispanic Sacramental Perspectives

THE "SACRAMENTAL" VISION OF REALITY

Among the salient features of Catholicism is its sacramental understanding of reality. By "sacramental," I mean that fundamental Catholic approach of relating what is human (e.g., language, human nature, historical experiences) to what is divine (e.g., Logos, grace, the reign of God). The Catholic tradition affirms that human reality, though fallen, is capable of participating in and revealing the mystery of God. What is human can serve as a sign of grace. As a result of this approach, Catholic theologians most often speak about the human in an analogical way.[1] That is, we affirm a "similarity-in-difference" between the human and the divine.[2] In the present chapter the sacramental approach to human reality, and the analogical way of conceiving the human and divine encounter, will be appealed to in connection with the various explicitly religious or symbolic expressions associated with U.S. Hispanic popular Catholicism, particularly the culturally rooted images, stories, and rituals associated with U.S. Hispanic Marian devotions.

Popular Catholicism is essential in understanding the religious ethos of U.S. Hispanics. Its various expressions mediate for U.S. Hispanics a sacramental encounter with "the gracious face of the divine." Popular Catholicism is also the primary sacramental means by which U.S. Hispanic communities remember, celebrate, and affirm their distinct Christian identity.[3] Indeed, while U.S. Hispanics may not be characterized as

---

[1]On the Catholic analogical imagination see David Tracy, *The Analogical Imagination: Christian Theology and the Culture of Pluralism* (New York: Crossroad, 1981), esp. 405-445.

[2]See Richard McBrien, *Catholicism* (New York: HarperCollins, 1994), 15.

[3]See Gary Riebe-Estrella, "Latino Religiosity or Latino Catholicism?," *Theology*

sacramental in the widely conceived sense of the term (e.g., with regards to the seven sacraments),[4] the widespread appeal of U.S. Hispanic popular faith expressions, and especially U.S. Hispanic Marian devotions, exemplifies in an explicitly religious sense the profound sacramentality and Catholic roots of U.S. Hispanic cultures. This sacramentality also serves as a source for understanding the socio-politically sensitive approaches to the encounter of grace.

THE SYMBOLS, MEANING, AND SACRAMENTALITY OF U.S. HISPANIC POPULAR CATHOLICISM

That popular Catholicism represents a sacramental locus for U.S. Hispanic theological anthropology, especially when we consider its symbols, liturgical actions, and stories, is widely accepted among Latino/a scholars.[5] Like most Catholic sacramental expressions (whether officially sanctioned or not), U.S. Hispanic popular Catholicism underscores the potential of created reality, and of human realities in particular, to mediate an experience of the sacred.[6] In this latter sense, U.S. Hispanic popular Catholicism can be characterized as an exteriorized form of the life of grace.[7] U.S. Hispanic popular Catholicism is the "*mística*," that is, the spirituality that expresses the U.S. Hispanic way of being in the world.[8]

As I have already noted in chapter one, although U.S. Hispanic popu-

---

Today 54/4 (1998): 513-514; and Patrick L. Malloy, "Christian Anamnesis and Popular Religion," *Liturgical Ministry* 7 (1998): 121-128.

[4]Note, however, that as Richard McBrien argues, "the Church lived through its entire first millennium and then some without ever having settled upon even a final definition of *sacrament*, let alone their precise number. On the contrary, there were literally hundreds of sacred rites (what we call today 'sacramentals') which were simply referred to as 'sacraments.' " See McBrien, *Catholicism*, 800.

[5]For instance see Orlando Espín, "Pentecostalism and Popular Catholicism: Preservers of Hispanic Catholic Tradition?" ACHTUS Newsletter 4, no. 1 (Spring 1993): 12; Allan Figueroa Deck, "Hispanic Catholic Prayer and Worship" in *¡Alabadle! Hispanic Christian Worship*, ed. Justo L. González (Nashville: Abingdon Press, 1996), 29-41; and Roberto S. Goizueta, *Caminemos con Jesús: Toward a Hispanic/Latino Theology of Accompaniment* (Maryknoll, New York: Orbis Books, 1995), 18-19.

[6]See Deck, "Hispanic Catholic Prayer and Worship," 34-35, and Sixto J. García, "United States and Mainstream Trinitarian Theologies," in *Frontiers of Hispanic Theology in the United States*, ed. Allan Figueroa Deck (Maryknoll, New York: Orbis Books, 1992), 93-98.

[7]See the following arguments which suggest this characterization: Orlando Espín, "Trinitarian Monotheism and the Birth of Popular Catholicism: The Case of Sixteenth-Century Mexico," in *The Faith of the People: Theological Reflections on Popular Catholicism* (Maryknoll, New York: Orbis Books, 1997), esp. 57-59, and Sixto J. García, "A Hispanic Approach to Trinitarian Theology," in *We Are a People!: Initiatives in Hispanic American Theology*, ed. Roberto S. Goizueta (Minneapolis: Fortress Press, 1992), 120-132.

[8]See Mark R. Francis, "The Hispanic Liturgical Year: The People's Calendar," *Liturgical Ministry* 7 (1998): 131-132.

lar Catholicism is similar to other popular Catholic religious expressions, one must also note its distinctiveness. Among other things, the particularity of U.S. Hispanic popular Catholicism derives from various interrelated factors that have shaped and continue to shape this religious tradition. The factors informing the particularity of U.S. Hispanic popular Catholicism include: 1) its medieval and baroque Spanish Catholic roots, 2) its Amerindian and African influences, 3) its emphasis on ritual, the arts, and drama as sign-bearers of the life of grace, and 4) finally and perhaps more significantly, the specific historical context of U.S. Hispanics.[9]

It is this specific historical context that qualifies what U.S. Hispanic theologians understand as the "popular" element in popular Catholic expressions of faith. An increasing number of U.S. Hispanic theologians conceive the "popular" element of popular Catholicism not so much in terms of what is universally present or common among the many. Rather, what is "popular" is associated with particular social, gender, cultural, and political human experiences. Thus, according to Orlando Espín, popular Catholicism is "'popular' not necessarily because it is widespread but because its creators and practitioners are the people, and more concretely, the marginalized people in society (e.g., those social sectors pushed against their will to the 'dispensable' or 'disposable' margins of society)."[10] This understanding, suggests Goizueta, does not exclude the fact that this religious experience is also a widespread phenomenon among Hispanics.[11] But any perusal of social data on U.S. Hispanics would be sufficient to confirm how "the people" in question are overwhelmingly underrepresented and marginalized with respect to both Church and society.[12]

U.S. Hispanic theologians have cautioned that the association of popular Catholicism with the marginalized, and its widespread appeal among the

---

[9]See Espín, "Popular Catholicism among Latinos," in *The Faith of the People*, 111-155; William A. Christian, "Spain in Latino Religiosity," in *El Cuerpo de Cristo: The Hispanic Presence in the U.S. Catholic Church*, ed. Peter Casarella and Raúl Gómez (New York: Crossroad, 1988), 325-330.

[10]Orlando O. Espín, "Popular Religion as an Epistemology (of Suffering)," *Journal of Hispanic/Latino Theology* 2/2 (1994): 66. Also cited in Goizueta, *Caminemos con Jesús*, 21-22. For an alternative Latino perspective see García-Rivera, *St. Martín de Porres: The "Little Stories" and the Semiotics of Culture* (Maryknoll, New York: Orbis Books, 1995), 12-14. For an alternative perspective that challenges Espín's definition see Robert E. Wright, "If It's Official, It Can't Be Popular? Reflections on Popular and Folk Religion," *Journal of Hispanic/Latino Theology* 1/3 (1994): 47-67. For a Latin-American perspective on this issue, see: Cristián Parker, *Popular Religion and Modernization in Latin America: A Different Logic* (Maryknoll, New York: Orbis Books, 1996), 35-38.

[11]Goizueta, *Caminemos con Jesús*, 22, footnote 10.

[12]Ibid. See also Espín, "Popular Religion as an Epistemology (of Suffering)," 73.

common people, does not mean that this religious expression should be taken as being inferior to other and perhaps more officially sanctioned forms of Catholicism. In fact, some of these theologians have accepted the reference of Latino Catholicism as being a form of "popular religion" with reservation. The point is made that such a characterization can undermine the fact that for most Latino/a communities, popular Catholicism is the primary sacramental Catholic form of self-expression and encounter with the life of grace. Thus, Riebe-Estrella notes:

> Even we U.S. Latino theologians may be conceding too much by calling our religious heritage and practices in the Americas "popular religion." Too often the term "popular" carries with it a connotation of inferiority or lack of education. Rather, what we have in Latino religiosity is a valid form of Catholicism, an alternative to that developed in the Northern Hemisphere and which is lay-led and not eucharistic-centered.[13]

Riebe-Estrella's comments are not intended to dismiss the importance of the Eucharist and the other sacraments in Catholic expressions of faith. Rather, what he suggests is that the centrality of popular Catholicism within U.S. Hispanic communities has to be understood in light of the social-historical influences that precipitated this particular way of being Catholic and impacted the way Latinos/as have received and carried forth the Catholic tradition.

Catholic traditions have often addressed issues of sacraments and sacramentality in tandem with symbolic approaches to reality. For instance, Karl Rahner argues that "the teaching *on the sacraments* is the central place in which a theology of the symbol is put forward in general in Catholic theology."[14] It is within the arguments associated with the sacramentality of U.S. Hispanic popular Catholicism that we can expect the emergence of a U.S. Hispanic theology of symbol.

THE SYMBOLS OF U.S. HISPANIC POPULAR CATHOLICISM

The theological significance of U.S. Hispanic popular Catholic symbols lies in the fact that they "strike a chord deep in the identity and collective memories" of U.S. Hispanic communities.[15] An analogical imagi-

---

[13]Riebe-Estrella, "Latino Religiosity or Latino Catholicism?," 514.

[14]Karl Rahner, "The Theology of the Symbol," in *Theological Investigations*, IV, trans. Kevin Smyth (New York: Crossroad, 1982), 241.

[15]Deck, "A Pox on Both Your Houses: A View of Catholic Conservative-Liberal Polarities from the Hispanic Margin," in *Being Right: Conservative Catholics in America*, ed. Mary Jo Weaver and R. Scott Appleby (Bloomington: Indiana University Press, 1995), 97.

nation undergirds an Hispanic understanding of symbols: U.S. Hispanic theologians view the various symbolic expressions of U.S. Hispanic popular Catholicism as capable of participating in and revealing the reality of the sacred. Through this participation, various subjects, contextually defined and associated with these expressions, image the life of grace.[16] Yet the similarity established between the human and the divine is always a "similarity-in-difference" since most Latino/a theologians are careful to avoid idealizations that would deny the necessary distinction between human and divine realities. This symbolic understanding, which enables Latino/a theologians to affirm popular Catholicism as a locus of human and divine self-revelation, suggests the theo-centric and anthropo-centric nature of this explicit expression of U.S. Hispanic religiosity.

The primary symbolic function of U.S. Hispanic popular Catholicism lies in its ability to mediate, to a lesser or greater degree, an experience of grace.[17] This type of symbolization is theo-centric in nature. The divine reality, or the "beyond" of the symbol, is encountered within the popular symbol itself.[18] Thus, by symbol, U.S. Hispanic theologians understand "an object, image, or action that reveals, mediates, and makes present what may be called the ineffable, the holy, the sacred, or the supernatural."[19] This definition can and has been interpreted, within U.S. Hispanic theology in a more general way, to include the stories and rituals of U.S. Hispanic popular Catholicism. The former are conceived as symbolic discourses, the latter as symbolic actions.[20]

The secondary symbolic function of U.S. Hispanic popular Catholicism is to mediate a specific U.S. Hispanic understanding of the human as a result of its relationship to the realm of the sacred. This type of symbolic mediation is anthropocentric in nature. This mediation results from the relationship conceived between the divine reality mediated by the symbolic expressions of U.S. Hispanic popular Catholicism, and the histori-

---

[16]See Roberto S. Goizueta, "U.S. Hispanic Popular Catholicism as Theopoetics," in *Hispanic/Latino Theology: Challenge and Promise*, ed. Ada María Isasi-Díaz and Fernando F. Segovia (Minneapolis: Fortress Press, 1996), 272. See also, Sixto García, "United States Hispanic and Mainstream Trinitarian Theologies," 97; García and Espín, "'Lilies of the Field' : A Hispanic Theology of Providence and Human Responsibility," *Proceedings of the Catholic Theological Society of America* 44 (1989), 84; C. Gilbert Romero, *Hispanic Devotional Piety: Tracing the Biblical Roots* (Maryknoll, New York: Orbis Books, 1991), 51-52.

[17]We say to a "lesser or greater degree" in order to acknowledge the various degrees to which the symbols of U.S. Hispanic popular Catholicism "participate" in the divine reality. For a number of theologically valid reasons U.S. Hispanic theologians, like most Catholic theologians, recognize different types of symbolic participation in, and representation of, divine reality.

[18]Goizueta, *Caminemos con Jesús*, 27, note 26.

[19]Ibid.

[20]Ibid.

cal reality of its practitioners.[21] The symbol itself, suggest U.S. Hispanic theologians, although a mediator of what lies "beyond" the human, necessarily identifies itself with a human reality. The symbol, especially in so far as it is materially constituted, is a cultural creation of a people that "speaks *their* word."[22]

In accordance with U.S. Hispanic understandings of what qualifies as popular, Latino/a theologians have judged the popularity of symbols to be a function of how well they can speak to and within the experience of U.S. Hispanics. Thus, U.S. Hispanic theologians would argue that the frequent appeal of symbolic expressions like the rituals and stories associated with the crucified Christ derives from the fact that these symbolic expressions resonate analogically with the socio-cultural experiences of marginalization and suffering experienced by U.S. Hispanics.[23] Through this identification and solidarity with a specific people, these symbols offer a sacramental word of grace and hope. García writes,

> The broken humanity of Jesus stands as a sacrament of the broken humanity of the body of the Hispanic communities. Jesus the Christ is our brother in sorrow and oppression, and we can touch him, mourn with him, die with him, and yes, also hope with him.[24]

THE SACRAMENTAL SIGNIFICANCE OF U.S. HISPANIC POPULAR SYMBOLS

The presence of U.S. Hispanic symbols permeates the private and public domains of U.S. Hispanic faith experiences. This sacramental vision, which has escaped for the most part the dualistic and secularizing tendencies of modernity, reflects an integral and all-encompassing approach with respect to the relationship between the human and the divine. Moreover, the revelation of the sacred or what is "of" the sacred (statues of Mary, Joseph, the saints, religious processions, and home altars) within

---

[21]Goizueta, "U.S. Hispanic Popular Catholicism as Theopoetics," 272. See also his *Caminemos con Jesús*, 27, note 26 where he states: "Narratives, or stories, and rituals are the primary ways in which a community generates and identifies with its symbols, by explicitly locating them within the community's own ongoing history."

[22]Orlando Espín, "The Vanquished, Faithful Solidarity, and the Marian Symbol: A Hispanic Perspective on Providence," in *On Keeping Providence*, ed. B. Doherty and J. Coultas (Terre Haute: St. Mary of the Woods College Press, 1991), 88. Note how this understanding is in agreement with the more sociologically minded approaches. For instance, see William Christian who has persuasively argued how symbols are "measures of belonging" or "cultural boundary markers" that "are virtually totem objects," embodying in some way the essence of the humanity of their devotees." See Christian, *Person and God in a Spanish Valley* (New York: Seminar Press, 1972), 100.

[23]See Goizueta, "U.S. Hispanic Popular Catholicism as Theopoetics," 272.

[24]Sixto J. García, "A Hispanic Approach to Trinitarian Theology," 118-19. Cited in Goizueta, "U.S. Hispanic Popular Catholicism as Theopoetics," 273.

places associated with the everyday experiences of U.S. Hispanics (the home, barrios, family-owned businesses),[25] and relative to particular persons (women, grandmothers, children)[26] not only points to the preferred places and subjects of U.S. Hispanic theological anthropology, but also serves as a sacramental means for understanding the U.S. Hispanic encounter of grace.

Speaking from a sacramental perspective, the parallel to Goizueta's argument that "*[l]o cotidiano* is at the very heart of that history into which Christ has been born, in which he continues to accompany us, and upon which it is the task of the theologian to reflect,"[27] is found in the religious symbols of U.S. Hispanic popular Catholicism. Their presence within the ordinary life of Latino/a experiences is a source for understanding how U.S. Hispanics conceive the encounter with grace. While the omnipresence of these symbols in private and public spaces suggests the universal presence of grace, the association of these popular religious symbols with marginalized places, persons, and communities points to the particular U.S. Hispanic way of qualifying the universal experience of grace.

Underlying the sacramentality of the central symbols of U.S. Hispanic popular Catholicism is an approach that affirms the universal yet preferential offer of grace to suffering subjects. The symbols of U.S. Hispanic popular Catholicism enable U.S. Hispanics to identify sacramentally "with" and participate "in" the life of grace. Grace, in this popular Catholic sacramental experience, is closely related to and flows from Christ's' suffering. Through Christ, God offers life to those who are vanquished.[28] The experience of Christ's vanquishment and its ability to relate to the present-day experiences of U.S. Hispanics is sacramentally suggested in the widespread appeal to symbols connected with this theme. Among

---

[25]See Elizondo, "Popular Catholicism as the Core of Cultural Identity," in *An Enduring Flame: Studies on Latino Popular Religiosity*, ed. Anthony M. Stevens-Arroyo and Ana María Díaz-Stevens (New York: Bildner Center for Western Hemisphere Studies, 1994), 116.

[26]See Romero, *Hispanic Devotional Piety*, 83-97; Isasi-Díaz, "On the Birthing Stool: *Mujerista* Liturgy," in *Mujerista Theology: A Theology for the Twenty-First Century* (Maryknoll, New York: Orbis Books, 1996), 174-175; Goizueta, *Caminemos con Jesús*, 116; Espín, "An Exploration into the Theology of Grace and Sin," in *From the Heart of Our People: Latino/a Reflections in Catholic Systematic Theology*, ed. Orlando Espín and Miguel H. Díaz (Maryknoll, New York: Orbis Books, 2000), 121-152; Goizueta, "Why Are You Frightened?," in *El Cuerpo de Cristo*, 61-62. For a sociological argument see Ana María Díaz-Stevens "Latinas and the Church," in *Hispanic Catholic Culture in the U.S.: Issues and Concerns*, ed. Jay P. Dolan and Allan Figueroa Deck (Notre Dame: University of Notre Dame Press, 1994), 244-248.

[27]Goizueta, "Why Are You Frightened?," 55.

[28]Espín, "The God of the Vanquished: Foundations for a Latino Spirituality," in *The Faith of the People*, 11-31.

these expressions, the following two are worth noting: 1) the iconographic centrality of the crucified Christ and 2) the devotion to the sorrowful mother.[29]

Perhaps more than any other U.S. Hispanic sacramental expression, it is the Marian symbol that expresses the ongoing accompaniment of grace in the lives of U.S. Hispanics. As Elizondo himself asserts at the beginning of his *Galilean Journey*, relative to one of these U.S. Hispanic Marian symbols, "Guadalupe is the key to understanding the Christianity of the New World, the self-image of Mexicans, of Mexican-Americans, and all Latin Americans."[30]

THE SACRAMENTALITY
OF U.S. HISPANIC MARIAN EXPRESSIONS

Most Hispanic theologians would agree that "common to all forms of U.S. Hispanic popular Catholicism . . . is the central place of Mary."[31] One would be hard pressed, however, to arrive at a theological consensus relative to the identity of this symbol. For instance, some theologians argue that the U.S. Hispanic "Marys" represent particular instantiations of a more universal Marian devotion (Goizueta, Elizondo).[32] Others see this symbol as an embodiment of the "feminine" face of God (Rodriguez, Deck).[33] Some Latino/a theologians have argued that Mary represents the cultural and semantic analogy of divine attributes (Espín),[34] or have claimed that she is "the hermeneutical key to the Trinitarian experience of the Spirit" (García).[35] Still, for others, this symbol is associated with more traditional, biblical, or Euro-centric understandings (Isasi-Díaz, Vidal, Aquino, Romero).[36]

---

[29]See Vidal, "Towards an Understanding of the Synthesis in Iberian Hispanic American Popular Religiosity," in *An Enduring Flame*, 80-83; Espín, "Tradition and Popular Religion: An Understanding of the *Sensus Fidelium*," in *Frontiers of Hispanic/ Latino Theology*, 70-71; Goizueta, "U.S. Hispanic Popular Catholicism as Theopoetics," 271-280; and García, "A Hispanic Approach to Trinitarian Theology," in *We Are a People!*, 118-119.

[30]Elizondo, *Galilean Journey*, 12.

[31]Goizueta, *Caminemos con Jesús*, 37.

[32]See Goizueta, *Caminemos con Jesús*, 70-76; and Elizondo, "Mary in the Struggles of the Poor," *New Catholic World* Nov/Dec (1986): 244-247.

[33]Rodriguez, *Our Lady of Guadalupe: Faith and Empowerment among Mexican-American Women* (Austin: University of Texas Press, 1994), 152; Deck, *¡Alabadle!*, 37.

[34]Espín, "Tradition and Popular Religion: An Understanding of the *Sensus Fidelium*," in *Frontiers of Hispanic Latino/a Theology*, 75.

[35]García, "United States Hispanic and Mainstream Trinitarian Theology," 95.

[36]Isasi-Díaz, "On the Birthing Stool," 175; Vidal, "Towards an Understanding of the Synthesis," 76; Aquino, "*El culto a María y María en el culto*," *FEM publicación feminista* 5/20 (1981-82): 42; and Romero, "The Bible, Revelation, and Marian

The U.S. Hispanic approach to the Marian symbol becomes even more complex when other theological factors related to the cultural face of grace are taken into consideration. For instance, Espín's reflections have gradually led him more and more to associate Guadalupe with the Holy Spirit, rather than with Mary, the mother of Jesus. [37] At present, while Espín recognizes the more traditional forms of Marian devotion in Hispanic culture,[38] he has drawn some provocative arguments relative to the devotion to Our Lady of Guadalupe:

> I am not implying that Mary of Nazareth (and, consequently, Marian devotion) might be just mediating the maternal or feminine face of God, as some theologians have suggested. And I am certainly *not saying* that Mary *is* the Holy Spirit. I am only asking whether it is possible that what we have here is not mariology but pneumatology, but in an unexpected and brilliantly achieved cultural mediation?[39]

The absence of a theological consensus relative to the identity of this symbol does not in any way undermine my central thesis that U.S. Hispanic popular devotion to Mary serves as a sacramental means of understanding how the "Hispanically" human encounters grace. The brief survey above clearly suggests how U.S. Hispanic theologians uphold the potential of this symbol to serve as a central locus of U.S. Hispanic theological anthropology. As one theologian points out, U.S. Hispanic Marian symbols "whether or not they originate in apparitions, are culturally based, because they manifest a people's identity and because of the historical, socio-political, and anthropological contexts of the people who express the devotions."[40] Thus, the Marian symbol "speaks," or more precisely, given the aesthetic nature of U.S. Hispanic popular Catholicism, relates in iconic and dramatic ways what is "of" God to what is *latinamente* human.

Two U.S. Hispanic popular Marian devotions in particular exemplify this theological anthropology:[41] the devotion to Our Lady of Guadalupe

---

Devotion," *Marian Studies* XLIV (1993): 26. Note, however, especially in Romero's discussion the preferred titles by which Mary is known within U.S. Hispanic devotion: *Nuestra Señora del Socorro* (Our Lady of Perpetual Help), *Nuestra Señora de la Soledad* (Our Lady of Solitude), and *Nuestra Señora de Dolores*(Our Lady of Sorrows).

[37] The clearest example of this evolution can be seen by comparing and contrasting his article "Tradition and Popular Religion: An Understanding of the *Sensus Fidelium*" and his article "Grace and Sin," 121-152.

[38] Espín, *Faith of the People*, 10.

[39] Ibid., 9.

[40] Romero, "Bible, Revelation, and Marian Devotion," 26-27.

[41] For an overview of other Marian devotions in the U.S., see Stephen Holler, "The Origins of Marian Devotion in Latin American Cultures in the United States," *Marian Studies* XLVI (1995): 108-127.

and the devotion to Our Lady of Charity. The former is an apparition, or as some have preferred to call it "an encounter,"[42] which is primarily associated with Mexicans and Mexican-Americans. The latter symbol revolves around the finding of a statue, and is primarily associated with Cubans and Cuban-Americans. We turn now to the symbols of Our Lady of Guadalupe and Our Lady of Charity, and to their symbolic oral and written stories.

THE SYMBOL AND STORY OF OUR LADY OF GUADALUPE

Guadalupe is popular, that is, she is "of the people."[43] The symbol itself, the central story, and the symbolic inter-actions associated with this symbol reveal her "popularity." Guadalupe's popular identification suggests the specific U.S. Hispanic anthropological focus on concrete subjects informed by their various social, cultural, and engendered contexts. To characterize Guadalupe as being "of the people" is to associate her with a specific socio-cultural reality. The concepts of *mestizaje* and marginalization provide specific U.S. Hispanic interpretations of this reality.

How U.S. Hispanic theologians understand the socio-cultural reality depicted by the image and described in the story of the *Nican mopohua*[44] grounds the basis of their analogical connections. Working within the contours of a U.S. Hispanic religious ethos, namely, story, drama, and icon, U.S. Hispanic theologians have sought to appropriate the meaning of the symbol and story of Guadalupe. Like Elizondo's socio-cultural re-reading and appropriation of the Gospel's identity of Jesus, the symbol and story of Our Lady of Guadalupe have been re-read and appropriated through U.S. Hispanic lenses. The symbol has been interpreted as a "ver-

---

[42]To affirm the "inter-active" nature of this devotion, Goizueta prefers to use the "encounter" instead of "apparition," which he sees as implying passivity on behalf of the protagonist (Juan Diego). See his *Caminemos con Jesús*, 75. Similarly see Elizondo, *Guadalupe: Mother of the New Creation* (Maryknoll, New York: Orbis Books, 1997), 25.

[43]Rodriguez, *Our Lady of Guadalupe*, 143.

[44]The *Nican mopohua* is the story that describes the encounter between Guadalupe and Juan Diego. It is believed to have been originally composed by Don Antonio Valeriano, an indigenous scholar and convert, well versed in Latin. The document was published in Náhuatl in 1649 by Luis Lasso de la Vega, then chaplain of the Indians. The origins of the *Nican mopohua* and its authorship remain highly contested. The recent controversial study of Stafford Poole has prompted renewed historical and theological inquiry into the origins of this popular devotion. See Stafford Poole, *Our Lady of Guadalupe: The Origins and Sources of a Mexican National Symbol, 1531-1797* (Tucson: University of Arizona Press, 1995). For an alternative view, see Richard Nebel, *Santa María Tonantzin Virgen de Guadalupe: Religiöse Kontinuität und Transformation in Mexiko* (Freiburg: Neue Zeitschrift für Missionswissenschaft, 1992).

bal icon"[45] capable of identifying with and imaging how U.S. Hispanics image themselves and the divine. [46] In turn, the story provides the literary landscape that suggests how to reconfigure the socio-political landscape of U.S. Hispanic communities.

Iconically, Guadalupe unveils the face of subjects who comprise the underside of history. Similar to the "Word made flesh," who identified with the marginalized, a "word" of God "made icon" identifies with a vanquished community by assuming a Náhuatl face, and communicating through the native cultural ethos of "flower and song."[47]

Like Elizondo's Galilean Jesus, Guadalupe reveals a "both/and" rather than an "either/or" humanity. Guadalupe's "brown skin" is a sign, which vacillates between two histories, and proposes a "new mestizo anthropology—an anthropology of inclusive and progressive synthesis."[48] Guadalupe's face is not only a sacramental sign of the past, but rather a sacramental sign of the present. She is not only one of the indigenous, but also one-with Latinos and Latinas.[49]

From the perspective of symbolic discourse, several U.S. Hispanic theologians have underscored the specific social and cultural history presented in the story.[50] For instance, the significance of the Náhuatl language of the story, and the cultural memory mediated by the story has been affirmed.[51] Attention has focused on how the symbols within the story, such as "the song of birds" that attracts Juan Diego to Guadalupe and the "flowers" that convert the bishop to belief in the authenticity of Juan Diego's religious experience, culturally situate the story, communicate the Náhuatl experience of truth, and reveal what was considered to proceed from the realm of the sacred.

Some U.S. Hispanic theologians have also noted how literary expres-

---

[45]For the use of this phrase this writer acknowledges his indebtedness to Nicolas Ayo, who uses the phrase as the title for one of his works on Mary.

[46]For what follows see Elizondo, *La Morenita: Evangelizer of the Americas* (San Antonio: MACC, 1980); and Rodriguez, *Our Lady of Guadalupe*, 16-30.

[47]Elizondo describes Guadalupe as an "image-word that is experienced through the beauty of *flor y canto* and then explained through the spoken (later written) words of Juan Diego." *Flor y canto* (flower and song) are fundamental symbols of Náhuatl culture used to connote truth or the presence of the sacred. See Elizondo, *Guadalupe: Mother of the New Creation*, 118.

[48]Elizondo, *Guadalupe: Mother of the New Creation*, 132.

[49]Goizueta, *Caminemos con Jesús*, 45.

[50]For a complete text of the *Nican mopohua* see Elizondo, *Guadalupe: Mother of the New Creation*, 5-22. For various scholarly juxtaposing translations of the Náhuatl text see Jesús Galera Lamadrid, *Nican Mopohua: Breve análisis literario e histórico* (México: Editorial Jus, 1991).

[51]See Elizondo, *Guadalupe: Mother of the New Creation*; Goizueta, *Caminemos con Jesús*, 37-46; Espín, "The Vanquished, Faithful Solidarity, and the Marian Symbol," 90-93; Sixto García, "Our Lady of Guadalupe: A Sign of Ecclesial Unity," *Marian Studies* XLIV (1993): 88-105; Rodriguez, *Our Lady of Guadalupe*, 31-46.

sions in the story, such as "when it was still night" and "when it was beginning to dawn," evoke an integral anthropology that includes the whole of creation. In other words, the story of Guadalupe recounts how in the process of Guadalupe's "conversation" or "interaction" with Juan Diega a re-creation occurs: The barren earth produces life (roses in December), and a marginalized person regains his subjectivity (Juan Diego).[52] Echoing the central motif of Genesis 2-3, the story of Guadalupe suggests a reversal of the distorted sinful relationships that turn human persons into objects, and render unjust and exploitative the entire economy of creation. The interaction of Guadalupe and Juan Diego reveals something about the particular U.S. Hispanic way of conceiving how human persons encounter the life of grace that enables the recreation of human persons and everything under their stewardship. In his "inter-action" with Guadalupe, Juan Diego encounters a "grace-bearing sign" that enables him to affirm himself as a person rather than as "dung," and in so doing he mediates a restoration of right relationship between the human, the divine, and all of God's creatures.[53]

Our Lady of Guadalupe is not just perceived to be "of the people." She is also perceived to be "of God," and, therefore, symbolically connected to the experience of grace. "Because she is one of the violated people," writes Elizondo, "she can understand brokenness; because she is of God, she can completely rehabilitate those who have been abused."[54] Guadalupe, argue other U.S. Hispanic theologians, is: 1) "God's self giving or grace,"[55] 2) "the poetry of the Trinitarian God,"[56] 3) a *mestizo* revelation of the divine,"[57] 4) a "projected symbol of Providence,"[58] and 5) a cosmic reconciler or healer of personal and social evils.[59]

Within U.S. Hispanic theological anthropology, Guadalupe represents a social and cultural expression of God's ongoing preferential identification with the poor. Guadalupe is not "God." She is not, as Jesus or the Spirit are, ontologically speaking, revealer of God. Rather, what can be argued within the U.S. Hispanic context is that the symbol of Guadalupe can be interpreted as an aesthetic and semantic mediator of what the Christian tradition understands by grace.[60] As symbolic expression, Guadalupe functions, in the words of one Latino theologian, as a "cul-

---

[52]Goizueta, *Caminemos con Jesús*, 44.

[53]See ibid., 77.

[54]Elizondo, *Guadalupe: Mother of the New Creation*, 67.

[55]Rodriguez, *Our Lady of Guadalupe*, 150.

[56]García, "Our Lady of Guadalupe: A Sign of Ecclesial Unity," 105.

[57]Goizueta, "U.S. Hispanic Popular Catholicism as Theopoetics," 282.

[58]Espín, "The Vanquished, Faithful Solidarity, and the Marian Symbol," 87.

[59]On Guadalupe's association with healing see Elizondo, *Guadalupe: Mother of the New Creation*, 73-77; Goizueta, *Caminemos con Jesús*, 42, and Rodriguez, *Our Lady of Guadalupe*, 42-44.

[60]Goizueta, "U.S. Hispanic Popular Catholicism as Theopoetics," 284.

tural analogy of some divine attributes."[61] It is in this sense that she can be characterized as an essential U.S. Hispanic sacramental mediator of grace.

Perhaps nowhere else in the Guadalupan tradition is this understanding better exemplified than at the beginning of the story of Our Lady of Guadalupe: Juan Diego, a marginalized subject, stops to "hear" a word of grace, and "gazing" upon this word recognizes the word as "beautiful," as proceeding from within his own social, cultural, and religious history.[62] The "word" Juan Diego sees, and the word that accompanies him, is the word which, as Goizueta argues, eventually leads Juan Diego to see himself as a human subject, that is as a person, "even in his abandonment."[63] Goizueta's interpretation of the Guadalupan event, especially his emphasis on the grace that Guadalupe mediates to Juan Diego through his "participation in" the ongoing experience of the cross, suggests how the sacramentality of U.S. Hispanic Marian devotions can be related to God's definitive offer of grace in Jesus Christ. Indeed, U.S. Hispanic popular devotions to Mary generally portray her in relationship to her Son. Mary is not just Mary, but the mother of Jesus.[64] Guadalupe is not just Guadalupe but the mother of the abandoned Juan Diego who like Jesus suffers the pain of abandonment.

The historical reality that gave rise to the symbol and story of Guadalupe is analogous to the historical reality of present U.S. Hispanic communities.[65] The symbol and its story emerged in the midst of, and bridged, social, cultural, and religious conflicts.[66] The symbol and story emerged within the ecclesial body of the poor,[67] especially the ecclesial body of conquered and raped women.[68] It is the memory of this history, sacra-

---

[61]For instance see Espín, "Tradition and Popular Religion," 75.

[62]See the text of the *Nican mopohua* in Elizondo's *Guadalupe: Mother of the New Creation*, 6-7.

[63]Goizueta, "U.S. Hispanic Popular Catholicism as Theopoetics," 284-285.

[64]Goizueta, *Caminemos con Jesús*, 70.

[65]See Jeanette Rodriguez, "Contemporary Encounters with Guadalupe," *Journal of Hispanic/Latino Theology* 5/1 (1997): 48-60; idem, "*Sangre llama a sangre*: Cultural Memory as a Source of Theological Insight," in *Hispanic/Latino Theology*, 117-133; Timothy M. Matovina, "Guadalupan Devotion in a Borderlands Community," *Journal of Hispanic/Latino Theology* 4/1 (1996): 6-25; Elizondo, "Guadalupe as a Cultural Symbol: 'The Power of the Powerless,' " *Liturgy and Cultural Religious Traditions*, ed. Herman Schmidt and David Power (New York: Seabury, 1977), 25-33; Goizueta, "U.S. Hispanic Popular Catholicism as Theopoetics," 280-288; and Andrés G. Guerrero, *A Chicano Theology* (Maryknoll, New York: Orbis Books, 1987), 96-117.

[66]See Elizondo, *La Morenita*, esp. 57-64; idem, *Guadalupe: Mother of the New Creation*, 25-33; and Rodriguez, *Our Lady of Guadalupe*, 1-46.

[67]Note García's understanding of Guadalupe as a symbol of the Church, and in particular of the poor and discriminated persons in the Church. See his "Our Lady of Guadalupe: A Sign of Ecclesial Unity," 100 and 104.

[68]See Guerrero, *A Chicano Theology*, 113-115.

mentally evoked by the symbol itself, that U.S. Hispanic theologians understand is capable of enabling the historical participation of present-day U.S. Hispanic communities. Thus, Elizondo writes:

> In these new places amid new languages and cultures, she continues to be a source of cultural-religious dialogue. She enables her children to adapt in new and challenging situations while not losing the deepest treasures of their ancient traditions. Her ability to unify contradictory expressions of life continues to bring new life out of the contradictions and struggles that Latinas/os encounter in the United States.[69]

This sacramental participation of U.S. Hispanic communities in the Guadalupan reality effects communal ties, legitimizes ethnic identity, and resists the diminishment of religious and cultural heritage.[70] Thus, Guadalupe functions as the bearer and preserver of the communal identity of Latinos and Latinas. More specifically, within the writings of U.S. Hispanic theologians she has been identified with immigrants and with her ability to empower women to overcome oppressive relationships.[71] Her all-encompassing sacramental presence in the barrios, homes, and businesses of Mexican-Americans suggests the ongoing life of grace within the ordinary experiences of marginalized persons.[72]

These arguments exemplify the correlation between Guadalupe's accompaniment of marginalized communities then, and her accompaniment of marginalized communities now. Just as she was found then in the midst of *lo cotidiano* (Juan Diego's routine walk to Church) and wished to remain within the places associated with the ordinariness of life ("home"),[73] she still abides, today within ordinary places.[74] Just as she was the reflec-

---

[69]Elizondo, "Guadalupe: An Endless Source of Reflection," *Journal of Hispanic/ Latino Theology* 5/1 (1997): 64.

[70]See especially, Timothy M. Matovina, who elaborates on this symbolic participation by drawing on various Guadalupan rituals and ceremonies. See his "Guadalupan Devotion in a Borderlands Community," 6-26.

[71]See Michael E. Engh, "Companion of the Immigrants: Devotion to Our Lady of Guadalupe among Mexicans in the Los Angeles Area, 1900-1940," *Journal of Hispanic/Latino Theology* 5/1 (1997): 37-47; Rodriguez, *Our Lady of Guadalupe*, 127-142.

[72]Rodriguez, "God Is Always Pregnant" in *The Divine Mosaic: Women's Images of the Sacred Other*, ed. Theresa King (St. Paul: Yes International Publishers, 1994), 113.

[73]See Elizondo who points out how Guadalupe requests the building of a dwelling place and uses the following words to describe this place: 1) hermitage (place for the homeless), 2) a home (place of affectionate relationships), and 3), a temple (place to encounter the sacred). See Elizondo, *Guadalupe: Mother of the New Creation*, 8, 101, 113.

[74]On this point, see especially Espín's chapter on "Grace and Sin" in *From the Heart of Our People*.

tion of the marginalized then, so is she still associated with the faces of contemporary "Galileans." I turn now to the symbol and story of Our Lady of Charity. Though less known than Our Lady of Guadalupe, with respect to both the academy and the Church, this devotion represents a similar yet distinct expression of what it means to be "Hispanically" human.[75]

THE SYMBOL AND STORY OF OUR LADY OF CHARITY

Referring to Our Lady of Charity, Espín argues that it is very interesting how "the fundamental intuitions and structures" related to this devotion "are so similar to Guadalupe's, even if the externals and details are different." Like its Guadalupan counterpart, the symbol and story of Our Lady of Charity reflects a similar socio-cultural reality. Like Our Lady of Guadalupe, the devotion to Our Lady of Charity is "popular" in the U.S. Hispanic sense of the term.

Unlike the Guadalupan story, however, the story of Our Lady of Charity is not primarily associated with a Marian apparition. Nor does this Cuban and Cuban-American tradition have a long-standing written source similar to the *Nican mopohua*. Rather, the story has been primarily transmitted by oral and iconic tradition. The story revolves around the finding of a statue of the Virgin Mary.[76] Only in recent times did the Cuban historian Leví Marrero, searching through the Archives of the Indies in Seville, Spain, uncover an important written source for this Marian tradition. What Marrero found was the sworn testimony of Juan Moreno given to Spanish authorities in 1687. Moreno claims to have been one of three

---

[75]My essay "Dime con quién andas y te diré quién eres," in *From the Heart of Our People,* provides the first engaged and prolonged reflection on the story and symbol of Our Lady of Charity. Other U.S. Hispanic theologians who have alluded to this tradition, and have partly incorporated it into their reflections, include: Alex García-Rivera, "Wisdom, Beauty, and the Cosmos in Hispanic Spirituality and Theology," in *El Cuerpo de Cristo,* 106-113; Espín, "The Vanquished, Faithful Solidarity, and the Marian Symbol," 93-95, and Roberto S. Goizueta, "U.S. Hispanic Popular Catholicism as Theopoetics," note 77.

[76]Written accounts are available, but such accounts are not the primary means through which this tradition has been communicated. For instance, see Onofre de Fonseca, *Historia de la aparición milagrosa de Nuestra Señora de la Caridad del Cobre* (Santiago de Cuba: Impr. del Real Consulado de Santiago de Cuba, por Loreto Espinel, 1830); Ismael Testé, *Historia eclesiástica de Cuba,* vol. III (Burgos: Editorial el Monte Carmelo, 1969), 346-412; Leví Marrero, *Los esclavos y la Virgen del Cobre. Dos siglos de lucha por la libertad de Cuba* (Miami: Ediciones Universal, 1980); Irene A. Wright, "Our Lady of Charity: Nuestra Señora de la Caridad del Cobre (Santiago de Cuba), Nuestra Señora de la Caridad de Illescas (Castilla, Spain)," *Hispanic American Historical Review* 5 (1922): 709-717; and, most recently, in Olga Portuondo Zúñiga, *La Virgen de la Caridad del Cobre: Símbolo de cubanía* (Santiago de Cuba: Editorial Oriente, 1995).

men who found the statue of Our Lady of Charity. In this testimony, he recounts the events that led to the finding of the statue and those that occurred thereafter.

Iconically, the image is that of a woman with the child Jesus in her arms. Some have seen in the complexion of the woman and the child an iconic representation of the coming together of the European and the African cultures. "The statue of Mary and her Child are so obviously mixed-race," writes Espín, "that no explanation but intentional choice could explain their color in seventeenth-century Cuba."[77] Others have noted how the image reflects the Amerindian or Taíno culture of Cuba.[78] In either case, similar to Guadalupe, the image of Our Lady of Charity evokes the socio-cultural history of particular relationships among Spanish, Amerindian, and African peoples.

The statue of Our Lady of Charity was found by Juan Moreno, an African slave, and two Indian brothers, Juan de Hoyos and Rodrigo de Hoyos. According to the testimony of Juan Moreno,[79] the statue was found floating in the bay of Nipe as he and his two other companions were going about their ordinary business of searching for salt.[80] Interestingly enough, over the years human imagination embellished this ordinary set of circumstances with the presence of the supernatural. The stillness of the waters was transformed into a storm. This was perhaps done in an effort to underscore the encounter with grace in the midst of life-threatening circumstances that affected human and other creatures at the time. Thus, by a kind of popular and intuitive faith-filled sense, a link was established among natural, human, and divine realities. The story, which is most often told in oral traditions, speaks of how three salt-gatherers were saved in the midst of a storm.[81] A number of contemporary iconographical representations of Our Lady of Charity also witness this popular religious imagination.[82]

---

[77]Espín, "The Vanquished, Faithful Solidarity, and the Marian Symbol," 94.

[78]See Anthony M. Stevens, "The Persistence of Religious Cosmovision in an Alien World," in *Enigmatic Powers: Syncretism with African and Indigenous Peoples' Religions among Latinos*, ed. Anthony M. Stevens-Arroyo and Andres I. Pérez y Mena (New York: Bildner Center for Western Hemispheric Studies, 1995), 124-129.

[79]The testimony of Juan Moreno was discovered in 1973 by Cuban historian Leví Marrero in the Archives of the Indies in Seville. See Archivo General de Indias, Audiencia de Santo Domingo, legajo 363. This document has been transcribed and printed in several places. For instance, see Mario Vizcaíno, *La Virgen de la Caridad, Patrona de Cuba* (Miami: Instituto Pastoral del Sureste, 1981), 10-27.

[80]The bay of Nipe is located in the easternmost province of Cuba, and just north of the region known as del Prado. In seventeenth century Cuba, this region became the site of Spanish mining.

[81]See my essay, "Dime con quíen andas y te diré quien eres," esp. 160-161.

[82]For García-Rivera's description of the image, which follows this imaginative evolution, see his "Wisdom, Beauty, and the Cosmos in Hispanic Spirituality and

The statue's inscription, *"Yo soy la Virgen de la Caridad"* ("I am the Virgin of Charity") suggests the central theological theme of this devotion: charity as solidarity with the poor and marginalized.[83] Those who found this statue, namely an African slave and two Amerindians, the first devotees of this popular Catholic devotion, provide the hermeneutical key that unveils this theme. As representatives of Cuba's most oppressed classes in the seventeenth century, these three "salt-gatherers" demonstrate God's preferential love of the poor. Thus, the recent Episcopal Cuban conference declares:

> The image of Mary of Charity was found by three representatives of the most poor and exploited classes: two Indians and a black slave whom she fills with the joy of her presence. They, the humble, will seal her solidarity and nearness because Mary brings with her the one who "has shown the might of his arm, who deposes the proud in their inmost thoughts, who has deposed the mighty from their thrones and raised the lowly to high places, and has given every good thing to the hungry and has sent away the rich empty."[84]

Similar to Our Lady of Guadalupe, the symbol of Our Lady of Charity is not only a revelation about a particular people, but also a revelation about God. Like Our Lady of Guadalupe, Our Lady of Charity, argues Espín, is a symbol of grace, a symbol of God's "faithful solidarity."[85] For Espín, the symbol and story of Our Lady of Charity is a symbol that speaks a word of grace, and in a social cultural way communicates what divine providence is. Our Lady of Charity, Espín notes, is the culturally authentic way by which Cubans and Cuban-Americans perceive, understand, and express God's nearness to them.[86]

Like its Guadalupan counterpart, the symbol of Our Lady of Charity effects communal ties, legitimizes ethnic identity, and resists the diminishment of their cultural heritage.[87] "Our Lady of Charity," Cuban-American exiles believe, "is one of us."[88] She is found in their barrios, homes, and businesses. Although she has taken on new meanings in light of the Cuban-American exilic conditions, she is still very much, as was the case with

---

Theology," 106. See also Espín, "The Vanquished, Faithful Solidarity, and the Marian Symbol," 94.

[83]Espín, "The Vanquished, Faithful Solidarity, and the Marian Symbol," 110; and Miguel H. Díaz, "Dime con quíen andas y te diré quien eres," 153-171.

[84]*Encuentro Nacional Eclesial Cubano: Documento final e instruccion pastoral de los obispos,* 1.9. My translation.

[85]Espín, "The Vanquished, Faithful Solidarity, and the Marian Symbol," 95-96.

[86]Ibid., 96.

[87]See Thomas Tweed, *Our Lady of the Exile: Diasporic Religion at a Cuban Catholic Shrine in Miami* (New York: Oxford University Press, 1997), esp. 83-142.

[88]Ibid., 104.

those salt-gatherers who first found her, associated with the working poor.[89] In a special way, women rank among her primary devotees.[90] Again, as is the case with the Guadalupan symbol, the symbol of Our Lady of Charity evokes the U.S. Hispanic preference for particular persons and spaces.

The imaginative transformation of the ordinary into extraordinary (the salvation of the salt-gatherers in the midst of a storm) has been associated semiotically with Our Lady of Charity's ability to depict, through cosmological signs, socio-historical realities. Thus, García-Rivera has argued that in La Caridad, "natural evil appears to symbolize all human suffering."[91] García-Rivera's arguments point to the concrete "dangerous memory" (in Metz's sense of the term) that founds this devotion. As Espín's arguments underscore, "faithful solidarity" with marginalized persons originally founds this Christian tradition. Though emphasizing different aspects of the symbol (one, the historical; the other, the cosmological), both Espín and García-Rivera's arguments invite a more historically sensitive interpretation of the symbol that precludes its spiritualization.

Just as Goizueta, following the interpretation of Clodomiro L. Siller-Acuña, points out how the Guadalupan devotion was spiritualized when it became an "object" of admiration, rather than a symbol mediating a "dangerous memory,"[92] so the symbol of Our Lady of Charity can undergo similar spiritualizations. The stormy waters that have become part of this symbol's cosmology may in fact suggest how cosmology replicates anthropology. Espín's understanding of Our Lady of Charity's as "faithful solidarity" reflects, however, U.S. Hispanic concerns to ground aesthetic experience in the preferential love of the poor and marginalized (Goizueta). This vision should continue to guide any future theological interpretations and pastoral implications of this devotion.[93]

LOOKING AHEAD: ENVISIONING NEW SACRAMENTAL MEDIATORS OF GRACE

The symbol of Our Lady of Charity presents some further challenges to U.S. Hispanic theologians. Recent sociological research by Thomas A. Tweed in Miami has demonstrated how generational differences must be

---

[89]Espín, "The Vanquished, Faithful Solidarity, and the Marian Symbol," 95. Note, however, Tweed's sociological research contradicts this conclusion. In our judgment, the problem with Tweed's research is the fact that he primarily derived his conclusions from data derived at the shrine of Our Lady of Charity in Miami. Tweed himself acknowledges the need to conduct further research. See *Our Lady of the Exile*, 65.

[90]Tweed, *Our Lady of the Exile*, 61.

[91]García-Rivera, "Wisdom, Beauty, and the Cosmos," 112.

[92]Goizueta, *Caminemos con Jesús*, 45-46.

[93]See my essay "Dime con quién andas y te diré quién eres," 153-171.

considered in popular Catholic devotions. According to Tweed, the symbol of Our Lady of Charity appears to stir personal and collective memories mostly among first generation Cuban-Americans.[94] Tweed argues that the symbol functions to "translocate" this first generation of Cuban-Americans across space and time, thereby putting them in touch with the roots of their secular and sacred history.[95] Tweed's conclusions, however, may need some qualifications in light of the recent events surrounding Elian González. The finding of the child at sea stirred deep memories related to the social, cultural, and religious mythos that has shaped the lives of Cuban-Americans in exile. The child became a symbol of communal self-identity and his "salvation" at sea was quickly attributed to Our Lady of Charity. Even more significant is that in the aftermath of this human tragedy, Cuban-American youth in Miami appear to be more interested than in the past to identify with and claim their socio-cultural and religious roots.

So far, U.S. Hispanic theology has been very mindful of social, cultural, political, and gender experiences. Generational issues, however, have entered little into the definition of its context. As new generations of U.S. Hispanics emerge, it will become necessary to re-visit the issue of U.S. Hispanic context and sacramental mediators of grace. How much effect will the ongoing exposure to Euro-Anglo Catholic experiences have on present-day U.S. Hispanics? How will the new generation of U.S. Hispanics conceive the experience and language of grace? To what extent should socio-cultural factors within each Latino/a community be taken into consideration in understanding differences in the appeal of traditional U.S. Hispanic popular Catholic expressions on new generations of U.S. Hispanics? What will be the primary sacramental means to the life of grace for this new generation of U.S. Hispanics? In the wake of this new generation of Latinos/as, U.S. Hispanic theologians will need to become even more conscious than they have been of the geographical and generational differences that constitute the subjects of their reflection. This new consciousness will undoubtedly impact the way future U.S. Hispanic theological reflections conceive what is "Hispanically" human in its relationship to the life of grace.

---

[94]Tweed, *Our Lady of the Exile*, 65.

[95]Ibid., 94. Note, too, how the central mural behind the altar in the Shrine of Our Lady of Charity in Miami, Florida, is basically an historical iconic representation of the religious and secular history of the Cuban people. See also Tweed, *Our Lady of the Exile*, 107-110.

4

On Being Human
From Rahnerian Perspectives

WHY KARL RAHNER?

Contemporary Catholic thought stands on the shoulders of giants like Karl Rahner.[1] Characterized as the "greatest Catholic theologian of the twentieth century,"[2] Rahner has been perceived as "the ticket to theology's agenda for the twenty-first century."[3] Rahner's ability to address a wide range of theological issues, his attentiveness to the thought of Thomas Aquinas, his appropriation of contemporary philosophical insights, his contributions to Catholic theology leading to and following the Second Vatican Council, and his increased awareness and openness to other theological traditions within and outside the Church have surely earned him a place of distinction within contemporary Catholic thought.

In light of the recent explosion of contextual theologies that have moved Christian reflection beyond the European hold and into a manifold of idioms, thought patterns, and cultures, one may legitimately ask: Why Karl Rahner? My reasons for engaging Rahner in a book that seeks to deepen an understanding of U.S. Hispanic theological anthropology revolve around the following: 1) Rahner's theological vision of the ordinariness of life; 2) his understanding of popular faith experiences as a privileged source for theological reflection; 3) Rahner's methodological insistence on maintaining an intrinsic connection between human experi-

---

[1] On the influence of Rahner on contemporary theology see Stephen J. Duffy, *The Graced Horizon: Nature and Grace in Modern Catholic Thought* (Collegeville: Liturgical Press, 1992), 226.

[2] Andrew Tallon, "Editors's Introduction" to Karl Rahner, *Hearer of the Word*, trans. Joseph Donceel (New York: Continuum, 1994), xviii. See also, Johann Baptist Metz, *A Passion for God: The Mystical-Political Dimension of Christianity*, trans. J. Matthew Ashley (New York: Paulist Press, 1998), 92.

[3] Tallon, "Editor's Introduction," xviii.

ences and Christian doctrines; 4) his spiritual, philosophical, and theological conversational horizon, which includes classical and contemporary sources; 5) Rahner's invitation to decentralize the European influences on the Church and theology in order to realize a more authentic global vision; and 6) the historical and open-ended understanding of his transcendental theology.

First, Rahner's theological anthropology can be characterized as an anthropology that underscores ordinary life experiences (*lo cotidiano*), as loci for encountering grace. Because he sees the human "always and everywhere" as the addressee of God's self-communication, for Rahner, all personal experiences contain at least an implicit, yet primordial, experience of God."[4] Similarly, U.S. Hispanic theological anthropology is also characterized by a focus on ordinary life experiences, and the grace encountered within those experiences. Differences between these two visions of humanity and the life of grace will be discussed. Rahner's concept of what is ordinary and what is grace-filled necessarily differs from emerging U.S. Hispanic understandings precisely because we are dealing with faith-filled theological responses that engage different contexts.

Second, and closely related to the above observations, is Rahner's appreciation of the faith of the people. In a post-Vatican II essay entitled "The Relationship between Theology and Popular Religion"[5] (a significant essay from the perspective of U.S. Hispanic theological emphases and concerns), Rahner argues that revelation is first and foremost always and everywhere "mediated by the concrete life of its hearers."[6] Rahner privileges the ordinary faith experience of the people over against what he terms "systematic, hence narrowing, theology."[7] While acknowledging the "countless deformations and corruptions of popular religion, Rahner maintains that "[t]he superiority of popular religion to theology . . . consists in the fact that popular religion is continually being unconsciously inspired and carried by original revelation."[8] "That is why," continues Rahner, "popular religion, borne by the power of grace, may spontaneously welcome and realize every human possibility, and, in that sense, have the courage simply to be human."[9]

---

[4]See Harvey D. Egan, *Karl Rahner: Mystic of Everyday Life* (New York: Crossroad, 1988), esp. 57.

[5]Rahner, "The Relation between Theology and Popular Religion," in *Theological Investigations*, XXII, trans. Joseph Donceel (New York: Crossroad, 1984), 140-147.

[6]Rahner, "The Relation between Theology and Popular Religion," 147. Note that among the characteristics of Rahner's later essays is a critique of institutional religion. This could partly help to explain the emphasis Rahner gives to popular religion in this essay. See Leo J. O'Donovan, "A Journey into Time: The Legacy of Karl Rahner's Last Years," *Theological Studies* (1985): 624.

[7]Rahner, "The Relation between Theology and Popular Religion," 145.

[8]Ibid.

[9]Ibid.

Rahner's essay underscores the fundamental importance of popular religion for theology (and not just the other way around) because in his view, popular religion is "closer to that first source of genuine religiosity and real faith that consists in God's universal standing invitation to accept divinization."[10] The ordinary faith experiences of a people, as that experience is socially and historically constituted, Rahner maintains, mediate at the most fundamental level the hearing and acceptance of God's Word.[11] Given the emphasis that U.S. Hispanic theology places on popular faith expressions, and their ability to mediate in social, cultural, and engendered ways the life of grace, Rahner's theology of grace, which as is evident from the arguments above underscores popular expressions of faith as fundamental loci of God's self-communication, is worthy of consideration.

Third, Rahner provides an example of and challenge to contextual theologians on how to explore human experiences from a foundational perspective, and how to relate these experiences to Christian doctrines. As James Bacik observes, "Standing behind this [Rahner's] methodology is the conviction that human experience and Christian doctrines are connected not simply logically and externally but organically and intrinsically."[12] Even after embracing the challenges of emerging political and liberationist visions, he cautioned that these theologies needed to engage much more in foundational matters. "If they are to be justified and to cover the whole of dogma," Rahner argues, "these theologies, too, need transcendental-speculative reflections . . ." because, according to Rahner, they run the "danger of becoming so enthusiastic about the novelty and urgency of their task that they are liable to forget difficult and absolutely imperative theological problems and tasks."[13]

Undoubtedly, U.S. Hispanic theology has been quite convincing in its attempts to point out the need to attend to the concrete experiences of the people of God. U.S. Hispanic theology runs the risk, however, of not sufficiently relating these concrete experiences to foundational concerns. Rahner's transcendental anthropology can help pave the way in this direction. His effort to correlate human experience and doctrine provides a heuristic example and challenge for U.S. Hispanic theologians to consider, as we continue to develop and articulate the relationship that our specific claims carry for re-envisioning Christian doctrines.

Fourth, because of Rahner's central conversational partners, entering into conversation with Rahner can broaden and deepen the conversa-

---

[10]Ibid.

[11]Ibid., 144 and 147.

[12]See James Bacik, *Apologetics and the Eclipse of Mystery: Mystagogy According to Karl Rahner* (Notre Dame: University of Notre Dame Press, 1980), 13.

[13]Rahner, "Foundations of Christian Faith," in *Theological Investigations*, XIX, trans. Edward Quinn (New York: Crossroad, 1983), 14-15.

tional horizon of U.S. Hispanic theological anthropology.[14] Thus far, partly as a result of the nature of their contextual project (e.g., dialogue with sources specific to the U.S. Hispanic experience), and partly as a result of the novelty of their project, U.S. Hispanic theologians have failed to engage in sustained, systematic, and explicit conversations with the central figures of contemporary Catholic thought. Engaging Rahner can contribute to this process and significantly expand the hermeneutical horizon of U.S. Hispanic theology.[15]

In a way, Rahner and his sources are already part of U.S. Hispanic traditions. Or perhaps, it is the other way around. When asked who were the most influential persons on his theology, Rahner readily recognized St. Ignatius of Loyola.[16] Without having to go into an extended discussion of this theme, it is prudent at the very least to point out how the incarnational principle that governs much of Rahner's theological anthropology (the discernment of grace in the ordinariness of life) stems from the kind of Spanish medieval spirituality that influenced the foundations and present orientations of Latino/a spirituality and theology.[17]

Fifth, Rahner envisioned a more genuine globalization of the Church and theology. Recognizing the historical limitations of his own European context, and anticipating the present era of philosophical and theological pluralism, Rahner increasingly welcomed other voices in theology.[18] While praising the accomplishments of the Second Vatican Council, Rahner continued to encourage pluralism within the Church. He challenged the Church to abandon its Euro-centric hold on theology and to embrace the spectrum of contextual visions even if that meant that such expressions

---

[14]See Thomas F. O'Meara, "Karl Rahner: Some Audiences and Sources for His Theology," *Communio* 18/2 (1991): 237-251.

[15]At least one U.S. Hispanic theologian has already perceived the need to engage Rahner's theology. See Claudio Burgaleta, "A Rahnerian Reading of Santeria: A Proposal for a Christian Recovery of the Syncretic Elements of Latin American Popular Religiosity Based on Rahner's Concept of 'Anonymous Christianity,' " *Apuntes* 13 (1993): 139-150.

[16]Paul Imhof and Hubert Biallowons, eds., *Karl Rahner: Faith in a Wintry Season: Conversations and Interviews with Karl Rahner in the Last Years of His Life*, trans. Harvey D. Egan (New York: Crossroad, 1991), 39.

[17]On this insight I am indebted to private conversations with Dr. Antonio Lopez, professor of philosophical theology at St. Vincent de Paul Regional Seminary. On Ignatius of Loyola's incarnational spirituality see the classic work by Joseph de Guibert, *The Jesuits, Their Spiritual Doctrine and Practice: A Historical Study*, trans. William J. Young (Chicago: Loyola University Press, 1964).

[18]See Rahner, "Possible Courses for the Theology of the Future," in *Theological Investigations*, XIII, trans. David Bourke (New York: Crossroad, 1975), 32-60; Rahner, "Reflections on a New Task for Fundamental Theology," in *Theological Investigations*, XVI, trans. David Morland (New York: Crossroad, 1979), 156-166; Rahner, "Reflections on Methodology in Theology," in *Theological Investigations*, XI, trans. David Bourke (New York: Crossroad, 1974), 68-114.

of faith would "at first" be alienating and "all but unintelligible."[19] For Rahner, theological pluralism was judged to be an essential implication of true Christian communion.

Sixth, although characterizations of Rahner's transcendental theology through the 1960s stressed his modern and idealist tendencies, Rahner's theology became more historically conscious in response to the changes initiated by the Second Vatican Council.[20] For instance, while in his writings after the Council Rahner still accepts the description of his theology as transcendental, he rejects the understanding that sees the human person as the subject of faith in an abstract transcendentality.[21] Rather, Rahner affirms that in his theology, transcendentality and history imply one another, that the immanent consummation of a history *is* its transcendent consummation.[22] For Rahner, transcendentality has to do with the mystery of salvation encountered "in," "with," and "under" historical realities. Thus, he writes:

In the last resort it must be shown that man's history is *not* something in which he is involved *over and above* his transcendentality to God as the absolute being and mystery, but that it is only *as* history of this transcendentality in freedom that history is actually history in which salvation can come about.[23]

Even though Rahner's transcendental theology increasingly became historically sensitive after the Council, he was still criticized for focusing too much on the private experience of faith, and not sufficiently attending to social issues.[24] Rahner himself recognized these criticisms but maintained that his theology was open to be developed in more socially and

---

[19]Rahner, *The Love of Jesus and the Love of Neighbor* (New York: Crossroad, 1985), 79. On the other hand note that Rahner also believed that European theology could act as a guardian of tradition and safeguard against dangers threatening other emerging theologies. See his "Aspects of European Theology," in *Theological Investigations*, XXI, trans. Hugh M. Riley (New York: Crossroad, 1988), 89-96.

[20]On the post-Vatican II changes that led Rahner to emphasize history over the previous existential focus in his thought see Thomas O'Meara, "Teaching Karl Rahner," *Philosophy & Theology* 12 (1998): 19.

[21]See Rahner, "Foundations of Christian Faith," 8.

[22]Rahner, "Immanent and Transcendent Consummation of the World," in *Theological Investigations*, X, trans. David Bourke (New York: Herder and Herder, 1973), 273-289.

[23]Rahner, "Foundations of Christian Faith," 8. Emphasis in original.

[24]On Rahner's tendency to privatize and intellectualize human experience see Johann Baptist Metz, *Faith in History and Society: Toward a Practical Fundamental Theology*, trans. David Smith (New York: Seabury Press, 1980), 230-231; Brackley, *Divine Revolution: Salvation and Liberation in Catholic Thought* (Maryknoll, New York: Orbis Books, 1996), 61-64; J. A. Colombo "Rahner and His Critics: Lindbeck and Metz," *The Thomist* 56/1 (1992): 91-96.

politically sensitive ways.[25] That such is the case is suggested by his understanding of what constitutes transcendental theology. For Rahner, "any *analysis fidei* implies some transcendental reflection" because in any such attempt fundamental questions must be raised and answered relative to the possibility of hearing and accepting God's Word and revelation.[26] Thus, what Rahner came to understand as "transcendental reflection" was not some kind of abstract Kantian analysis of faith experiences, but rather an incarnational vision of relating concrete human experiences to the ground of their existence. In fact, Rahner even abandoned the need for transcendental philosophy, and welcomed other tools and disciplines in theological explorations of faith.[27] Perhaps, it would be more accurate to describe Rahner's later thought as an exercise in fundamental sacramentality that is increasingly mindful of the ways that grace can be encountered in the plurality of historical experiences, especially in the experiences of the poor. Rahner never abandons his conviction of the ordinariness of grace, but as I will later point out, in the process of conversation and challenge he signals some qualifications.

Undoubtedly, objections can also be raised to the inclusion of Karl Rahner within a book that explores U.S. Hispanic theological anthropology. Some could fear that this option would take U.S. Hispanic theological anthropology on the path of European theological colonization. Others would argue that if the choice was made to engage a European theologian, why not engage someone like Johann Baptist Metz? Given the pronounced socio-cultural concerns of U.S. Hispanic theological anthropology, especially the focus on suffering subjects and on those who for various reasons are considered non-persons of the U.S. church and society, someone like Metz would make a more appropriate conversational partner. Indeed, some of the writings of various U.S. Hispanic theologians already exemplify the possibility of such conversation.[28]

---

[25]See "Foundations of Christian Faith," 14-15.

[26]See Rahner, ed., *Encyclopedia of Theology: The Concise Sacramentum Mundi* (New York: Crossroad, 1989), 1749.

[27]On Rahner's position regarding transcendental philosophy see his, "Possible Courses for the Theology of the Future," 45-46. On his embrace of other disciplines in theology see "On the Current Relationship between Philosophy and Theology," in *Theological Investigations*, XIII, trans. David Bourke (New York: Crossroad, 1983), 72-79.

[28]For instance see Roberto S. Goizueta, "U.S. Hispanic Popular Catholicism as Theopoetics," in *Hispanic/Latino Theology: Challenge and Promise*, ed. Ada María Isasi-Díaz and Fernando F. Segovia (Minneapolis: Fortress Press, 1996), 275; Sixto J. García, "A Hispanic Approach to Trinitarian Theology: The Dynamics of Celebration, Reflection, and Praxis," in *We Are a People!: Initiatives in Hispanic American Theology* (Minneapolis: Fortress Press, 1992), 107-111; Jeanette Rodríguez, "*Sangre llama a sangre*: Cultural Memory as a Source of Theological Insight," in *Hispanic/Latino Theology*, 122-126.

Yet, Metz, even after he distanced himself from Rahner's theology in the mid-sixties and proposed his own practical fundamental theology, continued to regard Rahner as "not only a teacher but also a father in faith"[29] and "a productive example of how to deal theologically with what is probably the most profound crisis facing contemporary Christianity: the crisis of passing on the faith to the next generation, from old to young."[30] While he did not believe that Rahner's central affirmation of theology as anthropology could "be simply repeated in a political theology of the subject," Metz argued that this affirmation was certainly capable of being made "more historically and socially evident"[31] within the parameters of his practical fundamental theology. In a similar way, while Rahner's anthropological starting point cannot be simply reproduced in U.S. Hispanic theology, his overall emphasis on anthropology as the starting point of theological reflection can be developed in a way that is more socially, historically, and culturally sensitive, and consequently, more in line with the concerns of U.S. Hispanic theological anthropology.

Others could also argue that given the emphasis U.S. Hispanic theological anthropology places on theological aesthetics someone like Hans Urs von Balthasar would be more appropriate to choose as a conversational partner. Some U.S. Hispanic theologians such as Roberto Goizueta and Alex García-Rivera have already initiated conversation along this path. Such efforts are welcomed and needed. I believe, however, that ultimately, Rahner's theological anthropology is more capable than Balthasar's of responding to the historical concreteness that informs U.S. Hispanic concerns. As Goizueta himself admits, Balthasar's project runs the danger of becoming an aestheticism because it is not "grounded in the historical praxis of oppressed communities."[32] Rahner may not have the aesthetical emphasis that one finds in Balthasar, but Rahner's theological anthropology does not lack this perspective. Moreover, partly as a result of his increased theological attentiveness to history, and, as I will later argue, partly as a result of his recognition of the social and practical dimension of history, Rahner's vision is more prone to enter into conversation with Latino/a theological concerns.

Finally, the choice of Rahner could be questioned on the basis of his marginal contribution to gender issues in theological anthropology. Since gender issues are an essential aspect of U.S. Hispanic theological anthro-

---

[29]See Metz, *A Passion for God*, 119.

[30]Ibid., 100.

[31]See Metz, *Faith in History and Society*, 64. See also Ashley's insightful reflections comparing and contrasting Rahner and Metz in *Interruptions: Mysticism, Politics, and Theology in the Work of Johann Baptist Metz* (Notre Dame: University of Notre Dame Press, 1998), 171-196.

[32]Goizueta, "U.S. Hispanic Popular Catholicism as Theopoetics," 271, note 21.

pology, Rahner's failure to speak to this human dimension could raise legitimate objections. Yet, just as feminist theologians have already begun a critical appropriation of Karl Rahner's thought,[33] the specific contributions in U.S. Hispanic visions of humanity that have emerged from the analysis of socio-gender experiences can also be brought into fruitful conversation with Rahner.

This chapter explores three central interrelated themes in Rahner's theological anthropology: 1) Rahner's theology of grace; 2) Rahner's theology of person and community; and 3) The social and practical character of Rahner's theological anthropology. This selection is not intended to represent all aspects of Rahner's theological anthropology. Rather, my purpose is to select elements in Rahner's thought that can enable a fruitful conversation with U.S. Hispanic visions. The selection, however, is not arbitrary.

In his arguments favoring popular religion as a fundamental means of revelation Rahner underscores the following three points relative to his theological anthropology: 1) God's universal will to save humanity; 2) the human person's essential constitution as addressee of God's self-communication; and 3) humanity as addressee, in its social, national, and historical context.[34] The first of these points suggests Rahner's theology of grace, especially his all-important concept of the supernatural existential. The second point suggests the anthropocentric nature of Rahner's theological anthropology. It focuses on the human person as recipient of God's grace. The third includes and is a development of the second, and signals Rahner's increased interest in the historical, social, practical, and political nature of God's addressee. Just as chapters two and three were structured to reflect the specificity of the U.S. Hispanic landscape—the central themes, language, theological concerns, and critical categories that comprise U.S. Hispanic theological anthropology—so does the present chapter reflect the specificity of the Rahnerian landscape.

RAHNER'S THEOLOGY OF GRACE

Central to Rahner's theological anthropology is his theology of grace, which emerges in response to two interrelated problems: 1) the problem of secularization, and 2) the overall problem of extrinsicism, characteris-

---

[33]On Rahner's appropriation within feminist thought see Mary Ann Hinsdale, "Heeding the Voices: An Historical Overview," in Ann O'Hara Graff, ed., *In The Embrace of God: Feminist Approaches to Theological Anthropology* (Maryknoll, New York: Orbis Books, 1995), 22-23. See also, Anne Carr, *Transforming Grace: Christian Tradition and Women's Experience* (New York: Harper & Row, 1988), esp. 131-32 and idem, "Feminist Views of Christology," *Chicago Studies* 35/2 (1996): 128-140.

[34]Rahner, "The Relation between Theology and Popular Religion," 144.

tic of neo-scholastic theologies of grace.[35] While in the former, the central problem tends to be more sociological in nature, namely, the "exiling" and "decategorizing" of God from the world of everyday experience,[36] the problem with the latter is more theological, namely, grace is conceived within its own sphere, penetrating human nature from outside "as little as possible."[37] Rahner's contribution lies in his ability to create an anthropological vision that addresses these social and theological concerns. Building upon the primary insights of contemporary philosophers (such as Immanuel Kant, Martin Heidegger, Georg W.F. Hegel, and Joseph Maréchal) and theologians (such as Pierre Rousselot and Henri de Lubac), and deeply informed by Thomas Aquinas's vision, Rahner's theological anthropology presents a sacramental approach to reality that underscores the gratuitous and all-encompassing presence of God in history.

The philosophical foundations for this theology of grace were established in his early work, *Geist in Welt* (*Spirit in the World*).[38] This work, which provides Rahner's metaphysics of human knowing, is an attempt to appropriate a Thomistic epistemology within modern categories of thought.[39] Human knowledge argues Rahner, occurs within the horizon of Being (and Being for Rahner is always identified theologically with the mystery of God).[40] Every act of knowledge involves an act of the senses (*phantasmata*), a turning to the world, and an anticipation (*der Vorgriff*) of Being, in and through worldly experience.[41] Every act of knowledge is characterized by the *reditio completa ad seipsum*. This " '[c]omplete re-

---

[35]On Rahner's theology of grace see Karl Rahner, "Concerning the Relationship between Nature and Grace," in *Theological Investigations*, I, trans. Cornelius Ernst (New York: Crossroad, 1974), 297-317; idem, "Some Implications of the Scholastic Concept of Uncreated Grace," in *Theological Investigations*, I, 319-346; idem, "Nature and Grace," in *Theological Investigations*, IV, trans. Kevin Smyth (New York: Crossroad, 1982), 165-188. On Rahner's understanding of the problem of secularization see "Theological Reflections on the Problem of Secularization," in *Theological Investigations*, X, trans. David Bourke (New York: Herder and Herder, 1973), 318-348; idem, "Theological Considerations on Secularization and Atheism," in *Theological Investigations*, XI, trans. David Bourke (New York: Crossroad, 1974), 166-184.

[36]See Rahner, "The Man of Today and Religion," in *Theological Investigations*, VI, trans. Karl and Boniface Kruger (New York: Crossroad, 1982), 11.

[37]Rahner, *Nature and Grace: Dilemmas in the Modern Church* (New York: Sheed & Ward, 1964), 117.

[38]Rahner, *Spirit in the World*, trans. William Dych (New York: Continuum, 1994).

[39]In *Spirit in the World*, Rahner engages in a thorough study of Thomas Aquinas's epistemology as found in the *ST*, Ia q 84, a.7. See Thomas Sheehan, *Karl Rahner: The Philosophical Foundations* (Athens: Ohio University Press, 1987), esp. 19-132.

[40]See Rahner, *Foundations of Christian Faith: An Introduction to the Idea of Christianity* (New York: Crossroad, 1990), 33-35 and 66-71.

[41]On Rahner's epistemology see Duffy, *The Dynamics of Grace*, 262-283; Sheehan,

turn to itself' means that a human being returns to its self-transcending state of self-absence in its reaching for God each time it knows a worldly entity."[42] Thus, "metaphysics spells out what human being already is: anticipatory movement toward the elusive, present but absent, ground of reality."[43]

In *Hörer des Wortes* (*Hearer of the Word*)[44] Rahner builds upon this metaphysics of knowledge and offers his philosophy of religion. Rahner's philosophy is driven by his theological conviction that the human person, in his/her historicity (a Heideggerian term used to connote temporality, worldliness, and human contingency) abides in the universal offer of grace. Rahner coins the term supernatural existential to describe this concrete human situation. Rahner's supernatural existential represents a significant breakthrough in the contemporary Catholic understanding of grace. It affirms the human reality, and by implication all the various concrete manifestations of this reality, under the offer of grace.

HUMAN CONTEXTS AND THE UNIVERSAL OFFER OF GRACE

Rahner proposed his concept of the supernatural existential as a response to an anonymous article (by "D") written in 1950, entitled "*Ein Weg zur Bestimmung des Verhältnisses von Natur und Gnade*."[45] Challenging the neo-scholastic separation between nature and grace and its corollary notion of pure nature, Rahner builds upon the fundamental insights of the *nouvelle théologie*,[46] and argues for the experience of grace as a permanent characteristic of the human condition. Borrowing Heidegger's understanding of human existentials,[47] Rahner's supernatural existential refers to an objective and ontological modification of "human world and history."[48] As a result of this permanent and fundamental modification, Rahner maintains that what is human exists "always and everywhere" under the *offer* of grace.

Karl Rahner: The Philosophical Foundations, 233-317; Andrew Tallon, *Personal Becoming* (Milwaukee: Marquette University Press, 1982), 30-71.

[42]Duffy, *The Dynamics of Grace*, 270.

[43]Ibid.

[44]Rahner, *Hearer of the Word*.

[45]In *Orientierung* XIV (1950): 138-141. Stephen Duffy argues that the so called "D" is Pierre Delaye. See *The Dynamics of Grace*, 295, note 75.

[46]The term *"nouvelle théologie"* refers to a theological movement in the 1840s and 1850s that attempted an historically minded retrieval of the thought of Thomas and that of the Fathers of the Church as a reaction to neo-scholastic theology. See Gerald A. McCool, *Catholic Theology in the Nineteenth Century: The Quest for a Unitary Method* (New York: Seabury Press, 1977), 251-267. See also Henri de Lubac's classic exposition of this theological movement in his *Surnaturel: Études historiques* (Paris: Aubier, 1946).

[47]On Heidegger's notion of human existentials see his *Being and Time* (New York: Harper & Row, 1962), 32-35.

[48]Haight, *The Experience and Language of Grace* (New York: Paulist Press), 125.

Rahner's concept of the supernatural existential overcomes the extrinsicism of neo-scholastic manual theologies. These theologies upheld a twofold finality of human nature (one that was purely natural, and the other supernatural), and consequently held a strict separation between human nature and the order of grace. Following the lead of the theologians of the *nouvelle théologie* (but avoiding the pitfall of intrisicism),[49] Rahner critiques this neo-scholastic teaching mainly for two reasons: 1) it conceives grace as a mere superstructure of human nature (something bestowed from "outside"); and 2) it understands the ordination of human nature to grace in purely negative terms, as mere non-repugnance.[50] While upholding the unexacted, unmerited, unowed, and supernatural character of grace, Rahner's supernatural existential bridges the order of nature with the order of grace in such a way that the two "always and everywhere" permeate one another, and do not exist apart from each other except as a theoretical possibility.[51] Simply stated, for Rahner, what is human is conceived as an "inner moment" of the life of grace.[52]

As a concrete characteristic of human existence, the supernatural existential conceptually describes the condition for the possibility of God's Triune self-communication in history, and in particular to the historical subject.[53] Rahner's language of grace is that of God's self-communication or uncreated grace, and his way of conceptualizing the impact of grace on the human person is through the notion of quasi-formal causality.[54] Rahner's language of nature goes beyond essentialist categories, and in-

---

[49]Intrinsicism is the opposite of extrinsicism. An intrinsicist position would make human nature inherently related to grace without also acknowledging the gratuitous and unexacted presence of grace. Such was the position condemned by Pius XII in his encyclical, *Humani Generis* (1950). Some of Rahner's commentators argue that Rahner's supernatural existential represents a middle point between extrinsicism and intrinsicism. See J. A. Colombo, "Rahner and His Critics," 76, and Duffy, *The Dynamics of Grace*, 303.

[50]Rahner, "Concerning the Relationship between Nature and Grace," 298; and idem, *Nature and Grace*, 115-116. On the neo-scholastic understanding of the relationship between nature and grace, the critique by the *nouvelle théologie*, and Rahner's nuancing of the latter position see Duffy, *The Dynamics of Grace*, 295-303; and J. A. Colombo, "Rahner and His Critics," 72-86.

[51]Rahner proposes the concept of pure nature as a residual concept (*ein Restbegriff*) to safeguard the gratuity of God's grace. For Rahner, pure nature is what would be experienced if God had not willed to make a concrete and universal offer of grace. See Rahner, "Concerning the Relationship between Nature and Grace," 312-315; idem, "Nature and Grace," 183-185.

[52]Rahner, "Philosophy and Theology" in *Theological Investigations*, VI, 73.

[53]On the trinitarian nature of grace see Rahner, *The Trinity*, trans. Joseph Donceel (New York: Crossroad, 1997), 88-98.

[54]The terms uncreated grace and quasi-formal causality describe Rahner's way of

creasingly embraces a more dynamic and historical understanding of the human reality. Indeed, Rahner moves the conversation on nature and grace beyond the static, ontological, and formal categories of neo-scholastic theology (e.g., grace as created, quality, and accident; nature as substance and permanent structure of being) into dynamic, historical, and personal categories (e.g., grace as love, intimacy, and self-communication; human nature characterized by freedom and self-determination).[55] Seen in light of these dynamic, historical, and personal categories, Rahner's supernatural existential carries enormous implications for contemporary Catholic thought, as evidenced in the writings of theologians even as diverse as those of Latin-American liberation theology.[56]

Because Rahner holds that what is human always exists under the offer of grace, he can affirm that one's realization in grace is also the realization of our natural capacities. In other words, although Rahner nuances his theological arguments and explicitly distinguishes (never separates) what is human (anthropology) from what is divine (grace), his concept of the supernatural existential makes clear that the human and the divine imply and presuppose one another. Among other things, Rahner's proportional understanding of the relationship between nature and grace implies an openness to understand the "supernatural" or grace-filled character of manifold human contexts, experiences, and actions.

Beyond these theological implications, Rahner's supernatural existential also carries methodological implications. Just as he understands nature as being intrinsically connected to the life of grace, so does he understand philosophy as an inner moment of theology.[57] But as Rahner himself suggests, his argument, which sees philosophy as intrinsically connected

---

understanding the relationship between God and creature. In Scholastic theology, the creature's existence was conceived in light of efficient causality, that is, a kind of production derived from casual consequences. Moreover, Scholastic theologians emphasized created grace as an entative change in the creature that enabled the creature's relationship to God. Conversely, for Rahner, creaturely existence is conceived in light of a nuanced way of understanding formal causality. Coining the phrase quasi-formal causality, Rahner argues that the relationship between creature and God is not one that results from a mere "production *out* of the cause ['*ein Aus-der-Ursache-Heraus-stellen*'], but from a taking up into the ground ['*ein In-den-Grund-Hineinnehmen*']. This ground is none other than the very personal indwelling of God in the creature. See Haight, *The Experience and Language of Grace*, 122, and Joseph H.P. Wong, *Logos-Symbol in the Christology of Karl Rahner* (Roma: Libreria Ateneo Salesiano, 1984), 129-130. On Rahner's own discussion of this subject see his "Some Implications of the Scholastic Concept of Uncreated Grace," 329-330.

[55]See Rahner, "Concerning the Relationship between Nature and Grace," 316.

[56]For instance, see Gustavo Gutiérrez's appropriation of Rahner's concept of the supernatural existential within his integral understanding of salvation as liberation. See Gutiérrez, *A Theology of Liberation* (Maryknoll, New York: Orbis Books, 1988), 44-45.

[57]See Rahner, "Philosophy and Theology," 72.

to theology can and should be extended, *mutatis mutandis*, beyond philosophy to include other disciplines as well.[58] Consequently, the importance of Rahner's supernatural existential lies not only in recognizing the supernatural character of a manifold of human experiences, but also in recognizing the supernatural or grace-filled character of a wide range of philosophical, sociological, and scientific approaches. Simply put, for Rahner there is neither pure nature, nor pure philosophy, nor pure human science. The supernatural existential makes clear that all human reality and endeavors are co-extensive with God's universal will to save.

JESUS CHRIST AS ORIGIN AND DESTINY OF ALL HUMAN CONTEXTS

According to Rahner, God's universal will to save has been concretely and irrevocably made manifest in Jesus Christ. In Jesus, God has become humanly other. Conversely, human nature, understood by Rahner as obediential potency for the hypostatic union, has reached its ultimate goal. Because the human person is self-transcendent, argues Rahner, human persons are essentially open to a union with God.[59] The Incarnation, he argues, is "the asymptotic goal of a development of the world reaching out to God."[60] Rahner's anthropology is, therefore, Christocentric. His theological anthropology converges from above and from below on Jesus Christ.[61] In Jesus, humanity has reached its ultimate ascent and divinity its most perfect descent. Rahner captures this notion in his axiom: "Christology is the beginning and end of anthropology. And this anthropology, when most thoroughly realized in Christology, is eternally theology."[62]

In order to avoid an understanding of his transcendental anthropology as capable of being reduced "*a priori*" to a kind of Kantian speculation, that is, independently of the revelation of its *de facto* existence,"[63] and in order to safeguard the uniqueness of Christ, Rahner argues: 1) While the transcendence of the human person suggests unlimited possibilities, there can be no deduction or exigency of its fulfillment in a definitive union with the mystery of God; and 2) even though human nature is

---

[58]Note specifically Rahner's arguments in "On the Current Relationship between Philosophy and Theology," esp. 70-75.

[59]Rahner, "On the Theology of the Incarnation," in *Theological Investigations*, IV, 110.

[60]Rahner, "Christology in the Setting of Modern Man's Understanding of Himself and of His World," in *Theological Investigations*, XI, 227. See also Rahner, *Foundations of Christian Faith*, 209.

[61]On the descending and ascending moments of Rahner's theological anthropology see John M. McDermott, "The Christologies of Karl Rahner," *Gregorianum* 67 (1986): 104-122.

[62]Rahner, "On the Theology of the Incarnation," 117; idem, *Foundations of Christian Faith*, 225.

[63]Rahner, *Foundations of Christian Faith*, 225.

essentially ready and adaptable, only in Christ has this potentiality been uniquely and definitively realized.[64] Rejecting an extrinsic understanding of the relationship "between nature and world on the one hand and grace or God's self-communication on the other," [65] Rahner underscores that the possibility of human existence is grounded on the greater possibility of God's self-communication; or to use his precise terminology, human nature is "the grammar of God's possible self-expression." Rahner writes that

> we could define man [sic], driving him all the way back to his deepest and most obscure mystery, as that which comes to be when God's self-expression, his Word, is uttered into the emptiness of the Godless void in love. It is also for this reason that the incarnate Logos has been called the abbreviated Word of God. The abbreviation, the cipher of God himself is man, that is the Son of Man and the men who exist ultimately because there was to be a Son of Man. Man is the radical question about God which, as created by God, can also have an answer, an answer which in its historical manifestation and radical tangibility is the God-Man, and which is answered in all of us by God himself.[66]

Rahner uses the term cipher to designate how human persons in a primary and derivative sense are expressions of God's very-self. That is, whereas in Christ what is human is the direct result of God's exteriorization in the world for the rest of us, humanity is ontologically derivative and expressive of this event. Herein lies the central cue to understanding Rahner's Christocentric anthropology. As Joseph Wong has pointed out, "[i]n view of this relation between men as the Logos' potential, imperfect expressions, and Jesus as its perfect expression or *Realsymbol*, Rahner insists on the close connection between anthropology and Christology."[67]

Rahner's theology of symbol provides a way to deepen an understanding of his Christocentric anthropology.[68] According to Rahner, every being, in order to fulfill its nature expresses itself in something that is distinct from itself but yet one with itself.[69] A "symbol reveals the thing symbolized, and is itself full of the thing symbolized, being its concrete

---

[64]Ibid.

[65]Ibid., 223.

[66]Ibid., 224-225.

[67]Wong, *Logos-Symbol*, 135.

[68]Note Rahner's argument that "the whole of theology is incomprehensible if it is not essentially a theology of symbols, although in general very little attention is paid, systematically and expressly, to this basic characteristic." Karl Rahner, "The Theology of the Symbol," *Theological Investigations*, IV, 235.

[69]Rahner, "The Theology of the Symbol," 228.

form of existence."[70] A symbol is not an arbitrary representation or a conventional sign that ties together two realities.[71] Although Rahner recognizes different degrees of symbolization, a symbol is not something separate from that which is symbolized.[72] Rather, a "symbol is the reality, which is constituted by the thing symbolized, as an inner moment of itself."[73]

Rahner sees humanity in general, but more specifically and uniquely, Jesus' humanity as a symbol of divine life. Jesus' humanity is the distinct self-expression [Selbstäusserung] of God's self-emptying [Selbstentäus-serung] in the world.[74] Jesus' humanity reveals and makes concretely present the life of grace (i.e., the Logos). Because of his solidarity with all humanity, all other persons are also ciphers of this divine life. Indeed, Rahner's Christocentric arguments make clear that human persons and by extension all human contexts are not merely instruments of divinity. By avoiding the "notion of an assumption which presupposes what is to be assumed as already and obviously given,"[75] Rahner refuses any dichotomy between the human and the divine. As a result of their symbolic relationship, the two imply one another. Rahner does, however, make Jesus Christ definitive in this relationship. Thus, Jesus Christ concretizes in an absolute and ontologically causative sense what Rahner judges to be always and everywhere present and visible in the world, namely, God's offer of grace. Hence the following observations:

> The human person is Christ-oriented; in Christ is found what humans are searching for and tending to in their own being, a life caught up root and branch in the horizon that is the holy mystery. The incarnation as a symbolic event points up the fundamental fact that human transcendence is a transcendence into God. Such a Christology does not warrant a transcendental deduction of the Christ event from the side of anthropology. Human experience cannot lead to the deduction that God freely relates to human beings either in self-communication or rejection. The consequence of Rahner's position that grace is omnipresent is that Jesus is the full, definitive symbolic cause and expression of the divine-human interrelation

---

[70]Ibid., 251.

[71]Ibid., 225.

[72]Ibid., 234. Rahner argues that because the concept of being is analogous, "it displays the various types of self-realization of each being, and being in itself, and hence also the concept and reality of the symbol are flexible."

[73]Ibid., 251.

[74]Rahner, Foundations of Christian Faith, 224.

[75]Ibid., 222.

that is always already present from the beginning and capable of being acknowledged in a myriad of ways in diverse times and places.[76]

THE HUMAN AS "HEARER" OF THE WORD

Because what is human is concretely under the offer of grace (the supernatural existential), the human person is, for Rahner, constituted as hearer of the Word. Rahner sees the human person as someone whose turn to the world, and in and through this turn, to being as such, makes him or her "refer to God and thus to a possible revelation."[77] The world, history, and consciousness become the human loci where the hearing of God's message can occur. Thus, "[i]t seems axiomatic for Rahner that 'God can only reveal what man is able to perceive.' The human being is on the lookout for a *human* word in which God's word may be heard."[78]

In a certain way one can see how Rahner would accept the notion of human persons as necessarily contextual beings who encounter the activity of grace and perceive it as God's revelation "in," "with," and "under" specific human histories. Even in his earlier writings Rahner had already maintained that the turn to history is not an option, but rather a necessary dimension of being a transcendental and corporeal person.[79] Since human histories vary, however, Rahner's approach to revelation should be understood as being universal but not universalistic.[80] In other words, Rahner's approach presupposes not one hearer, but many hearers to whom God's Word is addressed, and not one human word, but many human words in which God's Word can be heard. Rahner's attentiveness to and embrace of ecclesial pluralism in his later writings unmistakably confirm this insight.

Rahner's metaphor of the human person as "hearer" also needs clarification in order to underscore the integral anthropology that the metaphor presupposes. "Hearer" can suggest for some a conceptualist approach to the experience of grace. This understanding is not what Rahner intends. Rather, for Rahner, "hearer of the word" functions as a root

---

[76]Duffy, *The Dynamics of Grace*, 310.

[77]Rahner, *Hearer of the Word*, 137.

[78]Duffy, *The Dynamics of Grace*, 268-269. Emphasis in original.

[79]Rahner, *Hearer of the Word*, 137-138.

[80]On Rahner's notion of grace, revelation, and history see Thomas F. O'Meara, "A History of Grace," in *A World of Grace: An Introduction to the Themes and Foundations of Karl Rahner's Theology*, ed. Leo J. O'Donovan (New York: Crossroad, 1984), 76-91.

metaphor (in the Ricoeurian sense of the term).[81] Understood in the latter sense, this metaphor simply describes how persons are constituted to experience and know divine self-communication.

Rahner's essay on "The Theology of the Religious Meaning of Images"[82] offers justification for interpreting him in light of this more holistic anthropological approach. Following his earlier Thomistic premise that we cannot come to the knowledge of anything "even the most spiritual, most 'transcendental,' most sublime," except "through a *conversio ad phantasmata*,' "[83] Rahner argues that knowledge "is necessarily reached by an intuition that depends on sensory, and therefore also historical experience."[84] However, instead of developing this premise in light of his classical understanding of "hearing" of the word, in this essay, which comes late in his career,[85] Rahner unveils an epistemology that includes all the senses.

Rahner argues that the Christian tradition favors an understanding of revelation and God's self-communication as occurring "fundamentally through the word and through the hearing of the messages conveyed by words."[86] In spite of the latter, he readily admits that "[i]t is not true that the divine reality which must penetrate into human beings can enter their existence fully and completely through the single gate of the ears, of hearing."[87] Rahner goes on to argue that all the senses, and not just the sense of hearing, constitute a person's experience of transcendence. Thus, Rahner writes:

> . . . every experience of an object, even though the object is always a single and finite one, is carried by an a priori pre-apprehension of the whole breadth of the formal object of the sense power. It is more than the grasping of the concrete single object that is being known. This is not true for hearing alone. It is not true only for the spirit as such with its unlimited transcendentality. It is true that the senses and the spirit differ from each other by the fact that the latter has an unlimited formal object, an unlimited a priori pre-apprehension, whereas this is not true for the senses. Yet, even so, every act of the sense powers as such implies some experience of transcendence.[88]

---

[81]See Paul Ricoeur, *Interpretation Theory: Discourse and the Surplus of Meaning* (Fort Worth: Texas Christian University, 1976), esp. 61-65.

[82]In *Theological Investigations*, XXIII, trans. Joseph Donceel and Hugh M. Riley (New York: Crossroad, 1992), 149-161.

[83]Ibid., 150.

[84]Ibid. In this statement Rahner provides a summary of his central thesis he defended in *Spirit in the World*.

[85]This essay was originally a lecture that Rahner delivered in Munich on November 10, 1983.

[86]Rahner, "The Theology of the Religious Meaning of Images," in *Theological Investigations*, XXIII, 154.

[87]Ibid.

[88]Ibid., 158.

The significance of Rahner's arguments could not be overstated. Even if one acknowledges those critics who have challenged Rahner for not sufficiently attending to the practical and social experience of grace, Rahner's arguments witness his holistic embodied approach to the encounter with grace. Indeed, Rahner's arguments exemplify how revelation for him is not only "the history of grace made verbal,"[89] but also includes, among other things, the history of grace made act and icon. Such an understanding can speak much more to theological visions that conceive the anthropological response to God's Word in light of aesthetic and praxiological approaches.

RAHNER'S THEOLOGY OF PERSON AND COMMUNITY

Rahner's theological anthropology, especially his metaphor of the human person as hearer of the Word, reflects his earlier tendencies to describe the relationship between the human and the divine in light of individual categories. Still, even if his earlier thought exemplifies the focus on the individual human person, Rahner's theology is not individualistic. Rahner's theological anthropology is profoundly contextual and communal. If in Rahner the human person stands "always and everywhere" as hearer of the Word, by that Rahner understands a historically situated and embodied person, and consequently, a person who is communally constituted. Furthermore, it is precisely this communal understanding of the self *in tandem* with the key insights of his theology of grace that enables Rahner to venture into a more social and practical theological anthropology in his later writings.

THE HUMAN PERSON AS SPIRIT-IN-THE-WORLD

Rahner's central notion of the human person is spirit-in-the-world.[90] As spirit, Rahner understands the human person as someone who is always more than his or her particularity. Having God as her or his referent, and characterized by an openness to and desire for union with God, the human person is always self-transcendent. Thus, what ultimately concerns the human person resides in yet, at the same time, escapes the breadth of worldly particularities. "In his *essence*, in his nature," writes Rahner, "man himself is the mystery, not because he is in himself the infinite fullness of the mystery which concerns him, which fullness is inexpressible, but because in his real essence, in his original ground, in his nature he is poor, but nevertheless conscious orientation to this fullness."[91]

---

[89]O'Meara, "A History of Grace," 87.

[90]On Rahner's notion of the person as spirit see James O'Donnell, "The Mystery of Faith in the Theology of Karl Rahner," *Heythrop Journal* 25/3 (1984): 302.

[91]See Rahner, *Foundations of Christian Faith*, 216.

Rahner's insistence on seeing the human person as spirit-in-the-world does not mean that he dismisses or undermines in any way the human reality. In other words, Rahner's anthropology while affirming the transcendental nature of human existence is not abstract or idealistic. What Rahner wants to avoid is the kind of humanistic reductionism that would define persons in purely scientific, social, or cultural ways.[92] As evidenced by the previous discussion on grace, and his understanding of the human reality as the *Realsymbol* of the Logos, Rahner takes very seriously human corporeality. This is why when he speaks of spirit, he often juxtaposes phrases such as world, body, and matter in order to underscore the embodied reality of persons.[93] Indeed, for Rahner, "spirit-body" is what a human person is.

This embodied anthropology can be furthered exemplified by Rahner's notion of human freedom. Rahner maintains that freedom is not an "identifiable datum of human experience,"[94] because "it always concerns the person as such and as a whole."[95] Freedom, for Rahner, is not the capacity to choose this or that historical object, no matter how valuable such an object may be. Instead, freedom is the capacity of the person, as spirit, to decide about his or her entire self. But Rahner underscores that human freedom does not live "*behind a merely physical, biological, exterior, and historical temporality of the subject. Rather it actualizes itself as this subjective freedom in a passage through the temporality which freedom itself establishes in order to be itself.*"[96] Thus, similar to the spirit-world dialectic discussed above, Rahner's dialectic between the transcendental and categorical exercise of freedom affirms and depends upon, yet does not reify, the human reality.[97]

Essentially, Rahner's theology of the human person holds in dialectical tension the transcendental and categorical aspects of human experience. What must be underscored is that Rahner distinguishes the more spiritual aspects of human experience from those that can be characterized as

---

[92]Ibid., 27-28.

[93]Ibid.

[94]Ibid., 95.

[95]Ibid., 38.

[96]Ibid., 94.

[97]Note that in spite of Rahner's stress on freedom exercised in and through the historicity and temporality of the subject, critics have charged him with the kind of anthropological reductionism that does not attend sufficiently to the subject, his or her history, and his or her social relations. Metz accuses Rahner of bypassing the social and historical struggles of human identity "by means of a late and diminished form of metaphysics . . . which compensates for its suspected dissociation from history by a weakened idea of the historicity of the subject." In the end, Metz parts from Rahner because he does not believe that Rahner takes sufficiently into account the changing conditions of the world. Thus Metz asks: "[D]oes this transcendental anthropology take into account the fact that man's anticipatory existence is a historical existence?" See Metz, *Faith in History and Society*, 63-65. See also Colombo, "Rahner and His Critics."

being more material in nature. Rahner's theology, however, does not separate these realities. Rahner's notions of spirit-in-the-world and of human freedom make clear that persons are integral beings composed of matter and spirit and as such are open to experience the more spiritual realities (spirit, grace, the reign of God) within their worldly realities (body, human nature, society).

As a result of Kantian influences, some have raised the question whether in Rahner the human encounter with transcendence occurs merely within human subjectivity.[98] From the beginning, however, Rahner's embodied notion of the human person as spirit-in-the-world already discourages such an understanding. It is true that after the Council Rahner's theology acquires greater historical sensitivity. But all things considered, Rahner's theological anthropology from the beginning points to an experience of transcendentality that does not lie either in a purely subjective dimension or outside historical and bodily realities. Rather, as Mary Catherine Hilkert points out, "[a]s spirit-in-the-world, the human person can experience an invitation [to the life of grace] at the spiritual depth dimension of existence (transcendental pole) only insofar as that offer is mediated or made known in and through the social, tangible, and concrete manifestations of one's body, one's relationships, the events that constitute one's history, and the world in which one lives (categorical pole)."[99]

THE HUMAN PERSON AS COMMUNAL

As spirit-in-the-world, as freedom actualized in a specific context, the human person is, for Rahner, essentially open to another. Because the human person is an embodied being, he or she is, to use Gerald McCool's words, "bound to the history of the world from whose matter his human body has evolved."[100] As such, McCool goes on to argue, the human person "can achieve his personal fulfillment only through interaction with the fellow-members of his culturally determined society."[101] Thus, Rahner

---

[98]See Brackley's discussion of how, according to Basque philosopher Xavier Zubiri, Kantian epistemology and anthropology is essentially dualistic because Kant fails to unite sensing and intelligizing in the subject. "For Zubiri," writes Brackley, "human beings are fundamentally *sensing* intelligence (or intelligizing sensitivity)." Brackley goes on to suggest how those critics who focus too much on the Kantian influences on Rahner tend to reduce Rahner's categorical pole of human experience to an experience of human subjectivity. Such critics, argues Brackley, may be disregarding Rahner's own re-appropriation and modification of Kantian categories, especially as evidenced in Rahner's last writings. See Brackley, *Divine Revolution*, 100-102.

[99]Mary Catherine Hilkert, *Naming Grace: Preaching and the Sacramental Imagination* (New York: Continuum, 1997), 31-32.

[100]Gerald McCool, "Person and Community in Karl Rahner," in R.J. Roth, *Person and Community* (New York: Fordham University Press, 1975), 69.

[101]Ibid.

rejects any opposition between person and community, and denies the fullness of humanity to those who are not in relation.[102] For Rahner, "Man *is* insofar as he gives up himself."[103]

Rahner's communal anthropology, like his theology of grace, is Christocentric in orientation. Just as Rahner understands Christ as the perfection of that which is always and everywhere encountered in the world, namely grace, Rahner understands Christ as the perfect expression of human nature. For Rahner, Christ has defined human nature as self-gift for, as openness to, and as love of another.[104] But because the human being is a social and corporeal being, such giving, openness, and love can only but occur in embodied and communal ways. Rahner locates the human-divine encounter (God's self-gift to us in Christ and our self-gift to an other, and in and through this other to God) within the corporeal, concrete, and communal reality of persons, and more specifically, the community of the Christian Church. Rahner writes:

> The ultimate triumph of interpersonal love is promised in the love offered to us in him, it is already given in hope, and is present in the church. The church of course would have to be or has to be actualized in the concrete local church, and in concrete interpersonal relations between believing and hoping Christians, and this includes the concreteness of everyday reality.[105]

Rahner argues against an understanding of the human person "as separated, isolated, and discontinuous from everything else."[106] For Rahner, individuality and the abundance of being occur through intimate unity and mutual participation with an other.[107] The individual person "is not characterized, primarily, by having others of the same sort 'along with' it, by being inserted in a mass of others of the same kind and then somehow divided off from them."[108] Rather, Rahner defines human persons as intrinsically interrelated and as he affirms, "in some sense '*for* one another'; neither would be what it is if it were not for the other."[109] Even if as a consequence of corporeal limitations, this interrelatedness manifests itself as a kind of being "along with" an-other, Rahner rejects a separatist and individualist understanding of human interrelatedness.

As others have already pointed out, in his communal notion of the self

---

[102]Tallon, *Personal Becoming*, 175.
[103]Rahner, "On the Theology of the Incarnation," 110. Emphasis in original.
[104]See Rahner, *Foundations of Christian Faith*, 217-222 and 225-226.
[105]Ibid., 399-400.
[106]Rahner, *The Christian Commitment* (New York: Sheed and Ward, 1963), 77.
[107]Ibid., 78.
[108]Ibid.
[109]Ibid., 76.

Rahner underscores the analogous and correlative nature of persons and community: 1) correlative because, for Rahner, the human person has been created for the sake of establishing community, yet (as he argues) community cannot take place without persons; and 2) analogous because a person cannot be defined merely as something which occupies a position within a discernible mass.

Rahner's understanding of persons and community as analogous and correlative seeks to uphold the uniqueness of each person, as that person exists defined within a communal context, without falling into individualism and collectivism.[110] For Rahner, no two persons are ever the same, nor are persons particular instances of a universal reality—what he characterizes as a "spatio-temporal nailing down" of some universal essence or idea.[111] Yet, as he points out in order to underscore his correlative notion of individual and community, "the member of the pack or herd finds itself as an individual precisely in its membership."[112]

Rahner's anthropology not only underscores the ontological significance of community but also recognizes the plurality of communities that humans participate in, the potential conflicts that can result from such participation, and the hierarchies necessary in discerning which communal values will predominate. Rahner envisions that "[be]cause man is, in himself, this plural reality, it is his valid, and difficult task to effect a reconciliation of the individual and universal at the different levels of his own being."[113] As I point out below, Rahner's theology of the Kingdom attempts to effect such reconciliation.

To be sure, Rahner's embodied and communal anthropology, like his theology of grace, contains elements that would enable many contemporary theologians, including Rahner himself, to move along the lines of a more practical and socio-political theology. In this sense, Rahner's final writings can be seen to "fill out," socially and practically speaking, the central insights of his earlier theological anthropology.[114]

ON BEING HUMAN
FROM SOCIAL AND PRACTICAL PERSPECTIVES

Much has been made of Rahner's writings in the last years of his life. Some of Rahner's commentators have suggested how the changing world situation and paradigm shifts in theology (namely, the consciousness of oppressed persons and the emergence of political visions) forced Rahner

---

[110]See McCool, "Person and Community," 75.

[111]Rahner, *The Christian Commitment*, 82-83.

[112]Ibid., 80.

[113]Ibid., 81.

[114]For a survey and thematic overview of Rahner's later essays, see O'Donovan, "A Journey into Time," 621-646, and Philip Endean, *"La théologie du dernier Rahner,"* *Etudes Théologiques et Religiouses* 71/2 (1996): 303-304.

to reconsider his transcendental method in light of more practical and social dimensions.[115] Rahner's own acknowledgment that Metz's critique of his transcendental theology was the only critique that he took seriously[116] does suggest the impact that these political theologies (which underscored social relationships, praxis, and self-realization in the world) may have had on Rahner's later thought.

In light of these challenges, Rahner's theological anthropology evolved to incorporate, much more than his earlier thought had, the practical and social mediation of grace. Thus, just as in the earlier Rahner nature is understood as an inner moment of grace, in the later Rahner social and political self-expression is more and more conceived as an intrinsic moment of personal existence, and consequently, of the presence of grace in the world. Rahner never gives up on the idea that nature can at best be distinguished from grace, but Rahner becomes increasingly convinced that human nature, even when considered under individual and private aspects, can at best be distinguished from socio-political realities.[117] Rahner's notion of the love of God and neighbor and his theology of the world and the Kingdom of God exemplify the practical and social evolution of his theological anthropology.

THE LOVE OF GOD AND NEIGHBOR

In his introduction to Andrew Tallon's *Personal Becoming*, Rahner acknowledges the evolution of his theological anthropology particularly relative to how he came to understand the turn to the "other" within more personalistic categories (recall the influence of Thomas Aquinas on Rahner's metaphysical epistemology). Aquinas' anthropology is defined by the spirit's act of turning to the other in order to become present to self and to God. In so doing every act of the subject leads not only to knowledge of worldly entities, but also to knowledge of God. Similarly, although Rahner fails to coin a specific will-word (something like Blondel's *volonté voulante*), his understanding of the dynamism of the human spirit (*der Vorgriff*) includes both cognitive and ethno-practical dimensions.[118]

---

[115]Note Ashley's argument: "Indeed, it may very well be that Metz provided not only some of the impetus for Rahner's further development but even some of the ideas that Rahner himself followed up on." In *Interruptions*, 175. Note also Rahner's comments in *Faith in a Wintry Season: Conversations and Interviews with Karl Rahner in the Last Years of His Life*, trans. and ed. Harvey D. Egan (New York: Crossroad, 1990), 158-159.

[116]Bacik, *Apologetics*, ix.

[117]See *A Faith in a Wintry Season*, 61, 63, 155, 159, and 164-166. Note too Rahner's affirmation that the experience of God is an experience which has full social and public significance. See Rahner, "The Experience of God Today," in *Theological Investigations*, XI,159.

[118]See Tallon, "Editor's Introduction," in *Hearer of the Word*, xvi.

Rahner's introduction to Tallon's work echoes this twofold understanding of the human spirit and exemplifies how Rahner came to prefer personal categories, rather than conceptual ones, in elaborating his transcendental anthropology.

Parting from Aquinas's teaching that understands the "other," through which finite spirit returns to itself as a neutral object [*der materiellen "Gegenstand"*], Rahner proposes instead to re-envision Aquinas's metaphysical epistemology in light of personalist categories. Rahner points out that Aquinas does not consider that "the other in the true sense [*das eigentliche andere*] is another *person* [*'der' andere ist*] whom the subject encounters in knowledge, freedom, and love, in genuine interpersonal history [*in echter interpersonaler Geschichte*]."[119] Rahner argues that Aquinas's formal and abstract framework must be "filled out" concretely, if it is to be appropriated in a more genuine anthropology. Rahner then offers the following observations that suggest how he saw himself filling out Aquinas's framework:

> Thus, my dear Professor Tallon, you have correctly seen that for me the other, which mediates the person to itself, ever more clearly emerges as the personal other ["der" *andere*], whom the person in knowledge and love encounters, and that the human environment is such only as a human and personal world in which man lives in order to come to himself, so that in love he abides with the other and thereby experiences what is meant by 'God,' who is the sphere and the ultimate guarantee of interhuman love.[120]

Rahner's theology after the Second Vatican Council, especially his treatment of the love of God and love of neighbor, reflects the evolution of his thought into more personal and socio-political categories.[121] Whereas the turn to the subject characterized Rahner's initial reflections, the turn to the other as person and the personal encounter with God through this historical other became characteristic of Rahner's later thought. Indeed, the neighbor became for Rahner the human word in which God's word could be heard. Radicalizing the scholastic understanding of the love of

---

[119]Ibid., 3.

[120]Ibid., 3-4. Although Rahner himself acknowledges a difference between his theology and that of Aquinas, some of his critics have not been so convinced. For instance see Ashley's discussion of Metz's critique of Rahner's understanding of the "other" in *Interruptions*, 79-80.

[121]See Rahner, "Reflections on the Unity of the Love of Neighbor and the Love of God," in *Theological Investigations*, VI, 231-249; idem, *The Love of Jesus and the Love of Neighbor*, originally published as *Was heisst Jesus lieben?* (Freiburg: Verlag Herder, 1982); and "The 'Commandment' of Love in Relation to Other Commandments," in *Theological Investigations*, V, trans. Karl-H. Kruger (Baltimore: Helicon Press, 1966), 439-459.

God and neighbor, in a way that precluded an understanding of neighbor as a mere instrument for love and knowledge of God, Rahner argues that to love neighbor *is* to love God, and to love God *is* to love neighbor. Thus, Rahner argues that the love of neighbor "is not merely a preparation, effect, fruit and touchstone of the love of God but is itself an act of this love of God itself. . . . "[122]

Building upon the central insights of his theology of grace, Rahner argues that "The act of personal love for another human being is therefore the all-embracing basic act of man which gives meaning, direction, and measure to everything else."[123] Rahner characterizes the essential *a priori* openness of a human person to another as the most basic constitutive aspect of the self, and of self-transcendence.[124] In fact, Rahner reasons that from a "more concrete point of view," the supernatural openness to grace "is precisely the transcendentality towards the other who is to be loved and who first of all is one's fellow man."[125]

Rahner's theology of the love of God and neighbor is not, however, without controversy. Among Rahner's sharpest critics are those who would admit that Rahner abandons the more (conceptualist) framework of thought to favor a more existential and personal one. Still, they would argue that Rahner is unable to escape the privatized nature of "I-thou" relationships. Moreover, such critics would also point out how Rahner's failure to begin with concrete historical and personal experiences (Rahner's starting point is human transcendentality) prevents him from embracing the more politically oriented aspects of the love of neighbor.[126] While such criticisms cannot be easily dismissed, Rahner's understanding of the love of neighbor does not lack social and practical sensitivity in the political sense of the term. The turn to the other in Rahner's later thought became the turn to a contextualized other, where context is understood more and more in light of political realities.

In his essay "Who Are Your Brother and Sister" ["Wer ist dein Bruder?"],[127] Rahner addresses the nature of, and explores some contemporary consequences of, the love of neighbor. Rahner points out that because of the historical nature of the human person, the love of neighbor will necessarily undergo various transformations. Rahner calls this "a genuine historicity of Christian love of neighbor."[128] Among these con-

---

[122]Rahner, "Reflections on the Unity of the Love of Neighbor and Love of God," 236.

[123]Ibid., 241.

[124]Ibid.

[125]Ibid., 243.

[126]For instance, see Metz, *Theology of the World*, trans. William Glen-Doepel (Herder and Herder, 1969), 53-55; idem, *Faith in History and Society*, 60-65.

[127]In *The Love of Jesus and the Love of Neighbor*, 63-98. This essay reproduces a lecture that Rahner delivered on November 10, 1980 at the Catholic University of Graz.

[128]Ibid., 73.

sequences that Rahner includes are the political dimensions of the love of neighbor. Rahner argues that our contemporary situation has led to the insight that "the very nature of Christian communion necessarily generates a political responsibility, generates politics, and hence generates a political theology."[129] Recognizing the changes that have taken place in society, and reacting, perhaps, against those who would interpret his transcendental thought through individualistic, conceptualist, and privatistic categories Rahner writes:

> But now we live in a society that has made social and sociopolitical transformation the proper object of its very reflections and activity. We not only define our private existence in terms of a system of societal coordinates, we refuse to see that system of coordinates as fixed, and we change it. But thereby Christian love of neighbor and communion acquire a field of responsibility for the social structures required for life worth human living, a life that is "Christianly possible," in a society of maximal unification to this end. . . . It is no longer a matter of simple deductive intelligence. It is a matter of freedom, in itself and as such.[130]

Rahner's comments clearly exemplify the practical and socio-political evolution of his thought. As is evident from Rahner's comments above, his later writings increasingly define charity, not in abstract and essentialist terms, but in light of responsible socio-political action and solidarity. Thus, Rahner comes to acknowledge more and more the socio-political context as a context of self-realization and encounter with grace. Rahner's later writings even begin to echo the language often associated with liberation theologies. Rahner's characterization of the love of neighbor in light of the preferential option for the poor and the critique of unjust social institutions exemplify this important evolution.[131] "Today," Rahner writes in one of these later essays, "we might perhaps think that we can and must follow Jesus concretely by a solidarity with the poor and downgraded, by a critical attitude to institutionalizations asserted by power in society and Church, by courage for conflict with the powerful."[132]

But Rahner did not and would not surrender his insistence on taking up the transcendental or theological pole of any anthropological reflection. Theology remained for him, always and everywhere, *anthropologia negativa*. That is why, whether he spoke of the love of neighbor in its personal or in its political dimensions, he always did so in light of its

---

[129]Ibid., 90.

[130]Ibid.

[131]See Rahner, *Faith in a Wintry Season*, 61-63.

[132]Rahner, "Following the Crucified," in *Theological Investigations*, XVIII, trans. Edward Quinn (New York: Crossroad, 1983), 159.

transcendental dimensions. And as we have already noted, by "transcendental" Rahner does not intend to convey either idealistic or abstract notions of human experiences. Rather, what he intends is a recognition of the spiritual and theologically concrete dimension of those experiences. In short, Rahner never failed to insist that the ultimate justification of any anthropological claims, no matter how politically or socially ordinary in nature those may be, needed to be rooted in the life of grace because grace and nature comprise an integral unity.

THE SOCIAL SYMBOL OF GRACE: RAHNER'S THEOLOGY OF THE KINGDOM

Rahner's theology of the Kingdom and its relationship to worldly reality and human actions have already been anticipated by his theology of grace, his embodied and communal anthropology, and his theology of the love of God and neighbor. Rahner's understanding of the universal offer of grace, and his increased attentiveness to the practical and sociopolitical anticipation and mediation of grace through the love of neighbor have a corollary in his teaching on the Kingdom of God and the kingdom of the world. Rahner's understanding of these two communal realities follows his overall principle of distinguishing, but never separating, the earthly from the divine. Rahner's teaching on the Kingdom can be understood as an attempt to understand the human and divine contexts for self-realization.

Partly as a result of the fact that Rahner's theology of grace seeks a general and universal affirmation of the activity of grace in the world, his theology of the Kingdom does not sufficiently attend to the intersection of grace with particular social institutions, especially "death-dealing institutions."[133] Notwithstanding the latter, Rahner's approach is open to this development. Indeed, Rahner's relentless belief in the universal experience of grace and his analogical way of relating the human and divine suggest that any opposition between worldly realities and those pertaining to the Kingdom must be rejected. While Rahner avoids material reductionism, his theology of grace makes clear that world and Kingdom relate to one another in a way similar to his economic and immanent trinitarian distinction.[134] Just as for Rahner the economy is the place that reveals but does not fully exhaust or reify the mystery of God, so is worldly reality the place where one encounters in a non-reductionistic way the social activity of grace, otherwise referred to in Christian tradition as the Kingdom of God.[135]

For Rahner, the Kingdom of God is not some reality that lies beyond

---

[133]See Brackley, *Divine Revolution*, 56.
[134]On Rahner's trinitarian economic-immanent distinction see *The Trinity*, 82-102.
[135]See Rahner, "Immanent and Transcendent Consummation of the World."

history, but rather the Kingdom, though not fully realizable in history, is nonetheless "to be thought of here, as elsewhere also in the history of nature and of the world, as the self-transcendence of history. . . ."[136] The Kingdom of God "does not take place solely in a secret inwardness of conscience, in meta-historical religious subjectivity, but in the concrete fulfillment of an earthly task, of active love of others, even of collective love of others."[137] Rahner underscores the importance of human praxis in his affirmation that "The Kingdom of God only comes to those who build the coming earthly kingdom."[138] And as I have already underscored, for Rahner, the work of the Kingdom of God increasingly entailed loving one's neighbor in the socio-political sense of the term.[139]

Rahner makes clear that the Kingdom of God and its effects, namely, salvation, are not to be seen as lying beyond worldly actions. Rejecting any dichotomy between "the spiritual subjective" and "the historically concrete bodily nature and incarnate historical reality," Rahner affirms salvation as an integral manifestation of the Kingdom.[140] Echoing his praxis-minded notion of salvation, Rahner argues that if one takes the solidarity of Jesus' incarnation seriously, then "one could also speak of a self-redemption of the world."[141] Rahner does not deny the gratuity of grace in any way.[142] But his theology of nature and grace from the beginning includes an attentiveness to the transcendental or salvific aspects of human praxis.

The important point to underscore is that while Rahner understands worldly reality and human praxis as the loci for encountering grace and the salvific fruits of the Kingdom of God, Rahner wants to avoid the kind of anthropological reductionism that objectifies and thereby undermines the giftedness and realization of the Kingdom within worldly reality and action. In other words, although Rahner affirms worldly reality and action as the context for encountering grace and the fruits of the Kingdom, the former can never circumscribe the latter. The Kingdom remains both

---

[136]Rahner, "The Theological Problems Entailed in the Idea of the 'New Earth,' " in *Theological Investigations*, X, 268-269.

[137]Rahner, "Church and World," in *Encyclopedia of Theology: The Concise Sacramentum Mundi* (New York: Crossroad, 1989), 239. Cited in Brackley, *Divine Revolution*, 56-57.

[138]Rahner, "Christian Humanism," in *Theological Investigations*, IX, trans. Graham Harrison (New York: Crossroad, 1987), 201.

[139]For a discussion of how Rahner's later writings stressed the coming of the Kingdom through the love of neighbor, socio-politically defined, see Brackley, *Divine Revolution*, 59-60.

[140]See Rahner, "The Christian Understanding of Redemption," in *Theological Investigations*, XXI, trans. Hugh M. Riley (New York: Crossroad, 1988), 242-243.

[141]Ibid., 251.

[142]Ibid.

gift and mystery. To this end it is worth noting his essay entitled "History of the World and Salvation History," in which Rahner establishes the following three principles: 1) salvation-history takes place within the history of this world; 2) salvation-history is distinct from profane history; and 3) salvation-history explains profane history.[143]

Undoubtedly, Rahner's theology of the Kingdom of God, and of the world could be complemented with a greater dialectical, political, and prophetic sensitive imagination, and a greater emphasis on the discontinuity between earthly and divine realities.[144] Without embracing a form of dualism between world and Kingdom that would abandon the Catholic analogical imagination, it is important to acknowledge the profound discontinuity that often exists between some aspects of worldly reality and the Kingdom of God. The latter, however, is not altogether absent from Rahner's thought.[145] In so far as Rahner's theology includes a teaching on human sin and suffering, his theology also includes a dialectical moment.[146] Even if his theology at first does not sufficiently attend to the socio-political dimension of sin and to its concrete manifestations in worldly experiences (i.e., Auschwitz and the like),[147] Rahner is well aware of the shortcomings of worldly reality, as his now oft-cited metaphoric description of living through a "wintry-season" suggests.

While it is true that Rahner tends to speak of sin in general terms, that is, as an existential of the human condition, his writings also include very concrete examples that suggest his practical and socio-political sensitivity. For instance, in a well known anecdote found in his *Foundations of Christian Faith*, Rahner reflects upon human sinfulness in light of concrete socio-political experiences. Rahner recounts the story of someone who buys a banana and fails to realize his or her participation in social sin by the mere fact that such purchase is tied to the injustices related to banana pickers and to centuries-old commercial policies.[148] Rahner's anecdote, which clearly suggests the socio-political dimensions of sin, demonstrates how Rahner's understanding of the "always and everywhere" presence of grace, and his teaching on the Kingdom is complemented in

---

[143]See Rahner, "History of the World and Salvation History," in *Theological Investigations*, V, 97-114.

[144]On dialectical theological discourse see Hilkert, *Naming Grace*, 19-29.

[145]Note Metz's essay "Karl Rahner's Struggle for the Theological Dignity of Humankind," in *A Passion for God*, esp. 116-120.

[146]See Rahner, "Following the Crucified," 157-170.

[147]Note, however, the theological analogies that Rahner derives from his experiences of being trapped for long nights in air-raid shelters during World War II, and his growing consciousness of suffering in the world, poverty, and oppression. See respectively, Rahner, *On Prayer* (New York: Paulist Press Deus Books, 1968), esp. 9-10, and idem, "Following the Crucified," 157-170.

[148]Rahner, *Foundations of Christian Faith*, 110-111.

his later writings with themes which we would today commonly associate with dialectical and politically sensitive theological traditions.

Rahner's later writings, therefore, affirmed the sacramentality or transcendental nature of worldly reality, including socio-political actions. Rahner, however, refused to embrace any form of worldly reductionism or idealism. [149] He was well aware not only of the potential to love one's neighbor and thereby contribute to the building of the Kingdom, but also of freedom's possibility to utter a "no" to God, to be co-determined by guilt, and to be subject to various forms of worldly manipulations. [150] Such limitations on human freedom meant that every concrete human action was not only "always and everywhere" under the influence of grace, but also "always and everywhere" under what he termed the aetiologically inferred and historically experienced acts of human sin.[151] Just a year before his own death, Rahner reminded us of how we will one day render an account of our actions in a way that includes socio-political and practical dimensions that have gone against the building of the Kingdom:

> Each of us has to answer before God questions of whether we have fulfilled our political task, whether we have loved our neighbor, whether we have respected people's freedom and treated them with justice. If this life of ours, with its unavoidable 'political' component, has been lived the right way, it will be gloriously harvested in our eternity.[152]

RAHNER'S THEOLOGICAL VISION OF HUMANITY: A VISION FOR THE TWENTY-FIRST CENTURY?

Rahner's theological anthropology is not without consequences for the emergence of contemporary contextual theologies. Rahner's anthropocentric turn in Catholic thought paved the way for contextual theologians to carry the turn further in light of various contexts, to consciously consider these contexts in their reflections, and to re-envision theological anthropology accordingly. Indeed, something that must be underscored, which follows from Rahner's theological vision, is that contextual theologies have taken very seriously that God can only reveal what particular and historical humanity can perceive. God speaks grace in human "language." And this "language" is always framed within and constituted by social, gender, political, racial, and cultural factors.

---

[149]Rahner, "Utopia and Reality: The Shape of Christian Existence Caught between the Ideal and the Real," in *Theological Investigations*, XXII, trans. Joseph Donceel (New York: Crossroad, 1991), 28.

[150]See Rahner, *Foundations of Christian Faith*, 97-115.

[151]Ibid.

[152]Ibid. Originally delivered as a lecture on February 27, 1983 in Bad Hamberg under

Contextual theologians have, in a sense, taken on the challenge to affirm how their particular contexts "always and everywhere" stand in relationship to God's universal offer of grace. In so doing, these theologians have turned to *their* ordinary human experiences and they have attempted to name the experience of grace within those experiences. In this process, these theologians have pointed to new areas of human experiences overlooked in the past, new accents on what was perhaps quickly glossed over, new symbols, new mediators, and new contexts that have given rise to new questions and new anthropological formulations.

Rahner's supernatural existential, his Christocentric anthropology, and his notion of the human person as "hearer of the Word" suggest his overall affirmation of the universal offer of grace (transcendental pole of revelation) and the manifold presence of human mediators (categorical pole). Rahner makes very clear that as a result of God's universal offer of grace, God's solidarity with all humanity in Christ, and the essential constitution of the human as hearer of the Word, all human activity, even if unthematic and implicit, is religious activity.[153] Indeed, for Rahner, grace can be experienced in and mediated by implicit and explicit forms of religious activity, official as well as popular faith expressions.

Rahner's theological conviction of the universality of grace was to be complemented and developed by his increased post-Vatican II sensitivity to a world-historical consciousness. In this regard Rahner came to emphasize much more than he had done in his first writings the communal, socio-political, and practical mediation of grace. In light of this world-consciousness, it is also interesting to note how Rahner's theological anthropology, without completely abandoning its Christocentric focus, begins to prophetically signal a new starting point for future conversations in theological anthropology, namely, pneumatology.[154] This focus on the Holy Spirit anticipated present-day efforts that seek new ways of naming and new symbols for the experience of grace (see for instance, Espín's recent arguments on Guadalupe as a symbol of the Spirit).[155] This pneumatological move also carries implications with respect to the ongoing efforts to explore and name the experience of grace outside Christianity.

Rahner's newly envisioned pneumatological starting naturally flows from his earlier affirmation that the various forms of human inter-com-

---

the title "*Christliche Welt- und Lebensgestaltung zwischen Anspruch und Wirklichkeit.*" Rahner passed away in Innsbruck on March 30, 1984.

[153]See Rahner, "The Theology of the Religious Meaning of Images," 159.

[154]On Rahner's argument that pneumatology might precede Christology in the full development of an historically sensitive theology, see O'Donovan, "A Journey into Time: Legacy of Rahner's Last Years," 629.

[155]See Orlando O. Espín, "An Exploration into the Theology of Grace and Sin," in *From the Heart of Our People*, ed. Orlando O. Espín and Miguel H. Díaz (Maryknoll, New York: Orbis Books, 1999), 139-140.

munications with God serve as the condition required for the possibility of the saving mediatorship of Christ.[156] Through the manifold ways of God's self-expression, the Spirit has been at work perfecting human contexts unto the image and likeness of Christ. Thus, Rahner did not view the various mediations and mediators of grace as "dependent subordinate modes of participation in the unique mediatorship of Christ." Rather, Rahner reversed the process and argued that the mediatorship of Christ is "the eschatologically perfect and consequently the highest, the unique 'case' of human intercommunication before God and of the solidarity in salvation of all men [sic]."[157] In that broader context of human mediation, Rahner recognizes specifically the mediation of Mary.[158]

Given Rahner's universal yet categorical affirmation of grace, it is most fitting to characterize his theological anthropology as a theology of ordinary life experiences and of an ordinary experience of grace. Characterizations of his spirituality already suggest this theological interpretation.[159] Rahner's social and theological context, namely, secularism and extrinsicism, led him initially to affirm the ordinary human subject, concretely always and everywhere under the offer of grace. As the social context changed, and post-Vatican II social and ecclesial realities began to emerge, the "ordinary" in Rahner took on more and more a social and practical face. Today in a context of globalization and the alienation brought about by those unable to participate in the hegemony of the culture of inter-communication, what is ordinary can now take on new specific cultural meanings. In particular, Rahner's affirmation of the various human-divine inter-communications as authentic expressions of solidarity with God's unique self-communication in Christ, can be both empowering and validating in affirming how "all cultures may receive the Word of God and be able in some measure to communicate with one another, despite real and legitimate differences."[160]

The first three chapters of this book have underscored how social, practical, and cultural dimensions of humanity lie at the heart of U.S. Hispanic theological visions of humanity. The final chapter initiates a conversation with Rahner around the question: What can Rahner's transcendental anthropology contribute to the ongoing emergence of U.S. Hispanic theological anthropology, and what can this contextual project contribute, both critically and constructively, to contemporary understandings of Rahner's transcendental anthropology?

---

[156]Rahner, "One Mediator and Many Mediations," in *Theological Investigations*, IX, trans. Graham Harrison (New York: Seabury Press, 1972), 174.

[157]Ibid., 173.

[158]Ibid., 172-173, and 182.

[159]For instance, see Declan Marmion, *A Spirituality of Everyday Faith: A Theological Interpretation of the Notion of Spirituality in Karl Rahner* (Louvain: Peeters, 1998); and Egan, *Karl Rahner: Mystic of Everyday Life*.

[160]Robert J. Schreiter, *The New Catholicity: Theology between the Global and the Local* (Maryknoll, New York: Orbis Books, 1997), 128.

5

A Conversation

Being Human from U.S. Hispanic-Rahnerian
Perspectives

CONVERSATION AS A RESPONSE
TO THEOLOGICAL PLURALISM

The present chapter concludes this book with a Rahnerian-U.S. Hispanic conversation in theological anthropology. To embrace conversation as a form of deepening theological understanding is an exercise that reflects much of the spirit of our times. While conversation is certainly not a product of the contemporary mind—indeed, it can be traced back in the West at least as far back as the Socratic-Platonic tradition—in our times philosophers and theologians have increasingly retrieved conversation as a valuable tool to engage the present-day inter-cultural hermeneutical context.[1] For instance, David Tracy building upon the insights of Hans-Georg Gadamer has emphatically endorsed conversation as the contemporary model for attaining cross-cultural understanding and interpretation.[2]

Recognizing the pluralistic context that we find ourselves in, Tracy argues that "[t]he need for conversation—expressed in the differing strategies of confrontation, argument, conflict, persuasion, and above all, concentration on the subject matter—should free the Christian theologian to the fuller contemporary possibility of an analogical imagination."[3] Af-

---

[1]For instance, see Robert J. Schreiter, *The New Catholicity: Theology between the Global and the Local* (Maryknoll, New York: Orbis Books, 1997), esp. 28-45.

[2]See David Tracy, *The Analogical Imagination: Christian Theology and the Culture of Pluralism* (New York: Crossroad, 1981), 101.

[3]Ibid., 446-447.

firming the need to allow for a spectrum of theological voices, Tracy goes on to observe that "[u]nder the rubrics of a comparative and critical hermeneutics, the real similarities and dissimilarities, the continuities and discontinuities present in the contemporary pluralistic situation should be allowed their necessary emergence."[4]

In any fruitful conversation, the question(s) asked are as important as the answers that one proposes.[5] The central question raised and explored in this chapter is twofold: What can Rahner's transcendental anthropology contribute both critically and constructively to the ongoing emergence of U.S. Hispanic theological anthropology? And what can the latter contribute, both critically and constructively, to Rahner's transcendental vision? The U.S. Hispanic contribution to this question will be explored by re-visiting the inter-related themes of U.S. Hispanic theological anthropology (chapter two), and their sacramental expression, namely, popular Catholicism (chapter three). The Rahnerian answer to the question above will be provided by revisiting the three themes covered in chapter four of this book.

I have already pointed out how the emergence of contextual theologies can be seen as a natural outcome of the Council's call to read the signs of the times, and re-envision Christian faith in light of the socio-cultural contexts of the people of God.[6] More specifically, and with respect to the purpose of the present chapter, Rahner's own writings already anticipated the emergence of anthropological arguments that would, as U.S. Hispanic arguments have done, challenge the Euro-centric dominance of theology. In so doing, contextual anthropologies like U.S. Hispanic anthropology have re-envisioned the scattered themes that inform Christian anthropologies, and have underscored new elements that have been ignored or glossed over in the past (e.g., emphasis on social and gender issues, cultural identity, popular Catholicism, etc.).

Today, few would deny Rahner's influence on Catholic theologies since the Council. U.S. Hispanic theologies in particular have benefited from and appropriated much of Rahner's thought, even if at times implicitly.[7] Despite this, few U.S. Hispanic efforts have been made to engage Rahner

---

[4]Ibid., 447.

[5]Note the centrality of posing questions in contemporary hermeneutics. See Tracy, *The Analogical Imagination*, esp. 99-153 and Bernard Lonergan, *Method in Theology* (New York: Crossroad, 1972).

[6]For instance, see Pastoral Constitution of the Church in the Modern World (*Gaudium et Spes*), nn. 5, 24, 44, 54, and 66.

[7]In the case of some U.S. Hispanic theological sources (e.g., the writings of Orlando O. Espín, Sixto García, María Pilar Aquino), the Rahnerian influence can be substantiated with explicit references. In the case of others, however, Rahner's arguments are either implied or at the very least can be shown to be commensurable to U.S. Hispanic thought (e.g., the writings of Virgilio Elizondo, Roberto S. Goizueta, Alex García-Rivera). Note that this modest claim respects the commonly held thesis that Rahner's

in a sustained and systematic fashion. By carrying out this task in the following conversation, I will argue that Rahner's thought, even if in need of being challenged from U.S. Hispanic perspectives, can contribute to the development of U.S. Hispanic theology. On the one hand, Rahner's theological anthropology can enhance the foundational basis for the specific Catholic claims of U.S. Hispanic theological anthropology. On the other hand, U.S. Hispanic theological anthropology extends the development in Catholic thought already initiated by and anticipated in Rahner's transcendental Thomism.

The challenge that Tracy and others have set out relative to the need to engage distinct, yet related, Christian voices will be taken up in the present Rahnerian-U.S. Hispanic conversation in theological anthropology. Because the Rahnerian themes that I presented in chapter four of this book represent three areas that any contemporary theological anthropology could be reasonably expected to address, they will be used to structure the present conversation. Thus, this conversation will revolve around the following themes: 1) theology of grace; 2) theology of person and community; and 3) the essential social and practical dimensions that must be considered with respect to the human reality and its encounter with grace.

This structure, although partly inspired by Rahner's theological vision of the human, accords well with U.S. Hispanic theological concerns. Grace is a central theme in U.S. Hispanic theological anthropology. And as the various U.S. Hispanic anthropological visions and sacramental expressions suggest, neither the reality of grace nor its recipient are conceived in individualistic terms (recall, for instance, the communal nature of U.S. Hispanic Marian symbols). "Community is the birthplace of the self." But the self and community are not primarily to be thought of as concepts, but as social and practical human realities. Thus, what is human is also necessarily political in nature. While the kind of reductionism that turns the human into a mere product of economic, social, or political forces needs to be avoided, Rahner as well as U.S. Hispanic theologians make it clear that today socio-political experiences cannot be neglected in theological explorations of what it means to be human.

The exercise of bringing these two contemporary visions into conversation cannot ignore methodological differences that exist between the theological anthropology of Rahner and that of U.S. Hispanic theologians. Rahner's transcendental project tends to accent the universal over the particular, ontology over historical particularities. Conversely, U.S. Hispanic theological anthropology has accented from the beginning the particular over the universal. Unlike Rahner, U.S. Hispanic theological

---

thought has had a wide influence on Catholic contemporary thought, even if we readily acknowledge that relative to U.S. Hispanic theologians, Rahner is not the most influential figure.

anthropology generally shuns making any universal and metaphysical claims relative to an experience of grace.[8] U.S. Hispanic theologians prefer the language of universal relevance rather than that of universal validity.[9] Rather than some abstract notion of human experience, concrete human experiences, especially those experiences of socio-cultural marginalization, have mapped the U.S. Hispanic vision.

These methodological preferences, however, do not represent irreconcilable differences. After all, as I have underscored, Rahner's writings after Vatican II were characterized by a growing emphasis on the categorical pole of revelation, including a greater socio-political and practical consciousness.[10] After the Council, Rahner's writings became more attentive to human particularity, or to borrow from his Heideggerian language, his writings became more conscious of the "existentiell" experience of God and the world.[11] Of interest, too, is the fact that Rahner himself attempted to avoid theological abstractions. For instance, relative to grace, he preferred to speak in terms of the graced human person, rather than reflect upon the experience of grace in the abstract.[12] In this latter sense, the particular and contextual methodological starting points of U.S. Hispanic theological anthropology can be seen as a further concretization consistent with Rahner's developing vision.

Thematically speaking, U.S. Hispanic theological anthropology is in continuity with Rahner's theological vision, even while concretizing further Rahner's theological anthropology. This similarity is primarily due to the fact that the U.S. Hispanic vision, while highly aware of and informed by dialectical and prophetic Christian traditions, primarily as-

---

[8]U.S. Hispanic theologians have generally avoided metaphysical claims. Some, however, even while carefully qualifying their arguments, have not been able to fully escape metaphysical presuppositions. One U.S. Hispanic theologian (García-Rivera) has proposed a Latino re-interpretation of the metaphysical tradition in light of cosmology. On various U.S. Hispanic metaphysical stances see, for instance, Goizueta, *Caminemos con Jesús: Toward a Hispanic/Latino Theology of Accompaniment* (Maryknoll, New York: Orbis Books, 1995), 77; García-Rivera, "The Whole and the Love of Difference: Latino Metaphysics as Cosmology," in *From the Heart of Our People: Latino/a Explorations in Catholic Systematic Theology*, ed. Orlando O. Espín and Miguel H. Díaz (Maryknoll, New York: Orbis Books, 1999), 54-83; and Ada María Isasi-Díaz, *En la Lucha: A Hispanic Women's Liberation Theology* (Minneapolis: Fortress Press, 1993), 68-79.

[9]See Espín, "An Exploration into the Theology of Grace and Sin," in *From the Heart of Our People*, 125.

[10]See Thomas F. O' Meara, "Teaching Karl Rahner," *Philosophy and Theology* 12 (1998): 19.

[11]Briefly stated, recall that within Heideggerian thought existential (*existenzial*) refers to that which is universally given and experienced, while existentiell (*existenziell*) refers to the concrete and contextual situation in which humanity finds itself situated.

[12]On Rahner's preference to speak of engraced persons rather than an experience of grace in the abstract see Ladaria, *Introducción a la antropología teológica* (Navarra: Editorial Verbo Divino, 1996), 28.

sumes like Rahner an analogical approach to the relationship between the human reality and the divine reality (or that which is perceived to come "from" the divine).[13]

Rather than propose Rahnerian answers to specific U.S. Hispanic concerns, or U.S. Hispanic answers to areas where we may deem Rahner inadequate, my aim is to pave the way into an *analogical appreciation* of these two distinct but interrelated Catholic theological anthropologies, and their respective contexts. Whenever appropriate as a result of the ensuing conversation, challenge and critique will be carried out from the contextual horizon of each conversational partner. In so doing, we hope to avoid falling into the error of what Raúl Fornet-Betancourt, a contemporary philosopher, has characterized as turning a specific categorical world into the center and horizon by which other worlds are accepted and understood. In Fornet-Betancourt's judgment, such a view "understands by assimilating and incorporates by reduction," but in the end fails "to recognize in the other a source of equal originality and dignity."[14]

Fornet-Betancourt's contribution in the area of post-modern philosophical conversations offers some helpful insights for engaging in the present Rahnerian-U.S. Hispanic conversation. While fully acknowledging a polyphonic presence of "voices of reason,"[15] Fornet-Betancourt argues that "far from seeing in that historical-cultural load—in that dimension of lived and projected history present in every form of rationality—an impediment to dialogue, we must assume it as the true possibility for non-dominant communication."[16] Fornet-Betancourt sees each rational voice, arising from his or her own context, not as something absolute in itself, but rather, as a reality that one must cross if one wishes to attain intercommunication.[17] "Our culture" he writes, "would be something like a bridge, which we cannot jump over, but must be crossed if we wish to get

---

[13]Note how this approach is in continuity with the Thomistic tradition which affirms an openness between nature and grace (and vice versa). This openness is perhaps best captured in the now oft-cited Thomistic axiom: *"gratia non tollit, non destruit, sed perficit naturam."* On the latter and its implications for contemporary Catholic theology, including the work of Karl Rahner, see Bernard Quelquejeu, "Anthropological Presuppositions of Christian Existence," in *Is Being a Human a Criterion of Being Christian?*, ed. Marcus Lefébure (New York: Seabury Press, 1982), 58-64.

[14]See Raúl Fornet-Betancourt, *Hacia una filosofía intercultural latinoamericana* (San José: Departamento Ecuménico de Investigaciones, 1994), 19. My translation.

[15]Fornet-Betancourt follows Habermas, who argues that authentic conversation can take place when there is a presence of a multiplicity of voices of reason. See Fornet-Betancourt, *Hacia una filosofía intercultural latinoamericana*, 16.

[16]Cited in María Pilar Aquino's "Theological Method in U.S. Latino/a Theology," in *From the Heart of Our People*, 11.

[17]Like most post-modern thinkers, Fornet-Betancourt attributes the failure of intercommunication in the West, among other things, to its metaphysical tradition. Fornet-Betancourt believes that this metaphysical tradition has prevented the true emergence

to the other side."[18] In the present chapter, the Rahnerian and U.S. Hispanic perspectives serve as bridges that must be crossed if we are to achieve any real sense of inter-communication.

Even if a conscious attempt is made to remain faithful to the context and theological language shaping each particular vision, and attempts are made to avoid turning any one vision into the perspective by which another vision is judged, some form of theological translation is inevitable to achieve conversation. In any authentic conversation, translation, hereby understood as the drawing of analogies between two or more distinct theological visions, must take place if cross-contextual communication is to succeed. Since we are all in some ways children of modernity—a wider cultural matrix that speaks and practices the language of exclusion, either/or categories, and individualism—this exercise in the Catholic analogical imagination may be viewed as the difficult task at hand.[19]

The analogical imagination, however, is the backbone to U.S. Hispanic method and theology. The first three chapters of this book have already pointed out how U.S. Hispanic theology has been predisposed to this imagination by the socio-cultural and religious experiences that have fostered among U.S. Hispanics an openness to the other.[20] Indeed, in the very experience of *mestizaje/mulataje,* U.S. Hispanics have discovered a relational anthropology that invites conversation with the other, and the recognition that created reality is comprised of distinct yet mutually related aspects. As González proposes,

> [A] variety of perspectives enriches everyone's appreciation of the landscape itself. If I stand on hill A, someone from hill B can point

---

of an historically realized universality because such universality has been hypothesized in a metaphysical idea of universality, conceived in Western logical terms. While the present writer acknowledges the validity of this critique, we believe metaphysics per se is not what is at fault in realizing an authentic universality. We believe that some metaphysical affirmation, albeit one that reconceives metaphysics much more in light of historical and contextual categories, is necessary not only in affirming a true universality, but also to avoid falling into individualism (at the personal or communal level). On Fornet-Betancourt's critique of Western metaphysics see *Hacia una filosofía intercultural latinoamericana,* 14.

[18]Fornet-Betancourt, *Hacia una filosofía intercultural latinoamericana,* 13. My translation.

[19]On modernity and post-modernity see Goizueta, "In Defense of Reason," *Journal of Hispanic/Latino Theology* 3/3 (1996): 16-26, and idem, *Caminemos con Jesús*: 132-172.

[20]For an argument that explores the implications of socio-cultural experiences in terms of achieving an authentic pluralism see Goizueta, "United States Hispanic Theologies and the Challenges of Pluralism," in *Frontiers of Hispanic Theology in the United States,* ed. Allan Figueroa Deck (Maryknoll, New York: Orbis Books, 1992), 13.

out features in the landscape that I would never have noticed on my own. If I am interested in the way light bounces off of rocks and rivers, I can contribute something to my neighbor, whose interest lies in the various shades of green in the forest below us. Through conversation, we can amplify each other's experiences of the landscape—and thereby we can enhance each other's lives. Thus, I affirm my own perspective, not in order to claim that it is only I who understand the landscape, but rather in order to enrich the entire community of observers around me. And I am also much impoverished if I do not listen to what they have to say about the landscape as they see it from their own unique perspectives.[21]

A theological conversation cannot be idealized. In the process of mutual challenge, re-appropriation, and even rejection of another's understanding, distortions can occur. Since theological visions, their interlocutors and those that engage them, are always informed by specific contexts and interests, and since the latter are never exempt from participation in human ambiguity and sin, no conversation is ever totally immune from ideological interests. Indeed, as we have been reminded recently, conversations can often assume a context of distortions and ideological manipulations that mitigate against the unfolding of truth and authentic human liberation.[22] Mindful of the latter, I acknowledge the shortcomings of the following conversation.

ENCOUNTERING GRACE FROM U.S. HISPANIC AND RAHNERIAN PERSPECTIVES

Context always shapes the experience and language of grace.[23] Certain human experiences and the language that they engendered have acquired over the course of time a special place in Catholic thought. This is not the place to question in systematic and critical ways how and why some of these Catholic traditions came to occupy this special role. That question would produce another book. Suffice it for now to recognize that specific traditions of the experience and language of grace have been privileged, and that such privileging is partly due to the fact that these traditions have been judged by various authorities to express at a founda-

---

[21]Justo L. González, *Santa Biblia: The Bible through Hispanic Eyes* (Nashville: Abingdon Press, 1996), 19-20.

[22]For instance see, Jürgen Habermas, "On Systematic Distorted Communication," *Inquiry* 13 (1970): 205-18; and idem, *Knowledge and Human Interests* (Boston: Beacon Press, 1971).

[23]The phrase "experience and language of grace," along with its understanding, has been borrowed from Roger Haight, *The Experience and Language of Grace* (New York: Paulist Press, 1979), 6-31.

tional level the Catholic way of relating the human to the divine. One such tradition is the Thomistic tradition and its contemporary appropriation in the work of transcendental Thomists like Karl Rahner.

U.S. Hispanic theologies of grace, not unlike other contemporary contextual theologies, can and have drawn upon the central insights of this tradition. As Orlando O. Espín witnesses in his Rahnerian claim that human beings are, within their specific socio-cultural context, expressions of "God's self outside of the sphere of the divine" and as such "humanize" themselves through that context,[24] U.S. Hispanic theological anthropology has in various conscious and unconscious ways entered into conversation with this tradition.

The Human-Divine Relationship Revisited

Characteristic of Rahner's theological anthropology is an insistence on affirming grace in ordinary human experiences or contexts. The latter has also been referred to as his mystical approach to everyday life.[25] Rahner's early theology focused on the individual components of human experience (e.g., the intentionality of the thinking and willing subject), and his theology after the Council welcomed and underscored more and more socio-political and practical aspects. As Johann Baptist Metz points out, "[m]ore than almost anyone else he [Rahner] saw the concrete questions men and women had after the Council, and was without equal in the way he made himself accountable to them."[26]

In the previous chapter I noted how, socially speaking, Rahner's theology of grace emerges in response to the context of secularization—what Rahner characterizes as the alienation of God from everyday experience, whether individually or communally conceived. Theologically speaking, Rahner's theology of grace represents a response to the neo-Scholastic problem of extrinsicism. Rahner's supernatural existential overcomes the neo-Scholastic separation between nature and grace, and proposes instead a proportional understanding of these two realities.

Secularism and extrinsicism, however, are not unrelated contexts.[27] The two often imply and engender one another. That is, if, socially speaking, as Rahner argued, the main problem of secularism is the exiling of God

---

[24]Orlando O. Espín, "Grace and Humanness: A Hispanic Perspective," in *We Are a People!: Initiatives in Hispanic American Theology*, ed. Roberto S. Goizueta (Minneapolis: Fortress Press, 1992), 138.

[25]See Harvey D. Egan, *Karl Rahner: Mystic of Everyday Life* (New York: Crossroad, 1998), esp. 55-79.

[26]Johann Baptist Metz, "Do We Miss Karl Rahner?" in *A Passion for God: The Mystical-Political Dimension of Christianity*, trans. J. Matthew Ashley (New York: Paulist Press, 1998), 95.

[27]Note how one of the central theses of Henri de Lubac's work on the mystery of the

from everyday experience, a theology that sanctions an extrinsic under-standing of grace can only perpetuate the exile of God from wordly real-ity. With respect to the latter, it is interesting to note that while U.S. His-panic theology has emerged within a broader U.S. context of secularism, it cannot be conceived primarily as a response to extrinsicism or to secu-larism. In fact, the resilient Latin-American religious pre-modern ethos, which sees human and divine life as being intrinsically connected, has predisposed U.S. Hispanics to seeing their everyday and ordinary experi-ences, including the cultural and socio-political components of these ex-periences, as being closely intertwined with the life of grace.[28] This was particularly evident in chapter three's discussion regarding the sacramen-tal significance of popular Catholicism, especially the presence of reli-gious symbols within private and public places.

As a result of this religious predisposition or integral way of relating the human to the divine, U.S. Hispanic theological anthropology already affirms, even if implicitly, Rahner's key transcendental affirmation that conceives the human reality as "an inner moment of grace." If such is the case, we can with certain qualifications interpret U.S. Hispanic theologi-cal anthropology as a particularizing of Rahner's anthropological pre-supposition. This need not imply a causal effect relationship between Rahner and U.S. Hispanic theology whereby the latter is understood as merely instantiating the former. The methodological starting points and theological sources of U.S. Hispanic theological anthropology preclude one from drawing that relationship. In fact, if the religious and theologi-cal traditions that undergird U.S.Hispanic theologies are taken seriously into account (i.e., medieval Spanish Catholicism and its sacramental vi-sion of humanity), one may even hypothesize that in some ways these theological traditions anticipate Rahner's contemporary contributions. By affirming that U.S. Hispanic theology particularizes Rahner's theol-ogy we are simply arguing that the central themes that comprise U.S. Hispanic ways of understanding the human encounter with grace reso-nate with and indeed concretely exemplify and presuppose the kind of relationship between nature and grace that Rahner's theology proposes.

A "Rahnerian" reading of U.S. Hispanic theology could then see the following U.S. Hispanic visions of humanity as contextual expressions of the "always and everywhere" presence of grace: 1) Elizondo's Christo-centric notion of grace as implied in his notion of the Galilean identity of

---

supernatural is that theological extrinsicism contributes to secularism. See his *Surnaturel* (Paris: Aubier, 1946).

[28]See the various arguments of Joseph Fitzpatrick that bear upon this theme. For instance, see his *Puerto Rican Americans: The Meaning of Migration to the Mainland* (Englewood: Prentice-Hall, 1971), 116. See also Allan Figueroa Deck, *The Second Wave: Hispanic Ministry and the Evangelization of Cultures* (New York: Paulist Press, 1989), 110.

Jesus, and that of contemporary "Galileans"; 2) Goizueta's notion of divine accompaniment, and its relationship to the presence of grace within U.S. Hispanic places and persons; 3) Espín's socio-cultural understanding of humanization and of grace; 4) Isasi-Díaz's ethically and socio-culturally rooted notions of the kin-dom of God (*mestizaje*), and the love of neighbor (charity as solidarity); 5) Aquino's egalitarian, engendered, historical, and socially conscious notions of the human reality, which she sees intrinsically related to the life of grace (see the way she relates sacred and profane realities); 6) García-Rivera's affirmation of the diversity of creatures as a participation in the life of grace; and 7) García's notion of the trinitarian face of grace as encountered within the social-political, personal, and institutional experiences of U.S. Hispanics.

This Rahnerian reading deepens the foundational presuppositions of U.S. Hispanic theological anthropology by bringing U.S. Hispanic theology into conversation with the greater Catholic tradition, especially Aquinas's theology of grace. Rahner's notion of God's universal will to save presupposes an analogical understanding between nature and grace very much in line with Aquinas's thought. In his understanding of nature as an inner moment of grace, Rahner reflects Aquinas's classical Thomistic principle that grace does not surpass or destroy nature but perfects it.[29] This traditional Thomistic way of understanding the relationship between nature and grace, though not explicitly taken up in the arguments of U.S. Hispanic theologians, is implied, albeit in a more holistic anthropological manner.

But U.S. Hispanic theological anthropology can also challenge and suggest new paths of development in this Thomistic tradition. Within U.S. Hispanic theology, nature or that which is conceived to comprise an essential constituent of what it means to be human refers not so much to a formal "whatness" but, rather, to a very concrete personal, historical, and socio-cultural way of being in the world. Persons, to recall U.S. Hispanic understandings "are not just an idea or definition, but historical faces marked by space and time." In this sense, the human is not a "what" but a "who" responding to grace "in," "with," and "under" the impulse of historical experiences. With some modification that takes into account our modern-day historical consciousness, this dynamic notion of human nature can be brought into conversation with what Aquinas understood by nature. Nature in Aquinas is not simply the "what" of something, but most importantly, a principle of action that determines "how" something acts with respect to an end. Thus, "a nature governs the kind of actions performed by a being" and "generates behavior typical of its kind of being."[30] One can argue that U.S. Hispanic theologians have underscored

---

[29]For an excellent brief exposition of Aquinas's teaching on grace and nature, see Quelquejeu, "Anthropological Presuppositions of Christian Existence," 59-64.

[30]Roger Haight, "Sin and Grace," in *Systematic Theology: Roman Catholic Perspectives*, ed. Francis Schüssler Fiorenza and John P. Galvin (Minneapolis: Fortress Press, 1991), 127.

the historical reality of persons as that aspect of being human that intrinsically governs human acts and thereby generates and defines the "how"
of existence and the response to grace.

As a result of this more historically sensitive notion of what it means
to be human, U.S. Hispanic theologians do not simply speak of the graced
person, even if the latter, as is the case with Rahner's own development of
Aquinas's thought, is dynamically defined in terms of freedom, self-determination, and the like. Rather, drawing on a variety of contemporary
insights (especially those that derive from the social sciences), we have
gone further to specify those ordinary experiences that inform, partly
constitute human persons, and enable or hinder the mediation of grace.
As Elizondo's christological understanding of the Galilean identity of Jesus
witnesses, it is at this contextual level that U.S. Hispanic theological anthropology relates in a proportional or analogical way the human and
the divine. Elizondo's insistence on exploring the socio-cultural implications of Jesus' identity, and what his arguments imply in terms of a theology of grace, all presuppose this U.S. Hispanic analogical but particular
way of relating what is human to what is divine. In U.S. Hispanic theology, grace is not perceived as an "extrinsic" horizon of the self-in-com-
munity. Rather, in accordance with the popular Catholic analogical imagination of U.S. Hispanics, grace, as God's self-accompaniment, is perceived
as an ongoing and essential constituent of *lo cotidiano*.

Given the U.S. Hispanic theological concerns to affirm socio-cultural
identity against melting-pot ideologies and to denounce various forms of
socio-cultural marginalizations, it makes much sense to express the interaction between the human and the divine in terms of not only a Thomistic
nature/grace model, but also an older biblical and Augustinian tradition
that underscores a grace/sin model.[31] While the nature/grace model is more
consistent with an analogical effort to situate grace within the human,
the grace/sin model appeals more to the dialectical imagination that stresses
the discontinuity between the human and the divine. Context again is
important, and must be considered relative to the U.S. Hispanic experience and language of grace.[32] The notions of deculturali-zation (Espín),

---

[31]Note Duffy's observation: "Because of their philosophical heritage Western
students may find it odd that in the Christian Scriptures *charis* and the cognates are not
set in contrast to nature or creation (as the natural and the supernatural would be
contrasted in later theology) but to sin and helplessness (cf. Romans and Galatians)."
See Stephen J. Duffy, *The Dynamics of Grace: Perspectives in Theological Anthropology* (Collegeville: The Liturgical Press, 1993), 337. Similarly see also Stephen Bevans,
Models of Contextual Theology (Maryknoll, New York: Orbis Books, 1994), 38.

[32]For example, on the Latin-American perspective see José Ignacio González Faus,
"Sin" in *Systematic Theology: Perspectives from Liberation Theology*, ed. Jon Sobrino
and Ignacio Ellacuría (Maryknoll, New York: Orbis Books, 1993), 194-204; and José
Comblin, "Grace," in *Systematic Theology*, 205-215. On the U.S. Hispanic perspective
see Espín, "An Exploration into the Theology of Grace and Sin."

Latinas' efforts to critique sexism, the rejection of asymmetric relationships (García-Rivera), and the defacing of the trinitarian image in society (García) suggest why U.S. Hispanic theologians have gravitated to the grace/sin model. By way of contextual contrast, the nature/grace model makes much sense in light of Rahner's response to the secularizing tendencies of modernity's exiling of God.

These two models are not incompatible with one another. Rahner's analogical approach to the relationship between nature and grace can be very helpful in articulating some of the implicit foundational presuppositions of U.S. Hispanic theology (especially with respect to ongoing efforts to ground the universal—grace—in the particular—U.S. Hispanic experiences). Conversely, as a result of the contextual issues that accompany U.S. Hispanic perspectives, Rahner's theology can be extended much more than Rahner himself did in his later writings to include concrete experiences of the human reality under the impact of sin.

Similarly, Rahner's supernatural existential, though a valuable contribution to post-Scholastic understandings of grace, is not specific enough with regard to the details of the economy of salvation.[33] One is reminded of Johann Baptist Metz's question: "does this [Rahner's transcendental theology] take into account the fact that man's anticipatory existence is a historical existence?"[34] When concrete historical experiences are made the starting point of theological reflections, as they have been in the case of U.S. Hispanic theology, and when these experiences underscore suffering and sin (immigration, social injustices, gender exploitation), the confidence in the "always and everywhere" presence of grace is somehow shaken and the notion needs to be somewhat refined accordingly.

Because in U.S. Hispanic theological anthropology, concrete human experiences are more fundamental than in Rahner's theological anthropology, and because those experiences are often marked with various socio-cultural expressions of sin, the U.S. Hispanic understanding qualifies what could be characterized in Rahner's writings as an overly positive theological anthropology. The consciousness of sin and widespread efforts to reflect upon this experience among U.S. Hispanic theologians makes it necessary to qualify from a U.S. Hispanic perspective Rahner's ordinary and always-present experience of grace.

This does not mean, however, that U.S. Hispanic theological anthropology should be conceived, as Metz's theology has been conceived, primarily as a theology that embraces an experience of grace as "an interruption."[35] In my opinion, among other things, the focus on cultural

---

[33]Note Metz's critique that Rahner's theology does not attend sufficiently to the "dangerous memory" of the experience of grace.

[34]Metz, *Faith in History and Society: Toward a Practical Fundamental Theology* (New York: Seabury Press, 1980), 65.

[35]See Ashley's insightful reflections comparing and contrasting Rahner and Metz in

mediation and the sacramentality of Latino/a popular Catholicism precludes this line of interpretation. Even while very conscious of sin, U.S. Hispanic theological anthropology is fundamentally rooted upon the conviction that grace is experienced in and through created reality. Grace enters into, challenges, and changes the status quo, but always from "within." The principle is one of incarnating, of becoming one with the other, in order to change and transform the context that unites and defines the marginalized and the marginalizer. The sacramentality of U.S. Hispanic Marian popular Catholicism suggests my conviction.

Even after establishing points of intersection between Rahner's understanding and the U.S. Hispanic understanding of nature, sin, and grace, unresolved tensions still remain. The question can still be raised whether or not theological starting points, particular experiences and linguistic expressions of grace can ever be commensurable with other experiences.[36] In other words, can a given human context, and the particular linguistic expressions that arise therein, make conversation with another perspective difficult, if not impossible? As Stephen Duffy has remarked, "Social and linguistic patterns structure experience and make possible perception of one's inner life." Language, he goes on to argue, "is far more than a symbol system expressing the depths of one's inner life and experience. It shapes the experience itself."[37]

Duffy's observation cannot be easily dismissed. The face of the Galilean Jesus, the presence of grace in marginalized private spaces (the home and its subjects: women and children), and its sacramental manifestation in U.S. Hispanic popular Catholicism have established the hermeneutical lenses from which to tap into the U.S. Hispanic experience and language of grace. Indeed, social and cultural experiences (i.e., *mestizaje*, marginalization, and suffering) have been more than ordinary human experiences which in a Rahnerian sense of the term serve as mediators of grace. Compared to Rahner's theology, these experiences are within U.S. Hispanic theology much more fundamental in envisioning and constructing a theology of nature and grace.

As the symbols of U.S. Hispanic popular Catholicism witness (for instance, the crucified Christ, Our Lady of Guadalupe and Our Lady of Charity), cultural identity, marginalization, and suffering have become

---

Interruptions: Mysticism, Politics, and Theology in the Work of Johann Baptist Metz (Notre Dame: University of Notre Dame, 1998), esp. 171-196.

[36]Note the following observation by Gerald McCool: "In his later writings, he [Rahner] has shown a growing awareness of the culturally conditioned origin of human concepts and of the historical character of their content. Unlike Bernard Lonergan, however, he has done little to unite these two aspects of his writing on conceptualization in a single coherent position." In *Person and Community: A Philosophical Exploration*, ed. Robert J. Roth (New York: Fordham University Press, 1975), 83.

[37]Duffy, *The Dynamics of Grace*, 102.

the means from which to conceive the inclusive and preferential activity of grace.[38] These symbols are "popular" precisely not only because of their widespread appeal, but also because they embody sacramentally the experience of a great number of U.S. Hispanics, namely their cultural identity, their suffering, and their marginalization. This socio-cultural identification makes these symbols capable of "speaking" in a Rahnerian sense of the term, and of underscoring in a U.S. Hispanic fundamental sense that the word of grace that is always and necessarily mediated within specific human experiences, especially within the experiences of the poor and the marginalized.

U.S. HISPANIC MARYS WITHIN A CHRIST-ORIENTED EVOLUTIONARY VIEW OF THE LIFE OF GRACE

Rahner's understanding of the relationship between nature and grace finds ultimate expression in his ontological claim that makes Jesus Christ the beginning and end of our human existence. While Rahner understands Christ, as the source, paradigm, and end of human existence, his Christocentrism does not exclude, but rather presupposes other anthropological signposts. The latter can be attributed to his affirmation of the universal offer of grace. Since grace is universally offered in and through a manifold of mediators, and since Rahner understands all human mediation in relationship to Christ, there is the possibility of conceiving in continuity with Rahner's arguments other human expressions that delineate, in socio-cultural ways, the origin and destiny of human reality. Particularly important to recall, in light of the present observations, is Rahner's recognition of popular faith expressions, the pneumatological vision in his last writings, and his understanding of Marian devotions as authentic mediators of grace.

That Mary occupies a central place in U.S. Hispanic Catholic Christianity is something few would contest. The devotion to Our Lady of Guadalupe and that of Our Lady of Charity have already provided test cases in this book. These devotions, I argued, occupy a very special sacramental place in the religious experiences of U.S. Hispanics. They function as important symbols that mediate for U.S. Hispanics the relationship between their specific way of being human and the life of grace. Closely linked to the cultural and socio-political reality of specific Latino/a com-

---

[38]See Orlando O. Espín, "Popular Religion as an Epistemology (of Suffering)," *Journal of Hispanic/Latino Theology* 2/2 (1994): 55-78; and idem, "God of the Vanquished: Foundations for a Latino Spirituality," *Listening: Journal of Religion and Culture* 27/1 (1992): 70-83. Not all U.S. Hispanic theologians, however, would agree with this hermeneutical perspective. For instance, see Ada María Isasi-Díaz, "Elements of a *Mujerista* Anthropology," in *Mujerista Theology: A Theology for the Twenty-First Century* (Maryknoll, New York: Orbis Books, 1996), 130.

munities, these Marian devotions offer central sacramental sources for re-conceiving the presence of the divine.

Within U.S. Hispanic theology Mary is a symbol of grace. Whether understood as the female face of God (Rodriguez, Elizondo), a symbol of the Holy Spirit (Espín), the poetry of the trinitarian God (García), or the *mestizo* face of the divine (Goizueta), it is clear that U.S. Hispanic theologians understand Marian symbols as mediators of the life of grace, especially to and within the experience of the poor and marginalized. Such an understanding develops what is oftentimes found lacking in post-Rahnerian discussions of grace, namely, how the activity of grace can be imaged in more specific social, cultural, and engendered sensitive ways.

Conversely, Rahner's theology offers a way by which to deepen U.S. Hispanic Mariology. From Rahner's perspective, U.S. Hispanic Marys can be perceived as an expression of God's universal will to save and desire to accompany particular communities within *their* particular humanity. In allowing for a wide range of human mediators that stand in relationship to Christ, Rahner's theology of grace allows for possibly, indeed necessarily, different communal mediators of grace. Without compromising the fundamental Christocentric orientation of all human reality, Rahner's theology invites us to see how the U.S. Hispanic emphasis on Mary can be interpreted as a legitimate sacramental mediator of grace. Thus, within U.S. Hispanic contexts, Mary's special place suggests the ongoing evolution of the life of grace that originates in and climaxes with Jesus Christ, but is always humanly mediated. Rahner's perspective renders justice to the Catholic sacramental imagination and to God's universal offer of grace, while avoiding the stronger claim that Mary is the "incarnation" of grace.[39]

Rahner's theology also deepens the Catholic underpinnings of U.S. Hispanic theologies of Mary. So far, the anthropological arguments pertaining to U.S. Hispanic Marian devotions have avoided metaphysical overtones. Instead, U.S. Hispanic theologians have been content to point out how symbols such as Our Lady of Guadalupe and Our Lady of Charity function as semantic and cultural mediators of the life of grace. These religious expressions have been interpreted as cultural and social legitimate means that express in content and form Christian belief.[40] Since these symbols, however, relate in very concrete ways the human encounter with grace, their metaphysical underpinnings are unavoidable. Rahner's theology of grace, particularly in relation to his theology of symbol, of-

---

[39]This appears to be the theological impasse with Leonardo Boff's Mariology. See his *Trinity and Society* (Maryknoll, New York: Orbis Books, 1988), 210-212.

[40]See Espín, "Tradition and Popular Religion: An Understanding of the *Sensus Fidelium*," in *Frontiers of Hispanic Theology*, 75, and Jeanette Rodriguez, *Our Lady of Guadalupe: Faith and Empowerment among Mexican-American Women* (Austin: University of Texas Press, 1994), 149-158.

fers a way by which to render a more foundational approach to U.S. Hispanic Marian devotions.

For Rahner to be human is to be a grace-bearing symbol. Jesus is the "full, definitive symbolic cause and expression of the divine-human interrelation that is always already present from the beginning and capable of being acknowledged in a myriad of ways in diverse times and places."[41] As a result of God's self-expression in humanity, the human reality is iconic, "in a myriad of ways" of the life of grace. Thus, one can argue that the semantic and cultural expressions of U.S. Marian devotions truly communicate, in a contextually defined way, something about the origin and destiny of Latino/a reality, namely God. In this latter sense, the Marys of U.S. Hispanic popular Catholicism point to the beginning and end of an "Hispanically" human way of being in history in relationship to God. As I have underscored, this history includes social, cultural, gender, and political human experiences, especially those associated with the poor and marginalized.

U.S. Hispanic Marys are indispensable grace-bearing symbols that point to the divine-human interrelation of specific communities. Seen from this perspective, Rahner's Christocentric affirmation of human reality can be subjected within the particular sacramental experiences of U.S. Hispanics, to re-interpretation and appropriation without in any way undermining the uniqueness and paradigmatic function of Jesus Christ. To take seriously the wide U.S. Hispanic theological consensus on the importance of Marian devotions, and the predominant role that the latter have occupied in Latino/a anthropological reflections, means that Rahner's affirmation of Christology as beginning and end of anthropology can be culturally and socially qualified and appropriated from the perspective of U.S. Hispanic contexts. In these contexts, Mary's sacramental identification with her Son and the community of suffering persons identified with and embodied by her Son offers the key to such qualification and appropriation.

ENCOUNTERING GRACE IN THE "HEARING," "DOING," AND "SEEING" OF THE WORD

As a grace-bearing symbol, Mary serves as a reminder of the aesthetic nature of U.S. Hispanic theology. Indeed, U.S. Hispanic theology is as much a theology of content as it is a theology of form. With respect to the latter, it is worth recalling Goizueta's argument that one cannot speak "*about* God if we cannot speak *as* God speaks in our world, that is, if we are blind to the *form* of God's revelation. . . ."[42] Goizueta underscores the

---

[41]Duffy, *The Dynamics of Grace*, 310. Cited in chapter four.

[42]Roberto S. Goizueta, "U.S. Hispanic Popular Catholicism as Theopoetics," in *Hispanic/ Latino Theology: Challenge and Promise,* ed. Ada María Isasi-Díaz and Fernando F. Segovia (Minneapolis: Fortress Press, 1996), 265.

overarching aesthetic sensitivity of U.S. Hispanic theology in which the fundamental anthropological image can perhaps be best expressed by the notion of the human person as seer and doer of the Word.

Chapter four pointed out how Rahner's fundamental anthropological concept is that of the human person as "hearer of the Word." This concept is a corollary to his understanding of the supernatural existential. For Rahner, God constitutes persons "always and everywhere" in an offer of grace, and thereby essentially creates in them the universal condition for the possibility of God's self revelation. Rahner understands this human openness to revelation in a holistic anthropological sense. As Michael Fahey notes, Rahner "searches 'to find God in all things,' to discern through spirits within himself and in others how to become a better *hearer*, *seer*, and *doer* of the Word."[43]

Rahner's notion of the human person as hearer of the Word has its advantages and disadvantages. On the positive side, Rahner's rejection of neo-scholastic extrinsicism paves the way for a more integral understanding of human and divine realities, including socio-political dimensions. His affirmation of the "always and everywhere" offer of grace and its corollary understanding of the human person as hearer of the Word is an essential step taken in contemporary Catholic thought toward the recognition of the manifold ways in which God's offer of grace and self-revelation occurs. As such, Rahner's notion of the human person as hearer of the Word can be welcomed by U.S. Hispanic theologians in their relentless efforts to underscore *our* specific Hispanic way of "hearing" God's Word.

Since in Rahner the person is as much a doer or seer as he or she is a hearer of the Word, Rahner's theology of grace and revelation can provide a helpful partner in the development of U.S. Hispanic theology. Among other things, the underlying Thomistic affirmation in Rahner's theology of the human person as hearer of the Word, that Being is knowable and lovable in every act of sense experience (Rahner's *Spirit in the World*), can provide a bridge for U.S. Hispanic theologians to cross into conversation with Thomist traditions. This philosophical premise, which is central to Catholic theology, is something that U.S. Hispanic theologians have yet to address from U.S. Hispanic perspectives. Here I see an important contribution that U.S. Hispanic theologians can make to theological anthropology in line with Rahnerian anthropological presuppositions.

The U.S. Hispanic emphasis on the forms of revelation, which include the seeing and acting (praxis) of the Word, can complement and develop Rahner's transcendental experience of the human person. Not only do the notions of doer and seer of the Word convey a more embodied and communal anthropology in line with Rahner's own anthropological vi-

---

[43]Michael Fahey, "1904-1984, Karl Rahner, Theologian," in *Proceedings of the Catholic Theological Society of America* 39 (1984), 96. Emphasis added.

sion, but an understanding of the human person as seer and doer of the Word can mitigate against post-Tridentine biases, and German idealistic tendencies found in Rahner's earlier transcendental thought, and be more in line with the social-practical evolution of his thought.[44]

I have already noted how Rahner moves beyond Aquinas's metaphysics of knowledge to embrace the personal other as the preferred place of God's self-revelation and offer of grace.[45] Faintly echoing Blondel's *volonté voulante*, Rahner's notion of the love of neighbor established the love of a personal other as the human word in which God's Word can be heard. As Rahner was challenged by Metz and accepted the challenge to become more conscious of socio-political experiences, his transcendental notion of the love of neighbor acquired more socio-political dimensions. In light of the signs of his time, Rahner even began to speak the language of the preferential love of the poor.

In this respect, Rahner's transcendental theology came to reflect a more praxis-minded and preferential notion of the recipient or hearer of God's offer of grace and self-revelation—one that was perhaps closer to the U.S. Hispanic notion of the human person as "doer" of the Word on behalf of, and with, the poor and oppressed. Indeed, whereas in his early thought Rahner's deductive and conceptual logic offers little qualification to the subjects of revelation, in his writings after Vatican II, Rahner turns more and more from universal affirmations to inductive and practical arguments, from a universal hearer of the Word to a specific hearer of the Word. Thus, Rahner argued that "[t]he preference which Jesus showed and lived out for the poor and downgraded in society . . . cannot be deduced from an abstract and universal morality. . . . " Rahner's affirmation is important because of its qualification of the "always and everywhere" universal offer of grace and privileging of a specific group of persons as preferential recipients of God's offer.[46] Seen from this perspective, Rahner came close to the kind of preferential qualification that one finds in U.S. Hispanic theology with respect to the hearer of God's Word, and his or her social location.

PERSON AND COMMUNITY

Similar to Rahner, the U.S. Hispanic understanding of the recipients of the offer of grace presupposes an embodied and communal anthro-

---

[44]Recall Rahner's argument that God's self-communication occurs "*fundamentally* through the word and through the hearing of the message." See his "The Theology of the Religious Meaning of Images," in *Theological Investigations* XXIII, trans. Joseph Donceel and Hugh M. Riley (New York: Crossroad, 1992), 154.

[45]Note Rahner's comments in the introduction to Andrew Tallon's *Personal Becoming*, already discussed in chapter four.

[46]See Rahner, "Following the Crucified," in *Theological Investigations*, XVIII,

pology. U.S. Hispanic theology goes beyond Rahner's general affirmation of an embodied spirit (spirit-in-the-world) to explore and expand upon the following dimensions of human embodiment: 1) the relationship of the physical body to the social body; 2) the relationship between the private spaces of the body and its public spaces; 3) the relationship between female and male bodies; and 4) the interrelatedness of gender, race, and class and its effects on the physical and social body.

With respect to community, while both Rahnerian and U.S. Hispanic anthropological visions correlate personal and communal dimensions of human reality, Rahner stresses the individual, whereas U.S. Hispanic theology gives priority to community. The sacramentality of U.S. Hispanic popular Catholicism, and in particular, the collective memory recapitulated in U.S. Hispanic Marian symbols, clearly exemplifies this U.S. Hispanic communal emphasis. Conversely, Rahner's theological anthropology, as his Christology evidences, accents the relationship between one particular reality and another (e.g., the Logos and the humanity of Christ, Jesus Christ and all other human persons). These differences, although subtle, partly explain why U.S. Hispanic theological anthropology is more predisposed than Rahner's anthropology to the cultural and socio-political analysis of the self.

Rahner's approach to person and community (especially in his earlier thought) reflects his effort to bring transcendental Thomism into conversation with modernity's turn to the subject. James J. Buckley has rightly observed that Rahner's theological anthropology must be read in light of the turn to the individual subject who, as individual, necessarily expresses himself or herself in community, and in the public as a means of self-realization.[47] Rahner sees each individual person created in the image of the Triune God as inherently oriented toward a distinct other, in whom he or she finds self-realization and expression.[48]

Following the recent developments in the turn to the contextual subject, U.S. Hispanic theological anthropology has moved beyond the unsituated and neutral subject to embrace his or her social, racial, gender, economic, and political coordinates. Unlike Rahner, whose notion of person and community reflects philosophical continuity with the thought of Thomas Aquinas, U.S. Hispanic notions of person and community have

---

trans. Edward Quinn (New York: Crossroad, 1983), 160. See also 158-159 where Rahner's discussion takes on a very concrete and *a posteriori* starting point for his understanding of Christ and the ethical implications that follow from the latter. Note the similarities in Rahner's argument with Elizondo's notion of following the Galilean, and Goizueta's notion of accompaniment of the crucified Christ.

[47]See James J. Buckley, "On Being a Symbol: An Appraisal of Karl Rahner," *Theological Studies* 40 (1979): 470.

[48]See Rahner, "The Theology of the Symbol," in *Theological Investigations*, IV, trans. Kevin Smyth (New York: Crossroad, 1982), 235-236.

for the most part drawn on philosophical resources that have been judged to fall within or resonate with the cultural experiences of U.S. Hispanics.

The Embodied Self as Personal Mystery

Spirit-in-the-world characterizes Rahner's notion of the human person. This notion captures the tension and correlation that exists in Rahner's thought between the "spiritual" and "material" dimensions of human reality. Avoiding reified notions of created reality, Rahner conceives what is human, including its cultural and bodily manifestations, ultimately as mystery. Rahner's notion of spirit-in-the world underscores the self-transcendence of all reality, that is, the intrinsic relationality and other-oriented dynamism that in the final analysis reflects the trinitarian mystery of God.

This self-transcending and God-oriented approach to human person can invite a more "theological" development of U.S. Hispanic notions of the human person. The anthropological focus on *mestizaje,* accompaniment, solidarity, and on the human person as agent of struggle for change—which exemplify U.S. Hispanic efforts to address material, socio-cultural, and practical dimensions of the human person—can be developed in ways that make more explicit how these realities express and relate to the mystery of God. As Rahner's notion of the person as spirit-in-the-world underscores, the human person must ultimately be defined in reference to God, even if one readily acknowledges with Rahner that such referencing always takes place "in," "with," and "under" historical and embodied realities. The following observations already witness how such referencing has already begun to occur within the writings of U.S. Hispanic theologians:

> To love the poor preferentially is to make an *intentional choice* to be that which we already *are* through no choice of our own: individual persons defined by our *a priori* relationships to others, to humanity, to the universe, and, ultimately, to the Triune (i.e., intrinsically relational) God.[49]

Like Rahner's notion of the free subject, which presupposes self-realization in and through a worldly other, especially the personal other, U.S. Hispanic theological anthropology affirms self-realization through the accompaniment of worldly others, especially and preferentially women, children, the poor, and the places they inhabit. In so doing, U.S. Hispanic theological anthropology is concerned to affirm not only the "what" of person (e.g., person as relation, as self-transcendent), but also the "who," "where," and "how" of the person.

---

[49]Goizueta, *Caminemos con Jesús,* 179.

By emphasizing the accompaniment of specific marginalized subjects in the places they abide, U.S. Hispanic theological anthropology suggests a socio-cultural development of Rahner's notion of embodiment. This development takes very seriously, to use Rahner's language, the particularities that comprise the categorical pole of human experiences. While Rahner recognized readily that as spirit-in-the-world the person encounters self and God in and through his or her concrete ordinary communal life experiences, Rahner did not go far enough in terms of exploring the particularities of such encounter. If among the strengths of Rahner's theology is his theocentric affirmation of embodied reality, among the strengths one finds in U.S. Hispanic theological anthropology is the concrete socio-cultural and spatial implications of that reality. This embodied understanding partly explains why U.S. Hispanic theology, since its founding reflections on the Galilean identity of Jesus, has made as its starting point of theological reflection the concrete socio-cultural experiences of U.S. Hispanics. This concrete anthropological starting point also explains the importance the social sciences have played in the various efforts to critique neo-liberal, competitive, dualistic (with respect to the self and the places where the self abides), sexist, and individualistic notions of the human person.

Thus, U.S. Hispanic theological anthropology challenges and particularizes Rahner's notion of the self-transcending person as spirit-in-the-world. Rahner's notion, though *theologically* indispensable, comes across as being ethically neutral and lacking sufficient historical specificity. Still, one must be aware of the development that began to occur in Rahner's last writings. As a result of this development, these writings reflect a more qualified theological anthropology. For instance, Rahner's sensitivity to the preferential option and activity of grace in the lives of the poor suggests his openness to the idea that being a person, human or divine, being spirit-in-the-world, is not an ethically neutral activity. As Goizueta highlights, "to say that God's love is universal is not to say that God's love is neutral; indeed it is to say the very opposite. Only if God is identified preferentially with the poor, then, is God's love truly universal."[50]

Conversely, although the specific anthropological starting points of U.S. Hispanic theology can challenge contemporary appropriations of Rahner's anthropological vision, Rahner, in his relentless affirmation that ultimately reality has to be explained *theologically* (that is, in reference to the mystery of God), can challenge U.S. Hispanic theologians not to succumb to anthropological reductionism and to engage much more than they have in the past in a more explicit theological referencing of their anthropological claims. In other words, U.S. Hispanic anthropology must remain *theological* anthropology. Steps similar to the ones here undertaken must follow in order to continue to develop the theological basis of

---

[50]Ibid., 177.

our U.S. Hispanic visions. Rahner's challenge to make more explicit the transcendental foundation of human experiences, suggested in his notion of the human person as spirit-in-the-world, remains a valuable signpost to consider in Latino/a theology.

THE EMBODIED SELF AS COMMUNAL: FROM PERSON TO COMMUNITY OR COMMUNITY TO PERSON?

The embodied self is not only a personal mystery, but precisely because the body bridges, reflects, and participates in community, the self is also a communal reality. The Rahnerian and U.S. Hispanic ways of relating person, freedom, and community point us in this direction. Rahner's notion of freedom surfaces in connection with his notion of person as spirit-in-the-world. The U.S. Hispanic notion of freedom emerges within the U.S. Hispanic approach to community. In Rahner, the human as spirit-in-the-world is essentially defined by and in relationship to communal realities. In U.S. Hispanic theology, community is valued because this theology underscores that individuals are not merely relational and free beings, but members of wholes.[51] Or as Goizueta has succinctly expressed, in U.S. Hispanic theological anthropology, community is "the birthplace of self."[52]

The differences between Rahner's communal notions of person and freedom and the U.S. Hispanic notions are subtle, yet important in raising mutual challenges. While Rahner undoubtedly conceives personhood and freedom in communal terms, his anthropology remains focused on the individual subject and his or her self-expression in the world. In this regard, Rahner's ontology of symbol provides an essential hermeneutic for understanding his foundational presuppositions. The central premise of this ontology is that "Being *as* such, and hence *as* one (ens as *unum*), for the fulfillment of its being and its unity, emerges into a plurality—of which the supreme mode is the Trinity."[53] Thus, for Rahner, every person as a distinct and individual being for his or her fulfillment must open himself or herself up in freedom to and within community.

Whereas Rahner embraces a movement from individual to community, the opposite is the case with U.S. Hispanic theological anthropology. Thus, U.S.Hispanic anthropology accents the organic constitution of reality and underscores the individual as a unique expression of the whole. To recall the words of one Hispanic theologian relative to the communal basis of cultural identity, culture represents the "womb" from which there

---

[51]Ismael García, "A Theological-Ethical Analysis of Hispanic Struggles for Community Building in the United States," in *Hispanic/Latino Theology: Challenge and Promise*, 303.

[52]Goizueta, *Caminemos con Jesús*, 47-76.

[53]See Rahner, "The Theology of Symbol," in *Theological Investigations*, IV, (New York, Crossroad, 1982), 228. Emphasis in original.

is no birth because we are already born into it (Espín). The following image captures this U.S. Hispanic accent on the organic constitution of the self:

> In an organic anthropology, each person is not a mirror reflection but a unique refraction of the whole. Like glass prisms that, each cut in a different form, refract the light into uniquely structured, magnificent rainbows of colors, thereby making visible a light that would otherwise be invisible to the eye, each person is the unique refraction of that common Light which becomes visible only in the radiance of each unique, particular rainbow. Without the prisms, without their individual uniqueness, the Light would remain invisible.[54]

Although Rahner's theology is open to development in socio-political terms (indeed, that begins to occur in his later writings), the U.S. Hispanic communal starting point is more capable than Rahner's is of making a strong case for the socio-political constitution of the self. The emphasis on community predisposes U.S. Hispanic anthropology to consider more so than Rahner can with his individual starting point, those commonly shared experiences out which the self is born. The U.S. Hispanic theological focus on *pueblo*, the family, *mestizaje*, and the socio-political implications of these experiences exemplify my point. In all of these experiences the self is understood as a socially constituted self who exists and exercises his or her freedom not prior to or separate from, but within a given set of pre-existent relationships to others.

Like Rahner, U.S. Hispanic theologians with their communal approach to person have been somewhat mindful of the trinitarian underpinnings of Christian anthropology.[55] Whereas Rahner, however, seems to have appropriated a more Greek model of the Trinity, the overall U.S. Hispanic emphasis on community suggests a Latin model.[56] Although in recent times convincing criticisms have been raised relative to the communal starting point of trinitarian theology in the West,[57] there is much value

---

[54]Goizueta, *Caminemos con Jesús*, 76.

[55]Ibid., 179.

[56]Latin theologians have generally understood what is common in the one God (the divine substance) as being distinctly instantiated in a particular reality (the divine persons), while Greek theologians favor the person of the Father as the source of trinitarian life. For a comparison of Greek and Latin trinitarian thought see Catherine M. LaCugna, "The Trinitarian Mystery of God," in *Systematic Theology: Roman Catholic Perspectives*, 170-174. On Rahner's appeal to Greek trinitarian thought, see Gregory Havrilak, "Karl Rahner and the Greek Trinity," *St. Vladimir's Theological Quarterly* 34/1 (1990): 61-77.

[57]See specifically LaCugna's critique of Leonardo Boff's trinitarian theology in her *God for Us: The Trinity and Christian Life* (San Francisco: HarperCollins, 1991), 275-278.

in the Latin model from a socio-political perspective. Perhaps among the positive consequences that must be noted is the fact that it is in the West where one often encounters a more systematic treatment of Christian social teaching and the various theological challenges to social and political organisms from the perspective of communal trinitarian life.[58]

While Rahner's communal notion of person developed in a more socially conscious way in his later writings, the earlier emphasis upon the particular and its relationship to another particular (an "I-thou" relationship) makes Rahner's transcendental theology less oriented than is U.S. Hispanic theology to the cultural and socio-political anticipation of the trinitarian life of grace in society.[59] Notwithstanding the latter, Rahner's trinitarian reflections have served as point of contact with the more communal and socially conscious U.S. Hispanic starting point. García's Rahnerian-inspired reflections on the perichoretic activity in society of God's trinitarian life already exemplify some initial steps taken by U.S. Hispanic theologians to engage Rahner's thought in a more socio-culturally conscious way.[60]

Conversely, while U.S. Hispanic theological anthropology does not lack an attentiveness to the individual,[61] the communal emphasis of U.S. Hispanic theological anthropology has naturally led to underscoring the socio-cultural experience of sin and grace and the socio-political co-ordinates of human existence. Somewhat ironically, Rahner's attentiveness to the individual, particular, and unique self-expression of every being can challenge U.S. Hispanic theological anthropology to attend much more than it has to the particularity of U.S. Hispanic experiences, to the individual differences found within that particularity, and to personal responsibility for complacency in social sin. Three issues come to mind: 1) the need to attend much more than has been done in the past to the individual experience of grace and sin in U.S. Hispanic theological anthropology, and to the individual subjects that have been, for whatever reasons, marginalized from Hispanic faith communities; 2) the need to avoid romantic notions of communal experiences due to lack of attention paid to human particularity (e.g., the tendency to speak of family in the abstract and to idealize

---

[58]See, for instance, Leonardo Boff, *Trinity and Society* (Maryknoll, New York: Orbis Books, 1988), esp. 123-154.

[59]Note that in Metz's critique of Rahner, Metz does not deny the anticipatory character of the human subject. What Metz contests is "how" such anticipation occurs in Rahner's transcendental theology of the subject. See J.A. Colombo, "Rahner and His Critics: Linbeck and Metz," *Thomist* 56/1 (1992): 93.

[60]See García, "United States Hispanic and Mainstream Trinitarian Theologies," in *Frontiers of Hispanic Theology in the United States*, 88-103; and idem, "A Hispanic Approach to Trinitarian Theology," in *We Are a People!*, 107-132.

[61]For instance, note Goizueta who, in spite of his communal emphasis, also recognizes that "individual freedom is a prerequisite for authentic community." See his *Caminemos con Jesús*, 76.

this experience); and 3) the need to recognize generational differences, and how those differences may affect notions of freedom, community, and the human person.

ENCOUNTERING THE PRACTICAL AND
SOCIAL-POLITICAL FACE OF GRACE

Consideration of the practical and socio-political dimensions of human experiences and encounters with grace are unavoidable in U.S. Hispanic theological anthropology. The communal starting point of U.S. Hispanic theology naturally predisposes U.S. Hispanic theological anthropology to this type of consideration. Similar considerations are also possible with Rahner. As I have again and again noted throughout this book, Rahner himself increasingly reflected a more practical and socio-political approach in his last writings. While still favoring the individual as a starting point of his reflections, his Christo-centric understanding of individual self-expression (*Selbstaussage*) in and through community and the public domain enables Rahner to move into and explore more practical and socio-political dimensions. While Rahner's notion of the love of neighbor and his theology of the Kingdom can be particulaized and developed, Rahner can contribute toward a deepening of the U.S. Hispanic notion of solidarity with the oppressed and the theology of the Kingdom of God.

FROM CHARITY TO SOLIDARITY

Rahner's theology of the love of neighbor extends and radicalizes, existentially and ontologically speaking, the Scholastic notion of the supernatural theological virtue of charity (*caritas*).[62] Rahner saw his radical move to equate the love of God with the love of neighbor as being consistent with Catholic thought. Rahner noted how Catholic theology has already for a long time upheld the position that "the specific Christian love of neighbour is both in potency and in act a moment of the infused supernatural theological virtue of *caritas* by which we love God in his Spirit for his own sake and in direct community with him."[63]

But consistent with his own understanding of the supernatural and his rejection of a pure nature (existentially and historically speaking), Rahner moved beyond the Scholastic understanding to affirm that no human act

---

[62]See especially his argument already noted in chapter four of this book in his "Reflections on the Unity of the Love of Neighbor and the Love of God," in *Theological Investigations*, VI, trans. Karl-H. and Boniface Kruger (New York: Crossroad, 1982), esp. 236-237.

[63]Ibid., 236.

of love is ever immune from saving grace, and that, vice versa, no act of saving grace can ever be divorced from human love. Rahner accepted in theory (just as he accepts the possibility of a pure nature as a *Restbegriff*) the scholastic argument that charity can take the form of a mere human interpersonal experience with no theological referent.[64] Rahner critiqued scholastic theology, however, precisely for not being concrete enough—for being too theoretical.[65] Rahner pointed out that scholastic theology would acknowledge that at least formally speaking every act of charity, is even if implicitly, an act that involves the love of God.[66] But Rahner noted that scholastic theology, and most theologians today, would have a problem acknowledging the opposite.[67] Rahner summarized his position as follows:

> . . . wherever a genuine love of man [sic] attains its proper nature and its moral absoluteness and depth, it is in addition always so under-pinned and heightened by God's saving grace that it is also love of God, whether it be explicitly considered to be such a love by the subject or not.[68]

I suspect that most U.S. Hispanic theologians would readily accept Rahner's argument. As the arguments surrounding the theme of charity already exemplify, U.S. Hispanic anthropology has implicitly embraced with little or no qualifications Rahner's critique of and re-appropriation of the scholastic understanding. U.S. Hispanic theologians have taken very seriously the cultural, socio-political, and even spatial (private and public domains) mediation of love (Goizueta, Aquino, García). If any-thing, from the U.S. Hispanic perspective, Rahner's theology would be seen as not going far enough when it comes to concretizing, radicalizing, and specifying the scholastic notion of charity. As I have already pointed out in chapter two, love or charity is always understood in socio-political terms. Goizueta's approach to *mestizaje* and Isasi-Díaz and Espín's ap-proach to charity as solidarity exemplify how U.S. Hispanic theology has extended and particularized both neo-scholastic and Rahnerian ap-proaches to the love of neighbor. Thus, Isasi-Díaz writes:

> Solidarity, then, is a virtue. It is an attitude and disposition that greatly influences how we act. As a virtue solidarity becomes a way of life. It becomes the new way of living out "the love your neighbor as yourself" that up to now has been interpreted as giving out of our

---

[64]Ibid.

[65]Ibid.

[66]See *ST*, II-II, qq. 23-27 and *De Veritate*, q. 22, a. 2. ad. 1.

[67]Rahner, "Reflections on the Unity of the Love of Neighbor and the Love of God," 237.

[68]Ibid.

largesse. Given the network of oppressive structures in our world today that so control and dominate the vast majority of human beings, the only way we can continue to claim the centrality of love of neighbor for Christians is to redefine what it means and what it demands of us. Solidarity, then, becomes the new way of understanding and living out this commandment of the gospel.[69]

Reflecting the influence and appropriation of Latin-American liberation theologies, U.S. Hispanic theologians have extended notions of love and charity to include socio-political dimensions. Like its Latin-American sibling, U.S. Hispanic theology conceives charity as an act of solidarity with neighbor. This praxis for and with the poor is understood as a saving *and* liberative act. The opposite is also the case, that is, any reference to the love of God or to salvation in U.S. Hispanic theology necessarily presupposes a reference to solidarity with neighbor and the struggle for his or her integral liberation from oppressive human conditions. It is important to underscore that what is implied in the U.S. Hispanic notion of solidarity *is not* a reification of reality but rather, as Rahner would argue, a transcendental understanding or referencing of the love of neighbor understood from the perspective of practical and socio-political dimensions.

FROM THE KINGDOM OF GOD TO THE KIN-DOM OF MESTIZOS

Given the communal focus of U.S. Hispanic theological anthropology and the socio-cultural and political understanding of love of neighbor, these final reflections come as no surprise. Closely connected to communal experiences, the U.S. Hispanic notion of *mestizaje* and its sacramental expression in popular Catholicism provides a particular socio-cultural vision of the Kingdom of God. In this sense, this vision can be understood as affirming what Rahner holds relative to the relationship between the Kingdom of God and worldly experience, namely, that the Kingdom of God does not occur in "a secret inwardness of conscience, in meta-historical religious activity, but in the concrete fulfillment of an earthly task, of active love of others, even of collective love of others."[70]

This understanding, which underscores God's self-communication in the concreteness of history, is particularly reflected in García's notion of functional trinitarian relationships. García affirms the potential of concrete social structures and societies to image the divine perichoresis. For

---

[69]Isasi-Díaz, "Solidarity: Love of Neighbor in the Twenty-First Century," in *Mujerista Theology*," 101-102.

[70]Rahner, "Church and World," in *Encyclopedia of Theology: The Concise Sacramentum Mundi* (New York: Crossroad, 1989), 239.

García, modeling society after the divine perichoresis results in liberation, renewal, and hominization. Although García does not make the
specific connection to the U.S. Hispanic notion of *mestizaje,* the various
ways in which U.S. Hispanic theologians have already defined and understood this concept suggest that, within U.S. Hispanic theological anthropology, this concept exemplifies in a specific socio-cultural way this
perichoretic function. Thus Elizondo writes:

> *Mestizaje* is the beginning of a new Christian universalism. The depth
> of joy present in the *mestizo* celebration is indicative of the
> eschatological *mestizo* identity; they are the ones in whom the
> fullness of the kingdom has already begun, the new universalism that
> bypasses human segregative barriers.[71]

The work of several Latino/a theologians suggests a more critical reading of Elizondo's foundational reflections on *mestizaje* in order to avoid
romanticizing this communal symbol of grace. Similar to those of Rahner,
some of Elizondo's groundbreaking ideas have been subjected to further
critical refinement. Just as Rahner spoke of the intersection of the Kingdom of God in history, without offering much qualification of the latter
(especially in his early writings), so have Elizondo's past reflections spoken of the ability of *mestizaje* to manifest the Kingdom, without significant critical examination of those oppressive elements that comprise this
socio-cultural experience. This has undoubtedly led some to charge him
with anthropological idealism, and to question how it is that his thought
safeguards the eschatological dimension of the Kingdom of God.

Without rejecting totally Elizondo's analogical approach to *mestizaje,*
other U.S. Hispanic theologians have placed greater emphasis on examining the tension between worldly and eschatological reality. Building
upon but moving beyond Elizondo's initial vision, these theologians have
emphasized the kind of socio-political actions that are necessary for the
the Kingdom to be manifested "within" the socio-cultural experience of
Latinos/as (Isasi-Díaz, Goizueta). Only then, suggest these theologians,
will *mestizaje* be, as Elizondo believes, "the beginning of a new Christian
universalism."[72]

The above reflections exemplify how U.S. Hispanic theologians have
rejected a meta-historical religious understanding of the presence of the
Kingdom. Like Rahner, U.S. Hispanic theologians presuppose an analogical understanding that affirms: 1) the presence of the Kingdom as
occurring "within" historical realities; 2) the presence of the Kingdom as

---

[71]Virgilio Elizondo, *Galilean Journey: The Mexican-American Promise* (Maryknoll,
New York: Orbis Books, 2000), 124.
[72]Ibid.

being "distinct from" worldly realities; and 3) the presence of the King-dom as "explaining" worldy reality. Perhaps what is most unlike Rahner is that U.S. Hispanic theology adds a fourth dimension, namely, the pres-ence of the Kingdom not simply explaining but prophetically denouncing worldly realities. And as expected, the U.S. Hispanic notion of the King-dom of God is characterized by a greater focus on the specifics that define worldly realities.

The sacramentality of U.S. Hispanic Marian devotions exemplifies this fourfold characterization. The interpretation of U.S. Hispanic Marian symbols and narratives, such as Our Lady of Guadalupe and Our Lady of Charity, like Rahner, primarily falls within the Catholic analogical imagination. But these devotions also provide for U.S. Hispanic theolo-gians key theological loci that ground challenges to the present *status quo*. While analogical in nature relative to the cultural and religious iden-tity of U.S. Hispanics, U.S. Hispanic interpretations of these devotions also include dialectical elements that hinge upon practical and socio-po-litical experiences. In U.S. Hispanic theology, the association of Guadalupe with Juan Diego or *La Caridad* with Juan Moreno suggests the encounter with the life of grace that assumes from within, prophetically challenges, and perfects the human person who has fallen victim to oppression and marginalization.

In this latter sense, U.S. Hispanic popular devotions offer a source for re-envisioning a new society in which the marginalized are preferred as the beloved of God. These devotions exemplify the all-important premise of U.S. Hispanic theological anthropology that affirms the coming of the Kingdom of God as a result of charity understood primarily (though not exclusively) as solidarity with marginalized persons.[73] In so doing, U.S. Hispanic theology is more attentive than Rahner was to the where and how of the Kingdom, that is, to the specific social, cultural, political, and gender relations that mediate the Kingdom in space, time, and history. To recall Elizondo and Goizueta's Christocentric arguments, to know who Jesus accompanied and where such accompaniment took place is essen-tial to understand the who and where of grace, and of our personhood.

Thus, within U.S. Hispanic theology, the Kingdom is present in worldly reality but it is most present in the experience of the marginalized. The Kingdom is distinct from worldly reality, but it is most distinct from those who marginalize. And finally, the Kingdom critiques worldly reality, but it is most critical of oppressive human reality. In U.S. Hispanic theologi-cal anthropology, the "Kin-dom," to borrow Isasi-Díaz's gender-inclu-sive and socio-political notion, concerns the salvation and liberation, the

---

[73]See Espín, "The Vanquished, Faithful Solidarity, and the Marian Symbol: A Hispanic Perspective on Providence," in *On Keeping Providence*, ed. Barbara Doherty and Joan Coultas (Terre Haute, Indiana: St. Mary of the Woods College Press, 1991), 84-101.

struggle and survival of particular persons and communities who experience various forms of marginalization from the kingdoms of this world.[74]

ENCOUNTERING GRACE WITHIN "THE NEW CATHOLICITY"

Karl Rahner once commented that the Christian of the future would be a mystic or no Christian at all. Indeed, Rahner believed that what was needed was an awakening to the pervasive presence of God in our lives. As his theology after the Council increasingly exemplified, Rahner was aware that such awakening could not bypass the socio-political realities that constitute our ways of being human. U.S. Hispanic theologians have underscored that if we are to avoid idealization and abstraction, the encounter with grace, the encounter with God's benevolent love, must be mediated by concrete human realities. While none of these realities can ever be equated with grace, while the Kingdom remains an absolute gift— as embodied spirits we cannot experience God's self-gift to us but "within" our ways of being human. Today we have come to realize the essential role that socio-political realities play in the constitution of the communal self. Indeed, the encounter with grace is always and everywhere a "human" encounter that includes socio-political dimensions.

The previous pages have brought into conversation U.S. Hispanic and Rahnerian visions of what it means to be human. My purpose has been to deepen an understanding of U.S. Hispanic Catholic visions of what it means to be human, and to demonstrate how these visions uniquely fit within the Catholic tradition, even while particularizing and developing parts of this tradition. The emergence of a global Church since the Second Vatican Council has led to what Robert Schreiter has characterized as the "new catholicity." This presence of a manifold of contextual theologies urges us to go beyond the present effort and invite others into our home. In our traditional Hispanic way of expressing hospitality, we say, *mi casa es tu casa!* Come into our home, sit at our table, hear our story, and share your story of what it means to be human, and how your humanity has encountered the experience of grace.

---

[74]See Isasi-Díaz, *En la Lucha*, 35-36.

Select Bibliography

Abalos, David T. *Latinos in the United States: The Sacred and the Political.* Notre Dame, Indiana: University Press, 1986.

Aquino, María Pilar. *Aportes para una teología desde la mujer.* Madrid: Edición Biblia y Fe, 1988.

———. "El culto a Mária y María en el culto." *FEM Publicacíon Feminista* 5, no. 20 (1981-1982): 41-46. México.

———. "Directions and Foundations of Hispanic/Latino Theology: Toward a *Mestiza* Theology of Liberation." *Journal of Hispanic/Latino Theology* 1, no. 1 (1993): 5-21.

———. "Doing Theology from the Perspective of Hispanic Women." In *We Are a People!: Initiatives in Hispanic American Theology.* Edited by Roberto Goizueta, 79-105. Philadelphia: Fortress Press, 1992.

———. *Our Cry for Life: Feminist Theology from Latin America.* Translated by Dina Livingstone. Maryknoll, New York: Orbis Books, 1993.

———. "Perspectives on a Latina's Feminist Liberation Theology." In *Frontiers of Hispanic Theology in the United States.* Edited by Allan Figueroa Deck. 23-40. Maryknoll, New York: Orbis Books, 1992.

———. "Women's Participation in the Church: A Catholic Perspective." In *With Passion and Compassion: Third World Women Doing Theology.* Edited by V. Fabella and M.A. Oduyoye, 159-164. Maryknoll, New York: Orbis Books, 1988.

Ashley, J. Matthew. *Interruptions: Mysticism, Politics, and Theology in the Work of Johannn Baptist Metz.* Notre Dame, Indiana: University of Notre Dame Press, 1998.

Bacik, James J. *Apologetics and the Eclipse of Mystery: Mystagogy According to Karl Rahner.* Notre Dame, Indiana: University of Notre Dame Press, 1980.

Bañuelas, Arturo J. Editor. "U.S. Hispanic Theology: A Bibliography." *Apuntes* 2, no. 4 (1991): 93-103.

———. *Mestizo Christianity: Theology from the Latino Perspective.* Maryknoll, New York: Orbis Books, 1995.

Bevans, Stephen B. *Models of Contextual Theology.* Maryknoll, New York: Orbis Books, 1994.

Brackley, Dean. *Divine Revolution: Salvation and Liberation in Catholic Thought.* Maryknoll, New York: Orbis Books, 1996.

Buckley, James J. "On Being a Symbol: An Appraisal of Karl Rahner." *Theological Studies* 40 (1979): 453-473.

Burgaleta, Claudio. "A Rahnerian Reading of Santeria: A Proposal for a Christian Recovery of the Syncretic Elements of Latin American Popular Religiosity

Based on Rahner's Concept of 'Anonymous Christianity,'" *Apuntes* 13 (1993): 139-150.

Carr, Anne. "Starting with the Human." In *A World of Grace: An Introduction to the Themes and Foundations of Karl Rahner's Theology*. Edited by Leo J. O'Donovan, 17-30. New York: Seabury Press, 1980.

———. "Theology and Experience in the Thought of Karl Rahner." *The Journal of Religion* 13 (1973): 359-376.

———. *Transforming Grace: Christian Tradition and Women's Experience*. New York: Harper & Row, 1988.

Casarella, Peter and Raul Gómez. Editors. *El Cuerpo de Cristo: The Hispanic Presence in the U.S. Catholic Church*. New York: Crossroad, 1998.

Colombo, J. A. "Rahner and His Critics: Lindbeck and Metz." *The Thomist* 56, no. 1 (1992): 91-96.

Costas, Orlando. "Hispanic Theology in North America." In *Struggles for Solidarity: Liberation in Tension*. Edited by Lorina Getz and Ruy Costa, 63-74. Minneapolis: Fortress Press, 1992.

Deck, Allan Figueroa. "At the Crossroads: North American and Hispanic." In *We Are a People! Initiatives in Hispanic American Theology*. Edited by Roberto Goizueta, 1-20. Minneapolis: Fortress Press, 1992.

———. Editor. *Frontiers of Hispanic Theology in the United States*. Maryknoll, New York: Orbis Books, 1992.

———. "Hispanic Catholic Prayer and Worship." In *¡Alabadle! Hispanic Christian Worship*. Edited by Justo L. González, 29-41. Nashville: Abingdon Press, 1996.

———. "The Hispanic Presence: A Moment of Grace." *The Critic* 45, no.1 (1990): 48-59.

———. "Hispanic Theologians and the United States Catholic Church." *New Theology Review* 3, no. 4 (1990): 22-27.

———. "Latino Theology: The Year of the 'Boom'." *Journal of Hispanic/Latino Theology* 1, no. 2 (1994): 51-63.

———. "Liturgy and Mexican American Culture." *Modern Liturgy* 3, no. 7 (1976): 24-26.

———. "A Pox on Both Your Homes." In *Being Right: Conservative Catholics in America*. Edited by Mary Jo Weaver and R. Scott Appleby, 88-104. Bloomington: Indiana University Press, 1995.

———. "Proselytism and the Hispanic Catholic: How Long Can We Cry Wolf?" *America* 10 (1988): 485-490.

———. "La Raza Cósmica: Rediscovering the Hispanic Soul." *The Critic* 37, no. 3 (1993): 46-53.

———. *The Second Wave: Hispanic Ministry and the Evangelization of Cultures*. New York: Paulist Press, 1989.

———. "The Spirituality of the United States Hispanics: An Introductory Essay." *U.S. Catholic Historian* 9, no. 1 (1990): 137-146.

De Guibert, Joseph. *The Jesuits, Their Spiritual Doctrine and Practice: A Historical Study*. Translated by William J. Young. Chicago: Loyola University Press, 1964.

Díaz, Miguel and Orlando Espín. *From the Heart of Our People: Latino/a Explorations in Systematic Theology*. Maryknoll, New York: Orbis Books, 1999.

Dolan, Jay P. and Allan Figueroa Deck. Editors. *Hispanic Catholic Culture in the*

U.S.: Issues and Concerns. Notre Dame, Indiana: University of Notre Dame Press, 1994.

Dolan, Jay P. and Gilberto M. Hinojosa. Editors. *Mexican Americans and the Catholic Church 1900-1965*. Notre Dame, Indiana: University of Notre Dame Press, 1994.

Dolan, Jay P. and Jaime R. Vidal. Editors. *Puerto Rican and Cuban Catholics in the U.S., 1900-1965*. Notre Dame, Indiana: University of Notre Dame Press, 1994.

Duffy, Stephen J. *The Dynamics of Grace: Perspectives in Theological Anthropology*. Collegeville: The Liturgical Press, 1993.

———. *The Graced Horizon: Nature and Grace in Modern Catholic Thought*. Collegeville: The Liturgical Press, 1992.

Egan, Harvey D. *Faith in a Wintry Season: Conversations and Interviews with Karl Rahner in the Last Years of His Life*. Translated and edited by Harvey D. Egan. New York: Crossroad, 1990.

———. *Karl Rahner: Mystic of Everyday Life*. New York: Crossroad, 1998.

Elizondo, Virgilio P. *Anthropological and Psychological Characteristics of the Mexican American*. San Antonio: MACC, 1974.

———. "A Challenge to Theology: The Situation of Hispanic Americans." *Proceedings of the Catholic Theological Society of America* 30 (1975): 163-176.

———. *Christianity and Culture*. Huntington, Indiana: Our Sunday Visitor, 1975.

———. "Elements for a Mexican American Mestizo Christology." *Voices from the Third World: Journal of the Ecumenical Association of Third World Theologians* 15, no. 2 (1989).

———. *The Future is Mestizo: Life Where Cultures Meet*. New York: Crossroad, 1992.

———. *Galilean Journey: The Mexican-American Promise*. Maryknoll, New York: Orbis Books; revised edition, 2000.

———. "Guadalupe: An Endless Source of Reflection." *Journal of Hispanic/Latino Theology* 5, no. 1 (1997): 61-65.

———. *Guadalupe: Mother of the New Creation*. Maryknoll, New York: Orbis Books, 1997.

———. *The Human Quest: A Search for Meaning through Life and Death*. Huntington, Indiana: Our Sunday Visitor, 1977.

———. "Our Lady of Guadalupe as Cultural Symbol: The Power and the Powerless." In *Liturgy and Cultural Religious Traditions*. Edited by David Power and Herman Schmidt. New York: Seabury Press, 1977.

———. "Mary and the Evangelization of the Americas." In *Mary: Woman of Nazareth*. Edited by Doris Donnelly, 146-160. New York: Paulist Press, 1990.

———. "Mary in the Struggles of the Poor." *The New Catholic World* 229, no. 1374 (1986): 244-247.

———. *Mestizaje: The Dialectic of Birth and Gospel*. San Antonio: MACC, 1978.

———. "*Mestizaje* as Locus of Theological Reflection." In *Frontiers of Hispanic Theology in the U.S.* Edited by Allan Figueroa Deck. 104-123. Maryknoll, New York: Orbis Books, 1992.

———. "Le Métissage comme lieu théologique." *Spiritus* 93 (1983). Paris, (1977).

———. *La Morenita: Evangelizer of the Americas*. San Antonio: MACC, 1980.

———. "The Mystery of Human Fulfillment." *Good Tidings* 7 (September-October) Manila, 1969.

————. "The New Humanity of the Americas." In *1492-1992: The Voice of the Victims*, in the *Concilium* Series 1990/6. Edited by Leonardo Boff and Virgil Elizondo, 141-147. Philadelphia: Trinity Press International, 1990.

————. "Religious Education for Mexican Americans." In *Beyond Borders: Writings of Virgilio Elizondo and Friends*. Edited by Timothy Matovina. Maryknoll, New York: Orbis Books, 2000.

————. *Virgen y Madre: Reflexiones bíblicas sobre María de Nazaret*. San Antonio: MACC, 1983.

Empereur, James L. "Popular Religion and the Liturgy: The State of the Question." *Liturgical Ministry* 7 (1998): 105-120.

Espín, Orlando O. *The Faith of the People: Theological Reflections on Popular Catholicism*. Maryknoll, New York: Orbis Books, 1997.

————. "Pentecostalism and Popular Catholicism: The Poor and *Traditio*." *Journal of Hispanic/Latino Theology* 3, no. 2 (1995): 14-43.

————. "Popular Catholicism: Alienation or Hope?" In *Hispanic/Latino Theology: Challenge and Promise*. Edited by Ada María Isasi-Díaz and Fernando Segovia, 307-324. Minneapolis: Fortress Press, 1996.

————. "Popular Catholicism among Latinos." In *Hispanic Catholic Culture in the U.S.: Issues and Concerns*. Edited by Jay Dolan and Allan Figueroa Deck, 308-359. Notre Dame, Indiana: University of Notre Dame Press, 1994.

————. "Popular Religion as an Epistemology (of Suffering)." *Journal of Hispanic/Latino Theology* 2, no. 2 (1994): 55-78.

————. *Religiosidad popular: Un aporte para su definición y hermeneutica."* *Estudios Sociales* XVII, no. 58 (1984): 41-56.

————. The Sources of Hispanic Theology. *Proceedings of the Catholic Theological Society of America* 43 (1988), 122-125.

————. "Tradition and Popular Religion: An Understanding of the Sensus Fidelium." In *Frontiers of Hispanic Theology in the United States*. Edited by Allan F. Deck, 62-87. Maryknoll, New York: Orbis Books, 1992.

————. "Trinitarian Monotheism and the Birth of Popular Catholicism: The Case of Sixteenth-Century Mexico." *Missiology* 20, no. 2 (1992): 117-204.

————. "The Vanquished, Faithful Solidarity, and the Marian Symbol: A Hispanic Perspective on Providence." In *On Keeping Providence*. Edited by Barbara Doherty and Joan Coultas, 84-101. Terre Haute, Indiana: St. Mary of the Woods College Press, 1991.

Espín, Orlando O. and Miguel H. Díaz, editors. *From the Heart of Our People: Latino/a Explorations in Systematic Theology*. Maryknoll, New York: Orbis Books, 1999.

Espín, Orlando O. and Sixto J. García. "Hispanic-American Theology." *Proceedings of the Catholic Theological Society of America* 42 (1987), 114-119.

————. "'Lilies of the Field': A Hispanic Theology of Providence and Human Responsibility." *Proceedings of the Catholic Theological Society of America* 44 (1989), 70-90.

Fiorenza, F.M. "Karl Rahner and the Kantian Problematic." In *Spirit in the World* by Karl Rahner, XIX-XLV. New York: Herder and Herder, 1968.

Flick, M. and Z. Alszeghy. *Antropología teológica*. Salamanca: Ediciones Sigueme, 1989.

Fornet-Betancourt, Raúl. *Haciauna filosofía intercultural latinoamericana*. San José: Departamento Ecuménico de Investigaciones, 1994.

Francis, Mark. "The Hispanic Liturgical Year: The People's Calendar." *Liturgical Ministry* 7 (1998): 129-135.

García, Sixto J. "A Hispanic Approach to Trinitarian Theology: The Dynamics of Celebration, Reflection, and Praxis." In *We Are a People!: Initiatives in Hispanic American Theology.* Edited by Roberto Goizueta, 107-132. Minneapolis: Fortress Press, 1992.

———. "Hispanic Theologians as Actors, Poets and Prophets of Their Communities." *Journal of Hispanic/Latino Theology* 6, no. 4 (1999): 5-18.

———. "Our Lady of Guadalupe: A Sign of Ecclesial Unity." *Marian Studies* XLIV (1993): 88-105.

———. "Sources and Loci of Hispanic Theology." *Journal of Hispanic/Latino Theology* 1, no. 1 (1993): 22-43.

———. "United States Hispanic and Mainstream Trinitarian Theologies." In *Frontiers of Hispanic Theology in the United States.* Edited by Allan Figueroa Deck, 88-103. Maryknoll, New York: Orbis Books, 1992.

García-Rivera, Alejandro. *The Community of the Beautiful: A Theological Aesthetics.* Collegeville, Minnesota: Liturgical Press, 1999.

———. "A Contribution to the Dialogue Between Theology and the Natural Sciences." *Journal of Hispanic/Latino Theology* 2, no. 1 (1994): 51-59.

———. "San Martín de Porres: *Criatura de Dios.*" *Journal of Hispanic/Latino Theology* 2, no. 2 (1994): 26-54.

———. *St. Martín de Porres: "The Little Stories" and the Semiotics of Culture.* Maryknoll, New York: Orbis Books, 1995.

———. "Wisdom, Beauty, and the Cosmos in Hispanic Spirituality." In *El Cuerpo de Cristo: The Hispanic Presence in the U.S. Catholic Church.* Edited by Peter Casarella and Raul Gómez, 106-133. New York: Crossroad, 1998.

Goizueta, Roberto S. "Bartolomé de Las Casas, Modern Critic of Modernity: An Analysis of a Conversion." *Journal of Hispanic/Latino Theology* 3, no. 4 (1996): 6-19.

———. *Caminemos con Jesús: Toward a Hispanic/Latino Theology of Accompaniment.* Maryknoll, New York: Orbis Books, 1995.

———. "The Church and Hispanics in the United States: From Empowerment to Solidarity." In *That They Might Live: Power, Empowerment and Leadership in the Church.* Edited by Michael Downey, 160-175. New York: Crossroad, 1991.

———. "In Defense of Reason: Dichotomous Epistemology and Anthropology of Modernity and Postmodernity Oppressive to Hispanics." *Journal of Hispanic/Latino Theology* 3, no. 3 (February 1996): 16-26.

———. "The History of Suffering as *Locus Theologicus*: Implications for U.S. Hispanic Theology." *Voices from the Third World: Journal of the Ecumenical Association of Third World Theologians* 12 (1989): 32-47.

———. "*Nosotros*: Toward a U.S. Hispanic Anthropology." *Listening: Journal of Religion and Culture* 27, no. 1 (Winter 1992): 55-69.

———. The Preferential Option for the Poor: The CELAM Documents and the NCCB Pastoral Letter on U.S. Hispanics as Sources for U.S. Hispanic Theology." *Journal of Hispanic/Latino Theology* 3, no. 2 (November 1995): 65-77.

———. "La raza cósmica? The Vision of José Vasconcelos." *Journal of Hispanic/Latino Theology* 1, no. 2 (February 1994): 5-27.

———. "Rediscovering Praxis: The Significance of U.S. Hispanic Experience for

Theological Method." In *We Are a People!: Initiatives in Hispanic American Theology*. Edited by Roberto Goizueta, 51-77. Minneapolis: Fortress Press, 1992.

———. "Theology as Intellectually Vital Inquiry: The Challenge of/to U.S. Hispanic Theologians." *Proceedings of the Catholic Theological Society of America* 46 (1991), 58-69.

———. "U.S. Hispanic *Mestizaje* and Theological Method." In *Migrants and Refugees* in the Concilium Series 1993/4. Edited by Dietmar Mieth and Lisa Sowle Cahill, 22-30. Maryknoll, NY: Orbis Books, 1993.

———. "U.S. Hispanic Popular Catholicism as Theopoetics." In *Hispanic/Latino Theology: Challenge and Promise*. Edited by Ada María Isasi-Díaz and Fernando Segovia, 261-288. Minneapolis: Fortress Press, 1996.

———. "United States Hispanic Theology and the Challenge of Pluralism." In *Frontiers of Hispanic Theology in the United States*. Edited by Allan Figueroa Deck, 1-21. Maryknoll, New York: Orbis Books, 1992.

———. Editor. *We Are a People!: Initiatives in Hispanic American Theology*. Minneapolis: Fortress Press, 1992.

González, Justo L. Editor. *¡Alabadle! Hispanic Christian Worship*. Nashville: Abingdon Press, 1996.

———. *Mañana: Christian Theology from a Hispanic Perspective*. Nashville: Abingdon Press, 1990.

———. *Out of Every Tribe and Nation: Christian Theology at the Ethnic Roundtable*. Nashville: Abington Press, 1992.

———. Editor. *Voces: Voices from the Hispanic Church*. Nashville: Abington Press, 1992.

Gracia, Jorge J. E. *Hispanic/Latino Identity: A Philosophical Perspective*. Malden, Massachusetts: Blackwell Publishers, 2000.

Guerrero, Andrés G. *A Chicano Theology*. Maryknoll, New York: Orbis Books, 1987.

Gutiérrez, Gustavo. *A Theology of Liberation*. Maryknoll, New York: Orbis Books, 1988.

Haight, Roger. *The Experience and Language of Grace*. New York: Paulist Press, 1979.

Hilkert, Mary Catherine. *Naming Grace: Preaching and the Sacramental Imagination*. New York: Continuum, 1997.

Holler, Stephen. "The Origins of Marian Devotion in Latin American Cultures in the United States." *Marian Studies* XLVI (1995): 108-127.

Isasi-Díaz, Ada María. " 'Apuntes' for a Hispanic Women's Theology of Liberation." *Apuntes* 6 (1986): 61-71.

———. Defining Our *Proyecto Histórico: Mujerista* Strategies for Liberation." *Journal of Feminist Studies in Religion* 9, nos. 1-2 (1993): 17-28.

———. *En la Lucha/In the Struggle: A Hispanic Women's Liberation Theology*. Minneapolis: Fortress Press, 1993.

———. "*Mujeristas*: A Name of Our Own." In *The Future of Liberation Theology: Essays in Honor of Gustavo Gutierrez*. Edited by Marc H. Ellis and Otto Maduro, 410-419. Maryknoll, New York: Orbis Books, 1989.

———. "*Mujeristas*: Who We Are and What We Are About." *The Journal of Feminist Studies in Religion* 8, no. 1 (1992): 105-125.

———. *Mujerista Theology: A Theology for the Twenty-First Century*. Maryknoll, New York: Orbis Books. 1996.

———. "*Mujerista* Theology's Method: A Liberative Praxis, A Way of Life." *Listening: Journal of Religion and Culture* 27, no.1 (Winter 1992): 41-54.

———. "Praxis: The Heart of *Mujerista* Theology." *Journal of Hispanic/Latino Theology* 1, no. 1 (1993): 44-55.

———. "Toward an Understanding of *Feminismo Hispano* in the USA." In *Women's Consciousness, Women's Conscience: A Reader in Feminist Ethics.* Edited by Barbara Hilkert Andolsen, Christine Gudorf, and Mary D. Pellauer, 51-61. Minneapolis: Winston Press, 1985.

Isasi-Díaz, Ada María, and Yolanda Tarango. *Hispanic Women: Prophetic Voice in the Church.* Minneapolis: Fortress Press, 1992.

LaCugna, Catherine M. *God for Us: The Trinity and Christian Life.* San Francisco: HarperCollins, 1991.

Ladaria, Luis F. *Introducción a la antropología teológica.* Navarra: Editorial Verbo Divino, 1996.

Langemeyer, George. "Theological Anthropology." In *Handbook of Catholic Theology.* Edited by Wofgang Beinert and Francis Schüssler Fiorenza, 691-693. New York: Crossroad, 1995.

Maldonado, David. "Doing Theology and the Anthropological Questions." In *Teología en Conjunto: A Collaborative Hispanic Protestant Theology.* Edited by José David Rodríguez and Loida I. Martell-Otero. Louisville: Westminster John Knox Press, 1997.

Malloy, Patrick L. "Christian Anamnesis and Popular Religion." *Theology Today* 54, no. 4 (1998): 121-128.

Mann, Peter. "Masters in Israel: IV. The Later Theology of Karl Rahner." *Clergy Review* 54 (1969): 936-948.

———. "The Transcendental or Political Kingdom? I and II." *New Blackfriars* 50 (1969): 805-812, and 51 (1971): 4-16.

Masson, Robert. "Rahner and Heidegger: Being, Hearing, and God." *Thomist* 37 (1973): 455-488.

Matovina, Timothy M. "New Frontiers of Guadalupismo." *Journal of Hispanic/Latino Theology* 5, no. 1 (1997): 20-36.

McCool, Gerald A. *Catholic Theology in the Nineteenth Century: The Quest for a Unitary Method.* New York: Seabury Press, 1977.

———. "Person and Community in Karl Rahner." In *Person and Community.* Edited by R.J. Roth, 63-85. New York: Fordham University Press, 1975.

———. "The Philosophy of the Human Person in Karl Rahner's Theology." *Theological Studies* 22 (1961): 537-562.

McDermott, John M. "The Christologies of Karl Rahner." *Gregorianum* 67 (1986): 104-122.

Metz, Johann Baptist. "An Essay on Karl Rahner." Foreword to Rahner's *Spirit in the World*, 1968, xiii-xviii.

———. *Faith in History and Society: Toward a Practical Fundamental Theology.* New York: The Seabury Press, 1980.

———. *A Passion for God: The Mystical-Political Dimension of Christianity.* Translated by J. Matthew Ashley. New York: Paulist Press, 1998.

O'Collins Gerald. *Retrieving Fundamental Theology: The Three Styles of Contemporary Theology.* New York: Paulist Press, 1993.

O'Donovan, Leo J. "A Journey into Time: The Legacy of Karl Rahner's Last Years." *Theological Studies* (1985): 621-646.

O'Meara, Thomas F. "A History of Grace." In *A World of Grace: An Introduc-*

tion to the Themes and Foundations of Karl Rahner's Theology. Edited by Leo J. O'Donovan, 76-91. New York: Crossroad, 1984.

————. "Karl Rahner: Some Audiences and Sources for His Theology." *Communio* 18, no. 2 (1991): 237-251.

————. "Teaching Karl Rahner." *Philosophy and Theology* 12 (1998): 12-24.

Parker, Cristián. *Popular Religion and Modernization in Latin America: A Different Logic*. Maryknoll, New York: Orbis Books, 1996.

Pérez, Arturo, Consuelo Covarrubias, and Edward Foley. Editors. *Así Es: Stories of Hispanic Spirituality*. Collegeville, Minnesota: The Liturgical Press, 1994.

Pineda, Ana María. "*Pastoral de Conjunto*." In *Mestizo Christianity: Theology from the Latino Perspective*. Edited by Arturo J. Bañuelas. 125-131. Maryknoll, New York: Orbis Books, 1995.

————. "The Challenge of Hispanic Pluralism for the United States Churches." *Missiology* 21 (1993): 437-442.

————. "The Colloquies and Theological Discourse: Culture as a Locus for Theology." *Journal of Hispanic/Latino Theology* 3, no. 3 (1996): 27-42.

————. "The Oral Tradition of a People: *Forjadora de rostro y corazón*." In *Hispanic/Latino Theology: Challenge and Promise*. Edited by Ada María Isasi-Díaz and Fernando Segovia, 104-116. Minneapolis: Fortress Press, 1996.

Pineda, Ana María and Robert Schreiter, Editors. *Dialogue Rejoined*. Collegeville, Minnesota: Liturgical Press, 1995.

Rahner, Karl. "Aspects of European Theology." In *Theological Investigations*. Vol. XXI. Translated by Hugh M. Riley, 89-96. New York: Crossroad, 1988.

————. *The Christian Commitment*. New York: Sheed and Ward, 1963.

————. "Christology in the Setting of Modern Man's Understanding of Himself and of His World." In *Theological Investigations*. Vol. XI. Translated by David Bourke, 215-229. New York: Seabury Press, 1974.

————. *The Church after the Council*. Translated by Davis C. Herron and Rodelinde Albrecht. New York: Herder and Herder, 1966.

————. "Church, Churches and Religions." In *Theological Investigations*. Vol. X. Translated by David Bourke, 30-49. New York: Herder and Herder, 1973.

————. "Concerning the Relationship Between Nature and Grace." In *Theological Investigations*. Vol. I. Translated by Cornelius Ernst, 297-317. New York: Crosroad, 1974.

————. "On the Current Relationship between Philosophy and Theology." In *Theological Investigations*. Vol. XIII. Translated by David Bourke, 61-79. New York: Crossroad, 1983.

————. "The Dignity of Man." In *Theological Investigations*. Vol. II. Translated by Karl-H. Kruger, 235-263. Baltimore: Helicon Press, 1963.

————. "Following the Crucified." In *Theological Investigations*. Vol. XVIII. Translated by Edward Quinn, 157-170. New York: Crossroad, 1983.

————. "Foundations of Christian Faith." In *Theological Investigations* Vol. XIX. Translated by Edward Quinn, 4-13. New York: Crossroad, 1983.

————. *Foundations of Christian Faith: An Introduction to the Idea of Christianity*. New York: Crossroad, 1990.

————. *Hearer of the Word*. Trans. Joseph Donceel. New York: Continuum, 1994, xviii.

————. "History of the World and Salvation History." In *Theological Investigations*. Vol. V. Translated by Karl-H. Kruger, 97-114. Baltimore: Helicon Press, 1966.

———. "Immanent and Transcendent Consummation of the World." In *Theological Investigations*. Vol. X. Translated by David Bourke, 273-289. New York: Herder and Herder, 1973.

———. *The Love of Jesus and the Love of Neighbor*. New York: Crossroad, 1985.

———. "The Man of Today and Religion." In *Theological Investigations*. Vol. VI. Translated by Karl and Boniface Kruger, 3-20. New York: Crossroad, 1982.

———. *Mary, Mother of the Lord*. Translated by W.J. O'Hara. Glasgow: The University Press, 1963.

———. *Nature and Grace: Dilemmas in the Modern Church*. New York: Sheed and Ward, 1964.

———. "One Mediator and Many Mediators." In *Theological Investigations*. Vol. IX. Translated by Graham Harrison, 169-184. New York: Seabury Press, 1972.

———. "Possible Courses for the Theology of the Future." In *Theological Investigations*. Vol. XIII. Translated by David Bourke, 32-60. New York: Crossroad, 1975.

———. "Reflections on Methodology in Theology." In *Theological Investigations*. Vol. XI. Translated by David Bourke, 68-114, New York: Crossroad, 1974.

———. "Reflections on a New Task for Fundamental Theology." In *Theological Investigations*. Vol. XVI, 156-166. Translated by David Morland. New York: Crossroad, 1979.

———. "The Relation between Theology and Popular Religion," In *Theological Investigations*. Vol. XXII. Translated by Joseph Donceel, 140-147. New York: Crossroad, 1984.

———. "Some Implications of the Scholastic Concept of Uncreated Grace." In *Theological Investigations*. Vol. I. Translated by Cornelius Ernst, 319-346. New York: Crossroad, 1974.

———. *Spirit in the World*. Translated by William Dych. New York: Continuum, 1994.

———. "Theological Considerations on Secularization and Atheism." In *Theological Investigations*. Vol. XI. Translated by David Bourke, 166-184. New York: Crossroad, 1974.

———. "Theology and Anthropology." In *Theological Investigations*. Vol. IX. Translated by David Bourke, 28-45. New York: Crossroad, 1983.

———. "Theology of Freedom." In *Theological Investigations*. Vol. VI. Translated by Karl H. and Boniface Kruger, 178-196. New York: Crossroad, 1982.

———. "On the Theology of the Incarnation." In *Theological Investigations*. Vol. IV. Translated by Kevin Smyth, 105-120. New York: Crossroad, 1982.

———. "The Theology of the Religious Meaning of Images." In *Theological Investigations*. Vol. XXIII. Translated by Joseph Donceel and Hugh M. Riley, 149-161. New York: Crossroad, 1992.

———. "The Theology of the Symbol." In *Theological Investigations*. Vol. IV. Translated by Kevin Smyth, 221-252. New York: Crossroad, 1982.

———. *The Trinity*. Translated by Joseph Donceel. New York: Crossroad, 1997.

———. "The Unity of Spirit and Matter in the Christian Understanding of Faith." In *Theological Investigations*. Vol. IV. Translated by Karl-H. and Boniface Kruger, 153-177. New York: Crossroad, 1982.

Riebe-Estrella, Gary. "Latino Religiosity or Latino Catholicism?" *Theology Today* 54, no. 4 (1998): 512-515.

Rodríguez, Jeanette. "Contemporary Encounters with Guadalupe." *Journal of Hispanic/Latino Theology* 5, no. 1 (1997): 48-60.

———. "Experience as a Resource for Feminist Thought."*Journal of Hispanic/Latino Theology* 1, no. 1 (1993): 68-76.

———. "God Is Always Pregnant." In *The Divine Mosaic: Woman's Images of the Sacred Other.* Edited by Theresa King, 112-126. St. Paul, Minnesota: International Publishers, 1994.

———. "Hispanics and the Sacred." *Chicago Studies* 29, no. 2 (1990): 137-152.

———. *Our Lady of Guadalupe: Faith and Empowerment among Mexican-American Women.* Austin: University of Texas Press, 1994.

———. *"Sangre llama a sangre:* Cultural Memory as a Source of Theological Insight." In *Hispanic/Latino Theology: Challenge and Promise.* Edited by Ada María Isasi-Díaz and Fernando Segovia, 117-133. Minneapolis: Fortress Press, 1996.

———. *Stories We Live: Hispanic Women's Spirituality.* New York: Paulist Press, 1996.

Rodríguez, José David and Loida I. Martell. Editors. *Teología en Conjunto: A Collaborative Hispanic Protestant Theology.* Louisville: Westminster John Knox Press, 1997.

Romero, C. Gilbert. "On Choosing a Symbol System for a Hispanic Theology." *Apuntes* 1/4 (1981): 16-20.

———. *Hispanic Devotional Piety: Tracing the Biblical Roots.* Maryknoll, New York: Orbis Books, 1991.

———. *"Teología de las raíces de un Pueblo: Los Penitentes de Nuevo México." Servir* 15 (1979): 609-630. México.

———. "Tradition and Symbol as Biblical Keys for a U.S. Hispanic Theology." In *Frontiers of Hispanic Theology in the United States.* Edited by Allan Figueroa Deck, 41-61. Maryknoll, New York: Orbis Books, 1992.

Ruiz, Jean-Pierre. "Beginning to Read the Bible in Spanish: An Initial Assessment." *Journal of Hispanic/Latino Theology* 1, no. 2 (1994): 28-50.

———. "Naming the Other: U.S. Hispanic Catholics, the So-Called 'Sects,' and the 'New Evangelization.' " *Journal of Hispanic/Latino Theology* 4, no. 2 (1996): 34-59.

Sandoval, Moises. *On the Move: A History of the Hispanic Church in the United States.* Maryknoll, New York: Orbis Books, 1990.

Schreiter, Robert J. *Constructing Local Theologies.* Maryknoll, New York: Orbis Books, 1985.

———. *The New Catholicity: Theology between the Global and the Local.* Maryknoll, New York: Orbis Books, 1997.

Segovia, Fernando F. "A New Manifest Destiny: The Emerging Theological Voice of Hispanic Americans." *Religious Studies Review* 17, no. 2 (1991): 101-109.

———. "Two Places and No Place on Which to Stand: Mixture and Otherness in Hispanic American Theology." *Listening: Journal of Religion and Culture* 27, no. 1 (1992): 26-40.

———. "In the World But Not of It: Exile as Locus for a Theology of the Diaspora." In *Hispanic/Latino Theology: Challenge and Promise.* Edited by Ada María Isasi-Díaz and Fernando Segovia, 195-217. Minneapolis: Fortress Press, 1996.

Sheehan, Thomas. *Karl Rahner: The Philosophical Foundations.* Athens, Ohio: Ohio University Press, 1987.

Sosa, Juan. "Hispanic Liturgy and Popular Religiosity." In *El Cuerpo de Cristo: The Hispanic Presence in the U.S. Catholic Church*. Edited by Peter Casarella and Paul Gómez. New York: Crossroads, 1998.

Stevens-Arroyo, Anthony M. and Gilbert Cadena. Editors. *Old Masks, New Faces: Religion and Latino Identities*. New York: Bildner Center for Western Hemisphere Studies, 1995.

Stevens-Arroyo, Anthony M. and Ana María Díaz-Stevens. Editors. *An Enduring Flame: Studies on Latino Popular Religiosity*. New York: Bildner Center for Western Hemisphere Studies, 1994.

Stevens-Arroyo, Anthony M. and Andres I. Pérez y Mena. Editors. *Enigmatic Powers: Syncretism and Indigenous Peoples' Religions among Latinos*. New York: Bildner Center for Western Hemisphere Studies, 1995.

Stevens-Arroyo, Anthony M. and Segundo Pantoja. Editors. *Discovering Latino Religion: A Comprehensive Social Science Bibliography*. New York: Bildner Center for Western Hemisphere Studies, 1995.

Tallon, Andrew. *Personal Becoming*. Milwaukee: Marquette University Press, 1982.

———. "Rahner and Personalization." *Philosophy Today* 14 (1970): 44-56.

———. "Spirit, Freedom, History." *The Thomist* 38 (1974): 908-936.

Thompson, William M. "Rahner's Theology of Pluralism." *The Ecumenist* 11 (1973): 17-22.

Tracy, David. *The Analogical Imagination: Christian Theology and the Culture of Pluralism*. New York: Crossroad, 1981.

Tweed, Thomas A. "Identity and Authority at a Cuban Shrine in Miami: Santería, Catholicism, and the Struggles for Religious Identity." *Journal of Hispanic/ Latino Theology* 4, no.1 (1996): 27-48.

———. *Our Lady of the Exile: Diasporic Religion at a Cuban Catholic Shrine in Miami*. New York: Oxford University Press, 1997.

Vidal, Jaime R. "The American Church and the Puerto Rican People." *U.S. Catholic Historian* 9, nos. 1 and 2 (1990): 119-135.

———. "Popular Religion among the Hispanics in the General Area of the Archdiocese of Newark." In *Presencia Nueva: A Study of Hispanics in the Archdiocese of Newark*, 235-352. Newark: Office of Research and Planning, 1988.

———. "Popular Religion in the Origin of New York's Hispanic Population." In *Hispanics in New York: Religious, Cultural, and Social Experiences* II, 1-48. New York: Office of Pastoral Research of the Archdiocese of New York, 1982.

Vidal, Jaime and Jay Dolan. *Puerto Rican and Cuban Catholics in the U.S., 1900-1965*. Indiana: University of Notre Dame Press, 1994.

Wong, Joseph H.P. *Logos—Symbol in the Christology of Karl Rahner*. Rome: Libreria Ateneo Salesiano, 1984.

Wright, Robert E. "If It's Official, It Can't Be Popular." *Journal of Hispanic/ Latino Theology* 1, no. 3 (1994): 47-67.

———. "Popular Religiosity: Review of the Literature." *Liturgical Ministry* 7 (1998): 141-146.

Index

accompaniment, xv, 31-39, 56-58, 120

action vs. production, 35, 37

Amerindian culture, 75-76

analogical imagination, 115-17

Anglo-Protestantism, 4-5

anthropologies: instrumentalist, 35; subordinationist, 50

anthropology, theological (U.S. Hispanic Catholic): aesthetic component of, 43-44, 68-69; central themes of, xv; as dialogical, 49-50; and doctrine, 23-24; and individual, 134-35; as praxiological, 57-58; Rahner and, xiii-xvi, 58-59, 79-80, 112-17, 119-40; reductionism and, 131-32; sacramental aspects, 60-78

Aquinas, Thomas, 87-88, 101-102, 120-21, 128-30

Aquino, María Pilar, xv, 19-20, 49-52, 120

Archives of the Indies, 75

Augustine, 53, 121-22

Balthasar, Hans Urs von, 85

Caminemos con Jesús: Toward a Hispanic/Latino Theology of Accompaniment (Goizueta), 31-33

capitalism, 35

Charity, Our Lady of, 16, 69, 74-78, 125-26, 139

charity as solidarity, 48-49, 56-58, 120, 135-37

"Chicano/a" term, 11-12

communal identity: anthropology and, 128-35; and grace, 41-42; and human person, 98-100; language and, 13-14; theology and, 21-22

communication, non-dominant, 115-17

community: and option for the marginalized, 38-39; and person, xv-xvi, 32-33; as political, 113-14; romanticized, 134-35; sacramental participation and, 73; and Trinity, 42

contextual theology, 2-20, 54, 79-86, 112-17

conversation model, 111-13

cotidiano, lo (ordinary life experiences), 46-47, 51, 56-58, 66, 73, 80, 121

creaturehood, xv, 52-54

Cuban-American identity, 69, 75-76

cultural humanization, xv, 39-44

Deck, Allan Figueroa, 7-8, 43-44

dialogical relationships, 49-52

Diego, Juan, 70-74, 139

"Educación religiosa para el Mexico-Norteamericano" (Elizondo), 7-8

Elizondo, Virgilio, xv, 7-8, 19, 25-31, 73, 119-21, 138-39

153